Agusta 109 K2

DEDICATION

This book is dedicated to all of the individuals and organizations that have contributed to the advancement of the helicopter industry and to its great value to mankind.

Included in this dedication are:

The professionals who comprise the three key elements required for a successful helicopter operation: maintenance/engineering, management, and pilots. Each relies on the others for success, success includes safety — always the ultimate goal.

The manufacturers, without whom there would be no helicopters.

The members of HAI, many of whom have supported the association, and thus the industry, for many decades. "In Unity There Is Strength."

HAI's elected leaders, the Board of Directors. These individuals give unselfishly of their energy, talents, and time, with no compensation other than the knowledge that they are, through their efforts, working toward the common good.

The chairmen of HAI's committees, and all of the committee members, who, like the Board, serve without compensation from HAI.

HAI's dedicated staff, whose loyalty and productivity transcend the ordinary parameters of "employment."

All of these topnotch professionals and many others, including responsible government representatives, have worked in unison over the years, to make possible the safe and most admirable growth of the civil helicopter industry.

Helicopter
Association
International

Copyright © 1998 by the Helicopter Association International

Library of Congress Cataloging in Publication Data
  Francis G. McGuire
       Helicopters: 1948-1998
       A Contemporary History
       Includes index.
       ISBN 0-9630326-5-8

Book Design: Copeland Design, Inc.
Publisher: Frank L. Jensen, Jr.
Associate Publisher & Editor: Marilyn F. McKinnis
Helicopter Association International
1635 Prince Street
Alexandria, Virginia 22314-2818
Telephone: 703-683-4646
First edition

Spruce Goose escorted by a Bell 47B operated by Armstrong-Flint Helicopters, a founding member of HAI in 1948. Only helicopters could have provided an appropriate platform for the dozens of photographers who assembled for this November 2, 1942, one-minute flight of the Spruce Goose.

Hughes 500 D

Dauphin 2 SA-365N

HELICOPTERS

1948-1998

by Francis G. McGuire

A CONTEMPORARY HISTORY

Agusta A 109C

TABLE OF CONTENTS

BO-105

PREFACE

One would think that, especially since World War II, everything of significance in science, technology, and human events had been faithfully recorded and retained.

This is not the case. Without someone responsible for record-keeping, records are not always kept. Without necessary storage facilities and — most importantly — someone's interest in retaining records, they are discarded during housecleaning, reorganizing, or moving of any organization.

As a result, information is uneven over the years, with some periods well documented, and unfortunate gaps in the intervening periods.

Collecting, sorting, and filing of helicopter-related historic records is a daunting task in an industry where so much is going on in so many parts of the world at the same time.

This history would not be as rich in detail were it not for the leadership of the Helicopter Association International (HAI), which in 1982 created, and since then generously supported, the Helicopter Foundation International (HFI).

This HAI Golden Anniversary history interweaves the diverse flow of world events that carried the machines, people, and commercial enterprise of the helicopter industry through some of the most turbulent and rewarding years of the 20th century. That interaction affects all of us and the world in which we live.

Francis G. McGuire

Francis G. McGuire
Author

Bell 206L

ACKNOWLEDGEMENTS

*T*he publisher and the author wish to express sincere thanks to the following without whose generous assistance and cooperation this book would not have been possible: The companies whose profiles are featured in this book; their generous participation helped make this project financially possible. John M. Slattery, curator of the Helicopter Foundation International (HFI), for invaluable research and technical advice. Industry pioneers Carl Brady, Leon Plympton, Jim Ricklefs, Joe Seward, Carrol Voss, and Peter Wright, Sr. whose carefully preserved records and shared memories helped bring to life this fascinating history. And Marilyn McKinnis, who served as editor, business manager, and associate publisher; she most ably guided the volume from concept through initial drafts to its final form.

"If you are in trouble anywhere in the world, an airplane can fly over and drop flowers, but a helicopter can land and save your life."

Igor Sikorsky, 1947

FOREWORD

As this is written, about 21,000 civil helicopters are in use throughout the world, almost half of them in the U.S., with many new, better, and more versatile vertical-flight machines becoming available.

"Helicopters: 1948-1998" traces the growth of the civil helicopter industry worldwide, including increasingly safe and more capable machines and the dedicated professionals who manufactured, operated, flew, and maintained them.

Paralleling all this has been the growth of the Helicopter Association International (HAI).

The book is organized chronologically by decades and focuses on the people, the organizations, and the world events that — directly or indirectly — shaped the helicopter industry as it grew under the influence of some remarkably farsighted and courageous entrepreneurs.

Just as the field of medicine often improves dramatically during wartime, so it was that helicopters used during World War II and in Korea, Algeria, Southeast Asia, and other conflicts provided technical advances that benefitted the civil industry throughout the world.

Igor Sikorsky himself described the helicopter best in 1947 when he said, "If you are in trouble anywhere in the world, an airplane can fly over and drop flowers, but a helicopter can land and save your life."

Such benefits came with no guarantees of perfection, however, and helicopters of the early 1970s were experiencing about 30 accidents per 100,000 flying hours . . . a totally unacceptable rate by today's standards.

A principal goal of HAI is to achieve even greater safety in all aspects of helicopter activities. Largely through HAI-sponsored safety efforts, in concert with many organizations, helicopter safety has been greatly enhanced. Industry-wide safety experience during 1997 is about eight accidents per 100,000 flying hours, with many organizations achieving sustained, accident-free operations!

A perfect safety record is a worthy objective. But in order to be useful, helicopters must fly, and not always in the best of circumstances. Natural and man-made disasters, where helicopters are essential for humanitarian relief, do not always occur on sunny days. Many vital missions must be flown without regard to adverse weather or other detriments.

The helicopter has benefitted mankind in countless ways during its first half century, and with proper leadership, a reasonable regulatory environment, and modest incentives, it will continue to do so for many years.

It is impossible in these few pages to name and discuss each of the many persons and companies that have been responsible for the growth of this industry. Those mentioned and many others too numerous to mention have been true pioneers and are truly appreciated.

HAI is very pleased to sponsor "Helicopters: 1948-1998." We believe it fills a need for detailed but readable information on an exciting and productive half century. For helicopter professionals, this book should refresh your own recollections and possibly fill in some blanks in your memory.

For the non-industry readers, it is our hope that "Helicopters: 1948-1998" will open your minds to the true value of these incredible machines and this fascinating industry.

Frank L. Jensen, Jr.
President
Helicopter Association International

Air-Crane lifting Freedom Statue from
U.S. Capitol in Washington, D.C.

FRE

"Don't be afraid to take a big step if it is indicated. You can't cross a chasm in two small jumps."

David Lloyd George,
British statesman (1863-1945)

EDOM

FREEDOM

At dawn on May 9, 1993, helicopter pilots Dave Cox and Jon Long reached out and touched the switches.

Two turbine engines began to whine and the huge main rotor began to turn, picking up speed and accelerating the downward flow of air.

Aft-facing pilot Max Evans completed the crew.

The SkyCrane, also known as the Air-Crane, lifted off and flew unchallenged into Prohibited Area P-56 in the heart of Washington, D.C., the capital of free enterprise.

The machine was the property of Erickson Air-Crane Company.

Its 15,000-pound payload was the property of the people of the United States.

Above the dome on the house where laws are made, the SkyCrane defied the laws of gravity and gently lifted the Statue of Freedom from its pedestal atop the Capitol for the first time in 130 years.

It was gracefully lowered to the ground for cleaning and renovation.

Hundreds of onlookers cheered, and as it touched the ground a worker climbed a ladder, unhitched the web of protective straps, and kissed the bronze goddess on the cheek.

It was replaced in the same manner on October 23, 1993, under the watchful eyes of the president of the United States, the vice-president, cabinet officers, members of the Congress, and the world's media — this time with Larry Pravecek flying in the aft-facing pilot position. Conspicuous on the scene were countless TV technicians and reporters, recording every move of the SkyCrane.

In 1863, Freedom had been laboriously placed on its cast-iron pedestal in five sections by dozens of men using a steam engine, ropes, and pulleys. None had dared move it since.

Removing it in 1993 took the three men in the SkyCrane just 10 minutes.

This bronze classical female figure of Freedom, by American artist Thomas Crawford, was originally placed on top of the Capitol dome on December 2, 1863. It stands 19 feet 6 inches tall on a cast-iron globe encircled with the national motto, E Pluribus Unum ("Out of many, one.") and weighs approximately 15,000 pounds. Her crest rises 288 feet above the East Front Plaza.

When the project was complete, revitalized Freedom again towered over the Capitol.

It had been almost half a century since the summer when America and its allies restored freedom to much of the world at the end of World War II.

In a sense, both Freedom the statue and freedom the concept belong to the world as symbols and as goals.

Now a commercial helicopter — the only machine that could realistically have done so — took the big step to reach out and touch Freedom, the pinnacle of America.

Millions of television viewers around the world watched the dramatic event, marveling at this marriage of technology and human skill.

The link between helicopters and drama had, in fact, begun long before.

Some of the most enduring images of the late 20th century involve helicopters, and these glimpses of the whirly bird at work serve as bookmarks for the mind.

- The 1938 helicopter flights of 25-year-old Hanna Reitsch on the inside of a stadium in Berlin were among the most brilliant propaganda strokes in history.

- Igor Sikorsky as the world's most elegant test pilot . . . wearing a homburg but initially able to fly only sideways and backwards.

- Eleven years (1972-1983) of the TV show "M*A*S*H" opening with a Bell 47 arriving with wounded troops. It was fiction on the surface, truth just beneath.

- The nightly news from Vietnam, showing us the benevolently-named Huey; and eventually that war's crowning televised humiliation . . . the scramble to get on the last U.S. Marine helicopter lifting off the embassy roof. We wished that, too, had been fiction.

- The U.S. Park Police rescue in January 1982 of Air Florida crash survivors in the ice-choked Potomac River at Washington, D.C.

- Removal and replacement of the Statue of Freedom atop the Capitol by a commercial helicopter.

It is unfortunate that the world's introduction to helicopters came in a dazzling display of the Nazi swastika, which would have been a hundredfold more effective had global TV been available in 1938. More than half a century later, much of the world saw three civilians in a now-familiar machine quietly give a lift to Freedom.

The contrast reminds us again that man bends technology to his wishes.

Throughout the half-century-plus spanning these historic events, commercial helicopters have been bent to the wishes of those who make an inestimable contribution to our society.

Fundamentally, this is the story of those who have made the contribution.

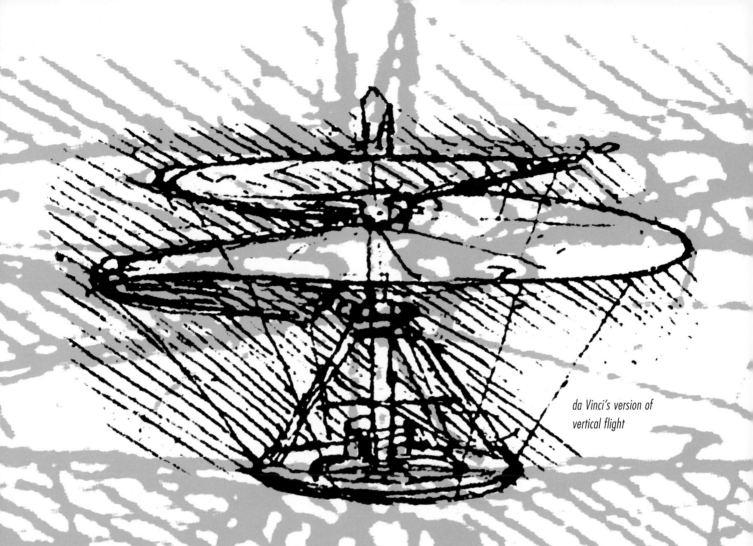

da Vinci's version of vertical flight

THE MACHINE

*"I find that if this instrument made with
a screw be well made . . .
and be turned swiftly, the said
screw will make its spiral in the
air and it will rise high."*

Leonardo da Vinci (1483)

Without a usable machine to leverage human strength, ideas are often futile.

Many inventors knew that air could be moved across a wing to create lift, not only by propelling an airplane down a runway, but also by rotating the wing around an axis. In fact, that concept preceded the airplane by at least a century, and far more efforts were aimed at developing a helicopter than developing an airplane.

It was called vertical lift, and naming it was the easy part.

The search for this vertical grail was well described by helicopter consultant Franklin D. Harris: "Man's flight within the atmosphere has progressed in five major steps as he sought to 'take off, fly, and land like a bird.' The first step occurred in 1745 when the Montgolfier brothers first ascended in a hot air balloon. Like a bird, the takeoff and landing was accomplished in a space about the size of the balloon . . . but they had very little control.

"The second step was accomplished by the Wright brothers in 1903 [and] while they had control of where they were going, they required nearly 10 times the airplane's size for takeoff and landing space. . . . Unfortunately, today's high-speed airplanes now require a space 50 times their size to take off and land.

"The third step came when Cierva demonstrated the autogiro [which] reversed the trend of required takeoff and landing space but was still far short of man's long-sought goal of bird-like capabilities. . . .

"The fourth step came at the onset of World War II when Focke, Flettner, and Sikorsky each developed producible helicopters."

The helicopter, noted Harris, has all the necessary attributes of bird-like flight except high speeds, and that is now in sight on the horizon with the emerging designs typified by the Harrier and the V-22 Osprey tiltrotor.

Before wondrous bird-like machines could become a reality, however, it would first become necessary to deal with engine power, blade angle, yaw, torque, fatigue, stability, ground resonance, vibration, controls, materials, and other less tangible aspects of the machine . . . including how to define useful work for the very first of the breed.

When thousands of World War II GIs saw the world's first production helicopters at work, it was inevitable that the wheels of inspiration would turn in many minds. After the war, that inspiration turned to finding useful civilian jobs for this machine with the unfamiliar name.

Igor Sikorsky with admirers

In the swirl of names surrounding the helicopter, some are more familiar than others. Bell, da Vinci, Hiller, Kaman, Kamov, Mil, Piasecki, Sikorsky, Westland, and their colleagues in many countries are forever linked with the machine.

Among the earliest and most familiar names was Leonardo da Vinci, whose notes in 1483 on aircraft totaled more than a hundred pages and included a helix for vertical lift. He speculated that man-powered aircraft could fly, a notion widely dismissed until the 1970s, when Dr. Paul Macready's designs took to the air.

What are less familiar than his helix drawings are da Vinci's efforts on engines (a steam-driven piston and a closed-loop convection-powered turbine), gears, pulleys, and other contributions to aeronautics, civil engineering, and military science, as well as mathematics, architecture, and art of nearly every form.

Many pioneers are not thought of in the context of helicopters, including Antonov, Berliner, Breguet, Brennan, Bristol, Cayley, Cierva, Cornu, de Bothezat, Ellehammer, Fairey, Flettner, Florine, Focke, Forlanini, Landgraf, Oehmichen, Pescara, von Baumhauer, and dozens of others, many of whom improved existing rotorcraft but did not create designs under their own names.

Paul Cornu and Florine tried tandem helicopters; Pescara, d'Ascanio, Breguet-Dorand, and Asboth designed coaxial types; de Bothezat and Oehmichen came up with quad-rotor designs; Anton Flettner invented the Flettner tab and the synchropter. Many contributed to the cause.

A story is told of the American interrogation of German rocket scientists at the end of World War II, when they were asked: What was the secret of the V-2 rocket engine?

"Why are you asking us?" came the puzzled reply. "We learned from the American . . . Dr. Robert Goddard."

It was a similar irony of genius-without-borders that saw one of the giants of American helicopter invention get his initial inspiration from an obscure book about a new kind of sailing ship. A young man named Arthur Young, eventual creator of the early Bell helicopter designs, read that the sailing ship used specially designed rotary drums to drive it across the Atlantic in 1927. The book was written by a German named Anton Flettner, soon to become an icon of helicopter design himself. Young decided that Flettner's idea could be applied to aircraft.

The most fundamental problem that defeated all early helicopter pioneers was a simple one: no engine was powerful enough to lift itself and an aircraft, and this situation prevailed until the first part of the 20th century. Before other problems could be attacked, obviously, the machine first had to get off the ground.

The Italian inventor Enrico Forlanini flew a steam-powered twin-rotor helicopter in 1877 to an altitude of 45 feet. It stayed there for one minute, but the limitations on the powerplant were abundant.

Paul Cornu built and flew a helicopter in France in 1907 that could take off vertically carrying a person, but after flying for 20 seconds about one foot off the ground, it unfortunately broke up upon landing. The next year, Louis Breguet built his Gyroplane, a four-rotor machine that rose 13 feet. All these aircraft had the same problem: "Until the arrival of the automobile," said Young, "engines hadn't been built that were powerful enough to meet the requirements of vertical flight. I also discovered that there were more attempts to make helicopters than airplanes."

Young, who had an independent income, set up a workshop and lab in a barn on his family's estate near Radnor, Pennsylvania. That's where he built flying models to check his ideas. In 1938 he bought an old farm near Paoli, Pennsylvania, and again converted the barn to an aeronautical laboratory.

Young attended the first Rotary Wing Aircraft meeting, where Igor Sikorsky presented a paper and showed a film. Young was impressed with what he saw.

"From then on, I was stuck on the tail rotor principle," he said.

Young began to experiment with hinged rotor blades and smaller models, seeking increased stability.

"This meant I had to have flights and have wrecks. Many earlier helicopters had received backing only to

Did You Know?

Developing helicopters can be hard on the nervous system, resulting in occasionally irrational behavior.

In 1909, a Russian designer named Tatarinov began construction of his Aeromobile. In the same year, Igor Sikorsky started work on his first helicopter while still a student in Kiev.

Tatarinov had received a grant from the Imperial Russian Ministry of War in St. Petersburg.

The Aeromobile had four large rotors turning at the ends of an X-formed beam, powered by a 25-horsepower engine, which also powered a five-bladed "centrifugal propeller."

Tatarinov thought development work on the Aeromobile was progressing well.

The Minister of War, Sukhomlinov, did not.

Funding for the project gradually fell to zero.

Tatarinov set fire to the only Aeromobile prototype, as well as the hangar in which it was housed.

There is no record of what happened to Tatarinov.

Enstrom F28F

crash on their trial run. The backers then backed out and the project collapsed. I felt you had to have the crack-ups before the initial flight, because these crack-ups were teaching you something."

Arthur Young tested a series of scale models that tipped from side to side and eventually crashed.

"After a series of unsuccessful flights I decided to try a stabilizer bar," he said, explaining the link between the bar and the main rotor. "With the addition of this device, the model performed remarkably, showing great stability."

The problem that had bedeviled Young for so long was now gone.

Everything seems so simple and obvious in hindsight, but such was the incremental nature of progress from the first flight of Juan de la Cierva's autogiro through the helicopter evolutions of slide-rule individuals like Heinrich Focke, Igor Sikorsky, and Arthur Young, then finally to the huge computer-aided engineering teams that generated production machines like Harrier and Osprey.

Worldwide efforts produced hundreds of design variations until finally the right combination of engine, rotor design, structure, control system, and good fortune occurred almost simultaneously in several places. The integrated design was then improved one feature at a time.

To this day, the helicopter industry depends on the right combination of those ingredients to make the machine do useful work on an economically sound basis.

Helicopters did not historically spring directly from the heritage of the airplane. Rotorcraft in the form of autogiros were an intermediate step and could do much of what later helicopters achieved. Autogiros could not take off vertically and could not hover. Because an autogiro's main rotor is unpowered, it must retain some forward motion on takeoff as well as in flight, though "jump-start" takeoffs are possible.

Those who pioneered rotorcraft were taking up the cause sparked by da Vinci centuries earlier — a cause that didn't bear realistic fruit until January 17, 1923, when Juan de la Cierva flew his C-4 design in Madrid, Spain. It was the first practical autogiro and used flapping hinges to handle unequal blade lift and gyroscopic precession.

As is often the case, others took the cue and within a short time there were many similar designs in the air.

Harold Frank Pitcairn licensed the Cierva C-8 and produced it, then designed and flew his PCA-2 autogiro in the U.S. in December 1928, winning the Collier Trophy as a result. Indicative of the multinational cross-pollination in any scientific field, he had based the PCA-2 on a British C-8 Mk IV airframe built by A.V. Roe in 1928, which Pitcairn had bought to develop his ideas.

It was the autogiro that first had to deal with flapping hinges and lead/lag hinges in the rotor system, as well as concepts of direct rotor control and cyclic pitch control. In 1938, the U.S. Army bought nine Kellett VG-1 autogiros and set up a school, laying the foundation for future rotorcraft operations.

Eventually, about 500 autogiros were produced in the U.S., England, France, Russia, Japan, Germany, and other countries. They were used for carrying the mail and delivering money to banks, high-priority courier work, photography, and other commercial uses, as well as the inevitable military applications.

On July 30, 1937, Gerard P. Herrick publicly demonstrated his Convertiplane. It was a biplane, but the upper wing could be rotated like an autogiro to provide unpowered vertical lift. Well, it was almost unpowered except for a jump start from a rubber bungee-cord system that set the upper wing spinning at 60 rpm, later reaching 200 rpm and serving as a rotary wing. The upper wing was all one teetering piece, not hinged.

The HV-2A aircraft, flown by test pilot George Townson, was successful as a flying testbed of the inventor's concepts. Unfortunately, Herrick died before completing the HC-6D phase of his development program, and interest in his approach died with him.

Still, autogiros and convertiplanes were not helicopters. Americans and Germans pursued war-driven helicopter research in the late 1930s. Other countries across Europe had programs under way as well. Some marginal success had been achieved.

Then it happened.

The initial public "working" flight of a new machine called the Fw-61 was a 67-mile trip from Bremen to Berlin on October 25, 1937. At the controls of the world's first practical helicopter was the world's first woman helicopter pilot, Hanna Reitsch. She was 25 years old and had just set several world helicopter records. The world's aviation community realized the importance of it immediately.

Politicians took much more notice of Hanna Reitsch and her Fw-61 the following February.

Reitsch stunned the world by flying the lateral twin-rotor Focke 61 helicopter around the inside of Berlin Deutschland Halle — an enclosed German sports stadium filled with 20,000 people — in a spectacular 1938 demonstration of an agile, fully controllable helicopter.

"Man wants
to fly like
a bird, not
like a bat
out of hell."

Lawrence Bell

Every evening for three weeks during the International Auto Show Hanna flew vertically, backward, forward, and sideways. She mastered the unpredictable eddies of turbulent air stirred up by the rotors' downwash, and controlled a machine whose engine was often oxygen-starved and near failure by the thousands of people in the stadium. . . . Adolph Hitler assigned her to give Charles Lindbergh . . . a demonstration flight.

The brilliance of the swastika-daubed helicopter flight as political propaganda almost overshadowed its demonstration of successful new helicopter technology.

(The diminutive and courageous Reitsch became one of the most renowned test pilots in Germany, and she flight tested every new aircraft design developed by Germany during the war. She was often the first pilot to fly any new type, including the extremely dangerous rocket-propelled fighter, the Me-163, and the usually unpiloted V-1 glide-bomb. Reitsch was to gain even more notoriety after she became one of Hitler's confidantes and virtually the last person to see him alive in his bunker in April 1945.)

Though Igor Sikorsky demonstrated the first practical single-rotor helicopter the following year, the Focke 61 is generally credited with being the breakthrough for powered-lift aircraft.

If da Vinci conceived vertical lift in the 15th century, and powered-lift efforts began a hundred years before the airplane flew, why did it take about 30 years after the development of the airplane to make a practical rotorcraft? The University of Maryland's Dr. Alfred Gessow explains: "To answer the question, we must go back to the hurdles that are inherent in all helicopter designs. These are complexity, high empty weight, complex stability and control, unequal lift experienced by the lifting blades in forward flight, unbalanced torque of the powered shaft, gyroscopic moments on the lifting rotor resulting from control moments, and the need for high power in hover and vertical flight."

While Paul Macready eventually demonstrated the feasibility of man-powered flight, that achievement required light structures. Like a lightweight, powerful engine, however, a lightweight, high-strength structure was quite elusive.

Rotor systems were developed in a variety of types. Single main-rotor systems (coupled with an anti-torque rotor) were eventually the most familiar design. There were tandem twin-rotor systems having the rotors at opposite ends of the fuselage, while other twin-rotor systems had the rotors on lateral outriggers flanking the fuselage. There were also coaxial designs, intermeshing types and variations on all of them.

Early efforts tended to use large quad rotors on the theory that their equilibrium was the most efficient way to counter the problems of torque and other control complexities. The numerous rotors, however, introduced their own complexities. Thus, after trying several approaches, Igor Sikorsky went to a single-rotor design, and used three smaller rotors for anti-torque and cyclic control.

To appreciate what early helicopter designers had to overcome to give the commercial helicopter industry of today a usable machine, Harris points out the crude technology and rudimentary analytical tools available to those designers.

"In the early 1900s, belt-drive transmissions were the most common means of reducing engine rpm to rotor rpm. As a result, as much as one-half of the engine's power never reached the rotors. And even with the use of gears and shafts, history recounts several instances when the engine did not deliver the manufacturer's claimed power. . . . Many early attempts to hover resulted in low, in-ground-effect altitudes.

"The pioneers had encountered a situation where (1) the rotors themselves were about 50 percent efficient relative to the ideal power calculated with available theory, (2) only one-half of the installed power was trans-mitted to the rotors, and (3) the benefit of ground effect reduced power required to hover by perhaps one-half. It appears that about 50 percent of the early inventors were, at best, in a marginal power — not to mention control — situation."

By the 1930s, rotor blades no longer featured "barn-door" geometry and began to look more like airfoils. Blades per rotor became fewer. Blades became narrower.

The results paid off in Germany shortly before the war broke out, and unfortunately for the U.S. and its allies, the successes were on the wrong side. France was almost the first, but work was also going on in England, Belgium, and Italy.

"The leap from Breguet's successful 'experiments' of 1936 to real, powered and controlled lift was accomplished by Heinrich Focke in Germany. His Fw-61 side-by-side rotor arrangement yielded a 2,200 pound-gross-weight helicopter that captured all the world rotorcraft records by 1939. The Fw-61 raised the altitude record from Breguet's 500 feet to 7,500 feet and then to over 11,000 feet; it could be hovered until the fuel ran out; it completed the first autorotation; it flew 230 kilometers non-stop in one hour, 20 minutes and it reached 76 miles per hour in level flight. In short, the Fw-61 astounded the world. The story goes that when Louis Breguet witnessed the Fw-61 perform, he shed tears of joy," said Harris.

With the outbreak of war, of course, every available machine on every side was pressed into military service.

The late 1930s and early 1940s ushered in a thriving era of war-borne tech-nology. Alongside technology-driven ideas, helicopters spurred human-driven ideas promising rescues, personal transportation, and industrial uses that would touch all our lives in the decades following the technology explosion of World War II.

The machine had such an uncommonly benevolent personality that it was called "Angel" by navy carrier pilots and "Angel of Mercy" by virtually anyone else in trouble, but it immediately found a head-scratching challenge: No one was really sure what to do with war technology after the war was over.

Few could cozy up to a nuclear weapon, but soon everyone imagined a heli-copter in the garage. The earliest headlines confirmed this personal link. At first even the pioneer helicopter manufacturers seemed to believe it, marketing their products with photos of small helicopters outside residential garages and debating whether they should make the machine look like a car or an aircraft. The heli-copter-in-the-garage vision quickly evaporated in the face of the realities involved.

The late 1930s and early 1940s ushered in a blossoming era of war-borne technology: helicopters, radar, turbine engines, rockets, nuclear weapons, computers, lightweight synthetic materials, and many other previously unknown terms. Scientific methods to perform more accurate analysis also came out of the war.

On April 8, 1945, Vice-President Harry S Truman visited the Bell plant in Buffalo, New York, and was shown Bell's developmental Model 30 helicopter.

Four days later, on April 12, President Franklin D. Roosevelt died of a cerebral hemorrhage in Warm Springs, Georgia, at age 63. Truman became president.

Americans and others in the indus-trialized world are often taken with the newness of a technology and fail to notice that early results may not be much different than the old technology. The fact that about 140,000 people were killed by the first atomic bomb amazed the same people who seemed unimpressed that an equivalent number of people were killed in Tokyo five months earlier in a "conven-tional" firebomb raid.

It was that new word "atomic" that made the difference.

With helicopters, the word "hover" made all the differ-ence over the autogiro.

President
Dwight D. Eisenhower

Soon everyone imagined helicopters in residential garages . . . a vision that quickly evaporated in the face of the realities involved.

Igor Sikorsky had flown the VS-300 on September 14, 1939, and in 1942 went into production for the army with the R-4, of which about 160 were built. On April 11, 1943, Frank Piasecki flew his single-main-rotor PV-2, America's second successful helicopter. It was said to be the first to have dynamically balanced blades and cyclic control. On the heels of these two designs came Stanley Hiller with a coaxial design, then his Model 360. Into the synchropter category came Kellett and Kaman.

By the end of the 1940s, however, only single-main-rotor and tandem-rotor designs were extant, the others having been quietly put away for the most part.

Within months after the end of the war, Piasecki had a U.S. Navy contract to develop a military helicopter with a larger-than-normal payload capability for the time. His tandem-rotor XHRP-X was the result, produced as the banana-shaped HRP-1. Descendants of Piasecki's banana design may still be seen in the Vertol 107 (military H-46) and the Chinook (military H-47).

Harris notes that of an estimated 90,000 helicopters produced between 1942 and 1994, 85,000 have been single-main-rotor designs.

Did the aviation community's own trade publications seem impressed with this versatile new aircraft? Not in the least. As "Flying" magazine described one of the early commercial helicopter operators in 1947, "Helicopter Air Transport's real contribution to the future of commercial helicopter operations is its exploration of specialized services for which the craft's flying peculiarities are ideally suited."

Flying peculiarities indeed. Helicopter pioneers didn't see it that way, believing that one observer's flying peculiarities are another observer's special capabilities, including no need for an airport.

As Bell's Arthur Young described it, the "Model 47 represented my best efforts in design after the experience of three experimental machines. I recall the great effort I made to design the whole rotor control and transmission fast so as to take advantage of forgings, etc. People talk about the virtues of hand made objects — but mass production, at least when not directed toward making things as cheap as possible, is an opportunity to get the prototype, which is sort of an ideal, after which you can't change it.

"I also recall about 30 minor changes (aside from redesign of the main components) which were made, of which about two-thirds had to be dropped. It gets harder and harder to improve after a certain point. The experimental Model 30 ship two was not as good as ship one. I put all the conservative ideas in ship one and all the innovative ideas in ship two — most of the latter didn't work. It is a mistake to try more than one innovative idea at a time. In any case, Model 47 was my pride and joy."

The cut-and-try approach of early helicopter development efforts led to some surprises in the outcome.

While Bell officials were immersed in an internal debate over the external appearance of the machine — that is, should it look like an automobile or an aircraft — they created what has become the most familiar helicopter profile in the world.

The early Model 47B-3 was an open-cockpit machine that had great visibility. Unfortunately, when it came to demonstration flights with potential customers, the open air visibility was too good. A way was needed to make customers feel more secure, so a method was developed to use hot air for shaping a large plexiglass sheet into a huge bubble that would cover the open cockpit.

When the original low-profile cowling was removed and the bubble installed, it was found that not only did customers feel better "inside" the helicopter, but the aircraft actually had better performance. Thus, most of the Model 47B-3 helicopters were modified to accommodate the bubble and doors, eventually leading to a new version called the Model 47D.

(A 50-year-old Bell Model 47B, Registration NC5H, was donated by Dr. Carrol Voss of AgRotors Inc. in 1996 to the American Helicopter Museum and Education Center near Philadelphia. It is one of only two in the world and is still flyable.)

25

The joy of creating a new machine . . . a new tool to do useful things . . . along with the self confidence of true inventors is clear in Arthur Young's comments, and the feeling was shared by many. "It seemed to all of us that if we could build it, we could fly it," said Stanley Hiller, whose first design (the coaxial XH-44) made its first free flight on July 4, 1944, in Palo Alto, California. He then designed and built the third production commercial helicopter certificated in the U.S., behind Bell and Sikorsky. The Hiller 360, noted for its remarkable stability, was certificated on October 14, 1948, and remained in production for decades.

In a sense, another certification occurred two weeks later when, on November 2, 1948, President Truman surprised political experts by being re-elected in a narrow upset over his Republican challenger, Thomas E. Dewey.

California's Landgraf Helicopter Co. produced a small outrigger H-2 model with a pair of three-bladed rotors supported by pylons that gave it a look remarkably like the later tiltrotor designs. It was the Landgraf H-2 that was the first helicopter flown by Jim Ricklefs, later founder of Rick Helicopters, in May 1946. Landgraf had rotor blade development contracts with the armed forces, but never got into production.

To be sure, much developmental work had been under way throughout the war by engineers at many helicopter endeavors, but most did not reach the public's attention until the war ended, and sometimes well after it ended.

It was not until December 1946 that the U.S. government disclosed that about a thousand German engineers and scientists were being brought to the United States for application of their expertise to America's technology needs. Their political leanings were of less interest to the government than their know-how.

It was part of Operation Paperclip that brought people like Wernher von Braun to the United States before Soviet forces could scoop them up for transfer to the U.S.S.R. With them came a half million documents and 5,000 tons of scientific equipment, all of which was expected to save United States taxpayers well over a billion dollars (in 1946 terms) in research and development costs. American research was accelerated from two to 10 years by taking advantage of German lessons and by avoiding any blind alleys they had discovered.

Many of the German scientists were later released for employment by private industry or universities in the United States. Most were re-located to Fort Bliss, Texas; White Sands, New Mexico; and Wright Patterson AFB, Ohio.

Among the scientists in the program was Baron Fritz Doblhoff, described by the War Department as inventor of the jet-propelled helicopter. In 1947, Anton Flettner also came to the U.S., and after a stint with the U.S. Office of Naval Research he launched an aircraft company with retired Adm. C.E. Rosendahl of airship fame.

The imported Germans may have saved the U.S. a billion or more in research, but large dollar signs still figured in the continuing development of the helicopter.

Homegrown U.S. helicopters were already making money in commercial service when Operation Paperclip was made public nine months after the Bell 47 was certificated.

On March 5, 1946, three days before the Bell 47 was certificated, former British Prime Minister Winston Churchill, in an address at Westminster College in Fulton, Missouri, spoke for the first time of an "Iron Curtain" stretching from the Baltic to the Adriatic.

Sikorsky SkyCrane completes a precision lift.

Two weeks later, on March 21, 1946, the new United Nations organization set up temporary headquarters at Hunter College in New York.

New commercial helicopter models of the day joined a newborn United Nations and a new "Iron
Curtain" in helping to shape a postwar world. They would all have a major impact — positively and
negatively — on that world for the next half century.

The capabilities of early helicopters impressed many people, mostly because no machine had ever
done such things.

Within the decade of the 1940s alone, the helicopter evolved from just one Sikorsky VS-300 and a handful of
scattered developmental models to hundreds of production-line Bell 47s, S-51s, and Hiller 360s routinely doing
useful commercial work around the world.

Solved in their most basic form were the technical problems that had stymied the helicopter visionaries for so
long after the concept was known. Now the challenge was to refine those solutions and improve the machine
bit by bit.

One of the biggest "bits" was the powerplant. It was one thing to barely get off the surface of the planet
and hover in ground effect. It was something else again to get out of ground effect, control the machine, and
still allow the pilot to think of doing useful work while he was up there.

Era's 1st "owned" hangar
Merrill Field, Alaska in 1959
S-55 is in the foreground

Did You Know?

In 1931, the first person to buy one of Pitcairn's aircraft (Serial Number 13) was John Miller, an engineer and pilot who flew parts of his career for Eastern Airlines, United Air Lines, and others.

That aircraft had been offered to Amelia Earhart, who turned it down in favor of a different serial number. She later flew her autogiro in a highly publicized flight across the U.S., but Miller had done the same thing without headlines two weeks earlier.

"She crashed it on the way out, then totaled it on the way back," Miller observed.

Miller also used the PCA-2 for personal flights and to demonstrate its capabilities over fixed-wing airplanes, even doing loops and rolls at air shows, to the amazement of other pilots who were not also engineers.

Miller knew very well what he was doing, and he had the shrewd, calculated-risk-taking engineer's perspective that would be demonstrated later by Igor Sikorsky, Arthur Young, Stanley Hiller, Joe Mashman, Les Morris, Frank Piasecki, and others.

Even engineers know how to say "Oops!" however, and Wallace Kellett's KD-1 autogiro nearly killed Miller during one 1937 test when it disintegrated violently before it left the ground. As Miller advanced the throttle for takeoff, the rotor blades ripped through the airframe, beginning with the tail section.

"It tore the aircraft to shreds. Pieces flew all over the airport. I just held on and tried to avoid getting decapitated. It was not a real healthy place to be."

Indeed. Miller suffered a cracked vertebrae but still completed the test program. In 1940, the Kellett KD-1 was the first wingless aircraft certificated in the U.S.

A Kellett autogiro went to the South Pole with Admiral Byrd in 1934, and the same model flew air mail from the roof of the Philadelphia Main Post Office to Camden and Philadelphia airports, demonstrating the capability in 1935.

Regular air mail flights were funded with $63,000 authorized by President Franklin D. Roosevelt, and began July 6, 1939, with Miller at the controls of the KD-1. Miller had convinced Eddie Rickenbacker to operate the flights at a loss by Eastern Airlines for the publicity value, which turned out to be a very good move.

The flights were flawlessly safe, but eventually the onset of war caused them to be suspended.

Kellett later sold the rights for his designs to Howard Hughes, who developed them into huge crane-category machines like the X-17, which never saw operational service but certainly proved a concept that is still in use.

As for John Miller, he retired from airline flying and at the age of 60 launched a commercial helicopter operation, using a Bell 47G. He sold that business in 1971 and flew as an active pilot well past his 80th birthday. Numerous awards were bestowed upon him for his contributions in the development of rotary-winged aircraft.

The early piston engines — the Franklins, Pratt & Whitneys, and others — did their job as best they could, but in too many cases that wasn't enough, and all helicopters were low-performance aircraft. A helicopter requires several times the power of an airplane of comparable weight. Piston engines needed clutches, gearboxes, cooling fans, mufflers, and other sub-assemblies. The early ones vibrated and had a staccato noise (the bigger the engine, the worse the noise), and they did not put out enough power to suit their developers.

To the rescue came military requirements, which easily flowed into the civil sector and provided great benefit to commercial operators.

A U.S. Army General Officer Board chaired by Generals Howze and Rodgers in the late 1950s looked at aviation's role in the future army and decided that all future helicopters should be powered by turbine engines. This brought with it a dramatic boost in power, reliability, and maintainability. The turbines burned more fuel, but that was considered an easy tradeoff to get their benefits, and it was a problem that could be tackled later.

The Wright R-1300 piston engine that powered the Sikorsky S-55 transport helicopter in 1949 weighed 840 pounds and generated about 800 horsepower. The T-53 turboshaft engine powering the UH-1 (Bell 204 class) in 1955 weighed 490 pounds and produced about 1,100 shaft horsepower (shp). The new T-800 class engine weighs less than 230 pounds and generates at least 800 shp.

There were many simultaneous efforts under way during those salad days of rotorcraft development. Ideas tumbled around and atop one another in their determination to bring a dream into flying reality. Sometimes the engineers at Bell, Hiller, Piasecki, Sikorsky, and smaller shops knew each other and knew what each was up to, but often they did not because the information vacuum was so difficult to overcome.

Arthur Young told of the first successful flights of Bell's Model 30 at the Gardenville, New York, plant in the summer of 1943 when the aircraft got up to 70 mph. This was well before the Model 47 was anywhere near reality and occurred at the height of the war. Within the small helicopter community of the day, word of the Model 30 got around and it eventually reached Igor Sikorsky, who arranged to visit Arthur Young that summer.

"Sikorsky wanted to see the aircraft's vertical engine mount. His entrance was made in a fleet of Cadillacs driven by vice presidents. I remember they all stood around the Model 30 in a circle. Finally, Sikorsky said to me:

"'I zee you use zee vertical engine.'

"'Yes, I use the vertical engine.'

"And that was the end of the conversation. They simply got into their Cadillacs and drove away."

Following the development of better powerplants to get the helicopter off the ground, the next priority of designers was to improve main rotor systems and their components. The dynamic systems of helicopters account for about 35 percent of the vehicle's empty weight and must deal with constantly changing conditions. Key improvements in this area have been of great benefit to commercial operators because — just as with engines — better reliability, maintainability, and performance of the dynamic systems all translate into lower costs and greater productivity.

Development of durable high-strength steel for gears, composite main rotor blades for unlimited life, improved ability to analyze and predict rotor loads, and better ways to design and test for fatigue all contributed to the bottom line for helicopter operators of all types. (The helicopter, indeed, has been called a "flying fatigue machine" by many engineers . . . especially those who design airplanes.)

Early fatigue testing was simple. A few specimens — perhaps only one, in some cases — were set up and tested until they failed. Analytical tools were crude at best and there was no other sure way to find out when a part would fail. Test-to-failure gave engineers some idea of the limits to be expected. Adjustments were made to the test results and that was the part's "in-service" rating.

(There was also, as some have pointed out, no product-liability case law at the time.)

"It seemed to all of us that if we could build it, we could fly it."

Stanley Hiller

The Stanley Hiller Family

It wasn't until 1952 that federal fatigue certification requirements appeared, as an appendix to requirements laid down in 1945 for helicopters.

Direct operating costs for helicopters were mostly dictated by big-ticket items like main rotor transmissions, main rotor blades, rotor hubs, and other rotating parts. Some transmissions had time-between-overhaul (TBO) limits as low as 400 hours, which prompted the army to have one designed with a 1,000-hour TBO rating.

Main rotor blades are the most distinctive part of any helicopter and the early versions used on commercial aircraft were usually circular steel tubes, wooden D-sections, or machined aluminum channel sections built up into airfoils using balsa wood, wood laminates, metal ribs, or doped fabric. Each type had advantages and disadvantages such as weathering, erosion from airborne sand, corrosion vulnerability, moisture absorption, or weight-and-balance variations.

Fatigue is a major enemy of rotor blades, just as it is of any dynamic component. Much effort has gone into the development of analytical tools to combat the problem.

In the 1950s and 1960s, notes Bell test pilot Floyd Carlson, "a variety of practices were developed and applied to improve the reliability of dynamic components. Experimental stress analysis techniques such as photo elastic models and 'stress coat' supplemented conventional stress analysis; pre-loaded bolt technology was reinvented and refined; rolled bolt threads replaced cut threads; and mechanical surface stressing such as shot peening, grit blasting, and 'bearingizing' were used to increase component endurance to limit and reduce scatter. Each manufacturer developed its own proprietary 'brew.'"

With the introduction of composite materials and analytical tools at an accelerating rate into the latter half of the century, coupled with reduction and control of vibration, the helicopter became a much more forgiving machine.

Helicopters and non-metallic composite materials epitomize the phrase "a marriage made in heaven." Because of its high empty weight fraction, the helicopter has always been a designer target for weight reduction. Some World War II aircraft used fiberglass materials in non-critical structures, and helicopters joined this trend in the late 1950s. The Hiller Hornet HJ-1 had a composite tail boom, but it was some time before primary structures for most helicopters used such materials, and main rotor blades were among the final holdouts. In the 1950s, however, tests on composite main rotor blades were done by Cornell Aeronautical Laboratories, Kaman Corp., Parsons, Vertol (originally Piasecki), and other firms. Vertol did some HUP-4 flight testing of fiberglass blades made by Prewitt in 1956.

Some disadvantages attended early composite structures, including cost, labor-intensive manufacture, and unique strength requirements for certain applications.

Western Europe has been ahead of the U.S. for the most part in applying composites to helicopter design, with composite-weight to airframe-weight ratios consistently ahead of the U.S. by 10 to 12 years. Messerschmitt-Bölkow-Blohm (MBB) flew composite main rotor blades on a BO-105 testbed in 1967, and such blades were production items on that model by 1971.

Eventually, glass was replaced as the embedded fiber by such materials as boron and graphite, and new epoxy matrices made the total product even more attractive.

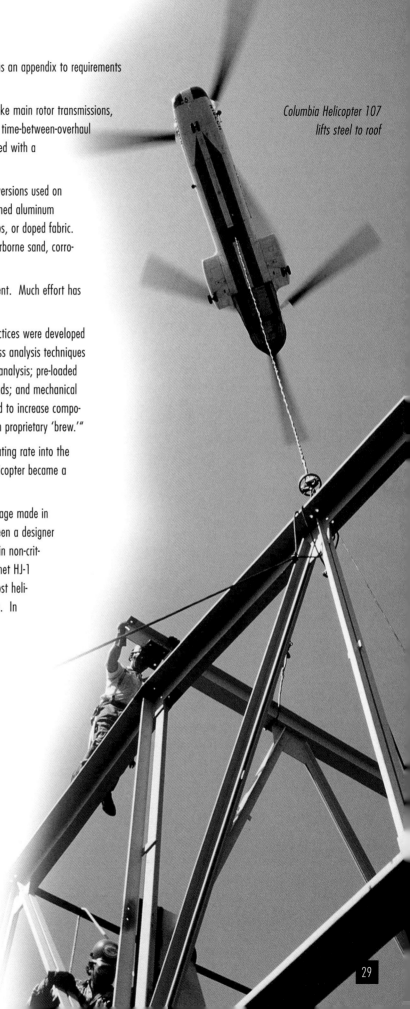

Columbia Helicopter 107
lifts steel to roof

Boeing Vertol tested composite main rotor blades on the CH-47 Chinook in 1974, then the CH-46, and Bell followed suit with such blades for the AH-1S, OH-58D, and UH-1 models. Their retirement life, technical performance, and cost accrued to the benefit of commercial operators, who now use such blades in many fleets.

In 1957, Lockheed — as others had done — began experimenting with teetering, hinged, and rigid rotor hub designs in an effort to determine the best concept for vertical takeoff and landing (VTOL) aircraft. Rotor hubs have been a perennial problem for helicopter engineers because of their complexity. The California company even had a 95-passenger, 300-mph compound helicopter on its long-term to-do list. (Piasecki, too, was developing the compound concept.)

By November 1959 Lockheed was test-flying its CL-475 testbed, and by 1962 it had a joint army-navy contract for more research. Development of the rigid rotor progressed in stages with various flight test models, and in 1965 the company showed the Model 286 four-blade rigid

EH101 Heliliner

rotor system. The rotor was on a 4,700-pound demonstrator aircraft that set a speed record of 206 mph in a shallow dive. In mid-summer 1966 it became the first rigid rotor certificated by the Federal Aviation Agency (FAA).

Lockheed never pursued its rigid rotor commercially, though it demonstrated the Model 286 to so many commercial operators that it seemed a civil version was being planned. The technologically related Cheyenne AH-56A military gunship was ordered by the U.S. Army, then canceled in 1969, and appears to have been Lockheed's last foray into helicopters.

What seemed to be a minor bit of the entire helicopter assembly was that whirling dervish called the anti-torque rotor. The tail rotor caused commercial as well as military operators no end of headaches by striking trees, wires, poles, the ground, other aircraft, people, and various other solid objects.

By the end of the 1960s, operators and manufacturers alike had enough experience to try to minimize the tail rotor's potential dangers. Into the prototypes of the day came fenestrons, ring-in-fin, directed engine exhaust, and other efforts to do the same job without the potential for trauma.

There were and still are other benefits aside from removing a physical danger. The tail rotor adds one more gearbox (and sometimes two) that needs maintenance; the tail rotor effect is distorted by main rotor downwash and by airflow around the fuselage; it requires constant pilot attention while on the ground and has a variable influence on the machine's aerodynamics when flying in a crosswind or quartering wind.

By the 1970s and 1980s, an increasing number of answers were in hand, and finally the decade of the 1990s saw many new helicopter models introduced with effective replacements for or enhancements of the tail rotor.

Names for the approaches were abundant: fantail, fan-in-fin, fenestron, ducted fan, fan-in-boom, and others.

Although the induced power is about the same, a ducted fan can be almost 30 percent smaller in diameter (or about half the total surface area) than the tail rotor it is replacing, due to aerodynamic efficiencies gained from the design of the fan and its enclosing shroud. It is also quieter than an exposed tail rotor.

The NOTAR (no tail rotor) system developed by Hughes Helicopters was the most successful design concept beyond placing a shroud around an otherwise conventional tail rotor. It involved a fatter, aerodynamically shaped boom, within which was a fan blowing air aft from the engine. The blown air exited the side of the helicopter and created additional sideward control forces by the tailboom's design.

The danger of ground resonance was just as invisible as the tail rotor was visible, and it made its presence known only when the machine was at the edge of destruction. The problem with ground resonance was that it was so difficult to visualize and comprehend. It had to do with the rotating mass of the main rotor blades acting on the fuselage mass and the stiffness of the landing gear. The rotation of the blades would set up a rocking motion in the aircraft that quickly became destructive and was almost impossible to stop once it began. Mathematical analyses finally got a handle on it, and when it was better understood, the engineers changed the way they designed the dynamic systems involved. Helicopters benefitted greatly from the experience of autogiros, which brought the problem to the forefront. Mathematical analysis showed the danger of interaction between helicopter dynamic systems and the ground itself via the landing gear.

Resolution of a large part of the ground resonance problem was accomplished through the introduction of dampers for rotor blades and landing gear. Even so, ground resonance damaged or destroyed tie-down test aircraft during development of the Sikorsky XR-4, R-5, and R-6, as well as

In order of importance from most to least, here are some of the rankings that helicopter historians place on various facets of helicopter development:

1. Cyclically controlled rotor
2. Invention of flapping hinges
3. Integration of the turbine engine
4. Demonstration of the Sikorsky VS-300
5. Production of the Sikorsky R-4
6. Aerodynamic theory of the rotor
7. Vibration control systems
8. Production of the first practical tandem-rotor helicopter, the Piasecki HRP
9. Electronic flight control and stability augmentation system
10. Development of the tiltrotor vertical/short takeoff and landing (V/STOL)
11. Hingeless/bearingless/elastomeric rotor hub system
12. Development of winged and wingless autogiro
13. Demonstration of Focke 61 lateral twin helicopter
14. Durable high-strength gear steels
15. Crashworthy structures, seating, and fuel systems
16. Unlimited-life composite rotor blades
17. Development and production of vectored-thrust Harrier V/STOL
18. First commercial helicopter licensing: the Bell 47
19. Development of see-saw pivoted two-blade rigid rotor
20. NOTAR and fantail anti-torque systems
21. Solution of ground resonance problem
22. Aerodynamically and structurally tailored cambered rotor blades
23. Digital and fly-by-wire/light flight control systems
24. Application of the lead-lag hinge
25. Integrated digital avionics systems
26. Demonstration of first vectored-thrust VTOL: the Bell Aero X-14
27. Development of modern helicopter simulation technology
28. Development and flight of the tilt-wing Vought XC-142 and Canadair CL-84
29. Development of aeroelastic scale-model rotor systems
30. Development of hydraulic control systems
31. Demonstration of the Flettner synchropter
32. Computerized 3-D databases, design methods, tooling, and manufacturing
33. Development of health and usage monitoring systems
34. Theory, analysis, and high-speed computational tools
35. Composite structures
36. Sensors
37. Distributed interactive simulation
38. Lightweight, air-cooled engine
39. Leonardo da Vinci concepts

the Hughes 269, Hughes XH-17, and the Piasecki H-21. The Soviet Union had similar engineering problems with the Yak-24.

One must learn to walk before learning to run, and this applied to early helicopter development as well.

The first helicopters capable of getting off the ground were considered successful if they merely did that and no more. Things like stability were secondary considerations.

This could not remain the case if the machine were to do useful work, however, and soon changes were made to airframes in an effort to correct excessive sensitivity in pitch and roll during hovering flight, along with pitch and yaw in forward flight. Eventually, electronic stability augmentation was brought to bear on the problem, which arose when pilots found that the smallest motion of the cyclic stick created high rates of pitch or roll.

Arthur Young's stabilizer bar was among the first solutions to the stability problem, followed by Stanley Hiller's "Rotormatic" variation using a similar principle to dampen pitch and roll. Other designers used main rotor blade devices such as tip weights, offset flapping hinges, and other devices. The effect of all of them was to reduce sensitivity of the main rotor system to control inputs.

By the 1950s, it was no longer considered adequate to apply mechanical solutions to stability, so electronic systems were developed that initially used high-speed gyros to measure the pitch and roll, then fed signals to the control system for damping. These approaches were supplemented by pilot-input signals that optimized the maneuvering responses, eventually resulting in electronic stability and control augmentation systems (SCAS). The next step was addition of radar altimeter systems and doppler ground-speed sensors so a helicopter could automatically hover at a fixed altitude over a given spot.

Surely, Juan de la Cierva would have been impressed.

The obvious question arises: why not add large stabilizing surfaces to helicopters just as the airplane designers used in the tail sections?

One explanation is that there are contradictory aerodynamic requirements for forward-flight performance and hover or near-hover performance by helicopters. When one regime is optimized, it degrades the other because airflow patterns change so dramatically during and after the transition. Horizontal stabilizers were initially put on the forward part of the tail boom to avoid the pitch disturbances during transition to forward flight. Later, designers tried variations such as T-tails, canted tails, stabilators, and other configurations.

Similar evolutions occurred with vertical stabilizers, which almost always required adjustments during development because of interactions with tail rotor airflow.

In addition to gyros that were eventually added to all axes of an aircraft's flight to improve both control and directional stability, sensors were incorporated to avoid too much of a good thing. Their function was to prevent excess control input from causing a catastrophe by limiting hard-over inputs to about 10 or 20 percent of full control travel.

Fly-by-wire stability control designs came into wide use during the 1980s and these sophisticated, computer-controlled systems had multiple sensors that allowed redundancy and other backup features, permitting high performance, reliability, and quick identification of defective parts.

What Euan Hooper called the last of the "Great Helicopter Problems" is familiar to anyone who has ever flown in one.

Vibration.

Hooper said, "It took Juan de la Cierva three years to find out why autogiros rolled over while going forward and to introduce the definitive solution in the form of a flapping hinge. It took about 20 years of struggling with inherent instability in hover before gyro stabilization was introduced to give hands-off stability. Fifty years later and the achievement of a 'jet smooth ride' for a new design is still an elusive goal."

Vibration levels for early rotorcraft, said Hooper, were "annoying but tolerable" because of the short duration of most flights and because pilots were often busy with other concerns.

Vibration was far more than an annoyance, however, and under the right (or wrong) circumstances could destroy the aircraft.

First the designers and manufacturers tried mechanical solutions by shifting parts of the structure around and adding mechanisms to reduce vibration. As with other engineering challenges, often the fix was found only after numerous modifications to the design both before and after flight testing had begun. From a certain historical perspective, this trial-and-error process had its humorous aspects.

"Early in 1939, then-engineering manager of the Vought Sikorsky Division of the United Aircraft Corporation [Igor] Sikorsky had on his drawing board the plans for an experimental rotary-wing framework, which by September of the same year had become an aircraft ready for its take-off trials.

"Nicknamed 'Igor's Nightmare' because of the number of changes it underwent during the development stage, it finally succeeded in making its first free flight in May 1940. It could climb vertically, hover, fly sideways, and even backwards, but it could not fly forward. Questioned about this, Sikorsky had a stock reply: 'That is one of the minor engineering problems we have not yet solved.' Later, when reminded about this, Sikorsky disarmingly confessed: 'The helicopter appeared so reluctant to fly forward that we even considered turning the pilot's seat around and letting it fly backward,'" according to Hooper.

On April 15, 1941, the VS-300 (V for Vought, S for Sikorsky) finally was persuaded to fly forward. It even broke the U.S. helicopter endurance record with a flight longer than an hour and five minutes.

But it was tough going for the people who had to produce results good enough to impress their peers. Sikorsky test pilot Les Morris described those early days by citing the mixed reaction of the crew chief, Adoph Plenefisch, as the hovering VS-300 moved a few feet off the ground above the ramp at the company's facility: "If you could only have seen us! Every time they would start down the ramp, we would run after them. Then they'd stop and back up and we'd run the other way. Back and forth, back and forth, until our tongues were hanging out a mile. But we could see that she was flying better every day. So we didn't care. We were proud of her. You should have heard the ragging we took, though. The other fellows in the shop couldn't see the purpose in it all."

Bell's chief engineer Bart Kelley explained why this apparently uninformed groping is so often the case in practical development of a new technology: "We made the helicopter so quickly, because we weren't too sure how to make it. It took longer when you knew all the things that had to be done right."

On June 26, 1943 — about 10 weeks after the April 11 first flight of Frank Piasecki's PV-2 — Floyd Carlson took the new Model 30 prototype on its first untethered flight through the meadow behind the Bell plant at Gardenville, New York. It flew quite well during its early flights until it got up to about 25 mph, when a horrendous vibration set in.

Carlson suggested they put a brace on the main rotor. They put a brace on the main rotor and when it worked they called the Carlson-inspired device a Swedish yoke.

It was Bart Kelley who devised and patented the flexible pylon as a vibration isolator in 1945 and the device was used on every Bell 47 and UH-1 helicopter. Then came the focal pylon invented in 1963 by Balke, Drees, and Lichten, and that was used on Bell 206A JetRanger models. Later, Drees came up with the nodal beam in 1974. It found a home on the Bell 206L LongRanger and other models.

All helicopter manufacturers have invented vibration isolation systems, but only Bell, Hiller, and Eurocopter (formerly Aerospatiale) have them as a standard part of production machines.

Makers of helicopters have used vibration absorbers and pendulums to reduce vibration, as well as more innovative solutions. In the Sikorsky S-61N, a spring-mass vibration absorber was installed under every seat. The

UH-2 used the battery as an active mass to control vibration. Kamov uses pendulums on the KA-27 lower rotor, while Mil and Sikorsky have used bifilars. Pendulums will also be used on production of the V-22 Osprey tiltrotor.

Many approaches have been tried to reduce or eliminate vibration, but none has been totally successful. Higher harmonic control (HHC) has been around as a theory for nearly the entire history of the helicopter but has yet to reach production levels. HHC ideally would feed computer-generated high-frequency signals into the rotor head, not only to reduce vibration but also to cut noise, structural loads, and required rotor power. HHC is one of those technology innovations that looks good on paper, but its problems prevent it from moving into a production mode.

Westland Helicopters has devised a variant of HHC called active control of structural response (ACSR). The results on an EH-101 testbed are so promising that it will be built into production models.

One approach to vibration reduction, especially for larger helicopters, is to increase the number of main rotor blades. The Sikorsky CH-53A mounted six main rotor blades and used no vibration reduction devices, neither does the seven-blade CH-53E or the eight-blade Mil-26. This approach, of course, is not feasible for smaller helicopters, but it should be noted that even Igor Sikorsky found a relevant difference in the number of blades on his first testbed, the VS-300.

Sikorsky also tested a two-bladed, in place of a three-bladed, rotor, and found that the simpler rotor mechanism produced performances comparable with those of the more complex one. However, Sikorsky did not pursue this line because he considered the vibrations caused by the two-bladed rotor to be excessive.

Subsets of all the problems facing helicopter inventors and designers are almost countless. They range from different methods for rotor blade retention to various improvements in flight control systems, avionics, and sensors.

The training of those who fly and maintain the machine has been vastly improved through the years by better simulation technology. Student pilots climbing into a real helicopter now are far better trained for their first flight than when the machine made its entry onto the commercial helicopter stage.

The rationale for all new technical developments is not to intellectually benefit scientists and engineers, but to produce useful work while keeping people safe. For obvious reasons, a dangerous machine does less work than a productive, safe machine.

As machines become more capable, of course, they are expected to meet more challenges. From the original fair weather machine that dared venture into the air only in full daylight over flat land, the industry began taking the helicopter into storms at sea to supply offshore rigs, at night into mountains on medevac missions, and into a tangle of wires, poles, and towering construction equipment on the job.

Each improvement in the machine prompted operators to say to the manufacturers: We want more. The reason was clear: Customers were saying the same thing to operators.

Improved avionics, better human engineering of the man-machine interface, stronger but lighter structures, better training due to the availability of computer-driven simulators, and many other considerations went into safer helicopters. Onboard diagnostics made problem analysis and solution practical, and flight data recorders became a realistic option for the first time.

What are not realistic options for the helicopter are the ejection seat and the parachute.

In the absence of those two common airplane features, the best option for helicopter designers has been to assume that accidents cannot be totally eliminated, and that the structure must therefore survive a crash with the occupants remaining inside.

Five criteria were established to make the machine safer:

- structural crashworthiness
- occupant, component, and cargo retention
- occupant strike hazards
- occupant deceleration
- post-crash hazards

New ways to avoid wire strikes in low-level flight, elimination of post-crash fires, and solutions to other hazards have steadily been developed to make flight safer. Fires after a crash were once a foregone conclusion in many cases, but "virtual elimination" of such fires has been achieved for new-design helicopters.

And so it has gone in the technology, safety, and productivity evolution of the helicopter for more than half a century, with vital commercial operator input to the manufacturers. From the earliest work done by pioneering entrepreneurs — such as New England Helicopter Service, Helicopter Air Transport, Central Aircraft, and others who saw the opportunity — the feedback from helipad to drawing board has been extremely helpful to designers.

Mainstream helicopter developments, however, have always been supplemented by another breed of entrepreneur: the product improvers — those ingenious inventors and engineers who see that the original helicopter designers missed an opportunity and perhaps discover a market for a better version. Their contribution to the evolution of the final product is too great to assess.

From the first verbal suggestions on agricultural spray attachments for the earliest Bell 47 model by Herman Poulin to the latest electronic devices for stabilization monitoring and navigation, aftermarket manufacturers have been extremely responsive to the needs of commercial operators.

And the machine gets better, often at the initiative of those who operate it in the private sector.

Erickson Air-Crane Co., the operator whose Sikorsky S-64 took the Statue of Freedom for a ride, began building the heavy-lift helicopter itself from scratch in 1997, after buying the rights from Sikorsky. The Central Point, Oregon, firm manufactured the first "new" S-64 Air-Crane (as renamed by Erickson) in more than 20 years. Why? Because there were no more SkyCranes around and they were needed. Erickson expects to build two of the giants each year.

What machine will commercial operators be adding to their fleets in the next 50 years? Will it indeed be the fifth step in man's search for a way to fly like a bird?

As Franklin Harris points out in his description of the five steps to bird-like flight: "The fifth step to a high-speed aircraft with true vertical takeoff and landing capability began shortly after successful helicopters were produced in the late 1930s and early 1940s. During the 1950s, 1960s, and 1970s, private industry and various world governments funded development of more than 60 different experimental high-speed VTOL configurations."

The rationale for all new technical developments is not to intellectually benefit scientists and engineers, but to produce useful work while keeping people safe.

Harris traces the history of the VTOL branch of the vertical lift family tree, concluding that tiltrotors are the wave of the future for commercial operators: "Growth in tiltrotor configuration technology over the next several decades should parallel that experienced by conventional fixed-wing airplanes as they matured. There is no fundamental size restriction, so 100- to 200-passenger civil tiltrotors can be expected to become a reality.

"Similarly, operational ranges of 1,000 to 2,000 miles at cruise altitudes from 25,000 to 40,000 feet are feasible. Cruise speed can be expected to exceed at least 0.6 and perhaps reach 0.7 Mach number (500 mph), given today's propulsion knowledge.

"Essentially, the tiltrotor has the capability to replace current commuter airplanes in the foreseeable future."

The next 50 years of development of this machine we now call a helicopter should be very interesting indeed.

As a flight attendant on the first commercial tiltrotor flight to a far-distant work site or branch factory is certain to say, "Please fasten your seat belts."

Bell-Boeing 609, the world's first commercial
tiltrotor aircraft, first flight scheduled for 1999

Charlie Kaman piloting a K-125 early experimental helicopter.

THE FORTIES & FIFTIES

*"History is
the record of
an encounter
between
character and
circumstances."*

Donald Creighton,
Canadian Historian (1902-1979)

Bell 47

Histry is not made by machines — history is made by people using machines; but first there must be a suitable challenge.

The helicopter was almost a cliché in the postwar years: a solution looking for a problem. The challenge was to find problems matching the helicopter's capabilities.

In the days following World War II, barely six years after the initial flight of Igor Sikorsky's first controllable helicopter, there were no precedents or guidelines for using the rudimentary machines.

There were more entrepreneurs searching for commercial applications of helicopters than many realize, however, and not all were in America. Those trying to employ the helicopter were so numerous and scattered that it is difficult to say who was first.

In England, Dr. W.E. Ripper, an entomologist with Fisons Pest Control Ltd., installed agricultural spraying equipment on a Sikorsky HSN-1 in September 1945.

In Rhode Island, Leon Plympton — in a remarkably farsighted demonstration of faith in a new machine that had not yet been certificated for civil use — incorporated New England Helicopter Service in January 1946 and bought a surplus Sikorsky R-6 from the army in March. It was the world's first privately owned helicopter, and Plympton was determined to use it effectively.

In Yakima, Washington, Herman Poulin and his associates at Central Aircraft Co. worked with Bell Helicopter and its experimental NX model to find the best way to spray crops. Already experienced with airplanes, they conducted commercial agricultural operations in early 1947 with a Bell 47B-3, trying to work out the best way of using it.

By early 1946, a company called Helicopter Air Transport, based in Camden, New Jersey, had been in business long enough that it was already the subject of aviation magazine articles describing its success.

In 1945 and 1946, the U.S. Department of Agriculture had one of its scientists, J.S. Yuill, working on a system to spray mosquitoes from a Sikorsky HSN-1, the same model used in England at about the same time. Earlier efforts in Connecticut by entomologist S.F. Potts had used an autogiro in 1938 to spray forests for insects.

And so it was that civilian helicopters first were applied to the problem of food production for a world that had had its social fabric torn severely by the war. Individuals were eager to join the excitement and find practical uses for this new technology.

People who asked about it after the war were sometimes surprised that a helicopter cost more than an automobile of similar size. In fact, one of the early design discussions at Bell Aircraft centered around the extent to which the Model 47 should look like an automobile. Larry Bell thought it would help sales; others disagreed. Eventually the automobile styling faded away after Arthur Young complained that management wanted the helicopter to "look like a Buick." The commercial helicopter industry began so soon after World War II that "Flying" magazine reported "the smallest commercial helicopter costs five times as much as the biggest black market automobile."

Even without knowing the year, that language gives away the era and the mindset.

The mechanized mindset of America was (and remains) betrayed by the fact that civilian gasoline and engine oil were removed from rationing lists within 24 hours after the announcement of Japan's surrender in August 1945, but it was two-and-a-half months before a civilian could buy a pair of shoes without a ration card.

Sikorsky S-51

The cost of this unfamiliar flying machine intimidated some, but not all. Many postwar entrepreneurs knew that capabilities and cost are inextricably linked and saw the helicopter as a key to their future economic independence.

The very newness of helicopter economics was one of the major obstacles of the new entrepreneurs, and aviation magazines of the time report that most of the businesses using helicopters failed.

One can almost hear the first helicopter customer asking the first helicopter salesman: "You mean it costs $50 to operate for only one day?" And the reply: "No, I mean one hour."

If nothing else, the persistence of these entrepreneurs bears testament to the personal vision that early helicopters prompted, and that made ex-GIs try their luck with the new machine.

When the great aircraft designer Kelly Johnson was interviewed by CBS's "60 Minutes" near the end of his long aviation career in 1982, he was inevitably asked about the future. What exotic, high-flying, hyperspeed aircraft would we see someday? What kind of aircraft would be most important to us?

Johnson smiled ever so slightly and said: Crop-dusters.

Cropdusters?

We need aircraft, Kelly continued, that are far more efficient for increasing food production than anything we have now . . . food production which will help feed the world's growing population.

It was hardly the space-age, right-stuff hypersonic answer that CBS expected, but it reflected instinctive awareness by aviation's movers-and-shakers about the real problems ahead. High altitude and high speed are exciting, but excitement does not inherently solve problems.

Helicopters help solve problems.

Perhaps without intentionally doing so, Kelly Johnson had closed a circle.

Having seen so much world hunger during the war, it was logical that the first application that ex-GIs envisioned for commercial helicopters was in agriculture. Wartime duties of reconnaissance and courier work hardly touched civilian needs, although medevac was clearly a common area of opportunity.

Elmer "Tug" Gustafson had worked for Pratt & Whitney at the East Hartford, Connecticut, maintenance base in the 1930s, and he saw Igor Sikorsky's flights in the VS-300. Gustafson became a salesman for both Bell and Sikorsky at various times and described the early search for a market during a recorded interview:

"The problem came down to the point: 'Where is the market for helicopters? What industry needs it every day?' Finally, we looked at oil, we looked at agriculture, and we looked at various industries. We finally came to the conclusion that the biggest industry in the world is feeding people."

Confidence is a fickle partner. Gustafson, then a new Bell Helicopter salesman, described a few of his Bell 47 sales demonstrations. The first was in 1947 to potato farmers in New York State:

Leon Plympton – One of the First of the Early Birds

In late 1945, Leon Plympton could see the future of the helicopter coming over the horizon, so in January 1946 he incorporated New England Helicopter Service (NEHS) in Rhode Island. That marked his claim to being the oldest helicopter-operating company in the world.

In March 1946 he bought a U.S. Army surplus Sikorsky R-6 helicopter, the first privately owned helicopter in the world. In January 1947 Plympton bought a Bell 47, even before it was officially certificated as the world's first commercial helicopter, and simultaneously opened the world's first commercial helicopter school.

In March 1947 — the same month Bell got its Model 47 certificated — NEHS was awarded an air taxi certificate by the Rhode Island Public Utilities Commission. In June Plympton received approval from the Veterans Administration for helicopter pilot training under the G.I. Bill, which he conducted throughout 1948.

School regulations indicate that Plympton and Chief Instructor Vin Colicci ran a tight ship.

In 1949, Plympton bought Air Crop Dusting Service Inc. and set up a base at Bradley Field, Connecticut, for agricultural operations. The following year he bought the assets of Eastern States Helicopter Service, Inc., which had charter and agricultural accounts.

His company set a record in 1951 for the most hours flown by two helicopters in flight training, averaging 200 hours per aircraft per month for three consecutive months.

Plympton bought New York Helicopter Corp. in February 1952 and in June won a half-million-dollar army contract for mapping services.

Also in June 1952 he established Canadian Helicopter, Inc.

Throughout 1953 his companies operated in Canada, Central and South America, and throughout the northeastern U.S. as far west as Chicago.

In 1954, the Plympton companies expanded agricultural operations by establishing a base in Gettysburg, Pennsylvania, and buying the assets of Helicopter Service, Inc., of Teterboro, New Jersey.

In 1956, Plympton moved his operations to Lakeland, Florida, changing the name of the parent firm to Helicopters International. By this time, the family of companies and affiliates included:

    Helicopter Agricultural Service — Gettysburg, Pennsylvania;
    Helicopter Sales and Service — New York and Miami, Florida;
    International Helicopters Inc. — Washington, D.C.;
    Dominion Helicopters Ltd. — Toronto, Ontario, Canada; and
    Helicopteros Latino-Americanos, S.A. — St. Petersburg, Florida.

1940 - One gallon of gasoline sells for 18¢ • Cincinnati wins World Series against Detroit •

"I felt so confident that I hired a competitor with his Stearman to demonstrate. . . . The Stearman came in, buzzed the field, and laid his dust down . . . I walked out with my megaphone and pointed out the corners he had missed, and so on.

"I forget my pilot's name, but he was a young Irish boy from Boston. I harped on him because the Polish entomologist I had hired had harped on me: be sure you get low, low, as low as you can and as slow as you can. We never practiced this . . . there was no rehearsal. There was nothing to practice, really, all you had to do was go low and slow.

"I said to the crowd through the megaphone: 'Now watch our helicopter.' So my pilot got up and the first thing he decided to do was show how the dust would boil up. As he's going across the field he was really right down on top of the potato crop, and his speed is maybe five miles an hour. There was about a 60-foot-wide swath of dust following him.

"I noticed as he got about halfway across the field, that every once in a while something dark would come floating out the top of the dust cloud. I'd say to myself: 'What the hell was that?'

"When we finished the demonstration and the dust had settled, we discovered we had uprooted every potato plant in a 60-foot-wide path across the entire field and what I had seen flying all over were potatoes. That was the end of the demonstration."

Gustafson took his Bell 47 and crew to Florida to sell the citrus growers, as well as truck farms that sent vegetables up north. On the way, Gustafson decided to land in Foley, Alabama, to demonstrate the helicopter's capabilities. The Gladiolus Growers Association got 500 people to come to a demonstration.

"This time we had agreed that we would fly much higher and much faster. I was absolutely certain that we would never uproot a gladiolus. But damned if we didn't put on the demonstration and we uprooted all the gladiolus plants. So I said to hell with this . . . I want nothing to do with agriculture ever, ever, ever again."

Despite that vow, Gustafson soldiered on, getting into more and more agricultural aviation experiments because the entire concept was so new that no one understood anything about techniques or results. It was all trial and error, and sometimes it seemed the errors were winning. With more successful techniques to apply chemicals from helicopters, however, the way to success was increasingly clear.

On March 16, 1942, Charles "Les" Morris, Sikorsky's chief test and demonstration pilot, had been issued the first commercial helicopter pilot's license by the Civil Aeronautics Administration (CAA) — predecessor to today's Federal Aviation Administration (FAA). Almost all aviation activity at the time was devoted to military needs, but by late 1945 that rapidly changed.

On October 5, 1947, in the first White House address ever carried on television, President Harry S Truman asked Americans to refrain from eating meat on Tuesdays and poultry on Thursdays so the U.S. could stockpile grain for starving people in Europe.

Early commercial helicopter pioneers were well ahead of the president's appeal. The first commercial helicopter model — a Bell 47 — was certificated on March 8, 1946, less than a year after the war ended. Almost at once, Bell began figuring out ways to hang hoppers and spray tubes on it. The Bell 47 was the first helicopter licensed for agricultural work.

On April 17, 1947, the Sikorsky S-51 received commercial helicopter certification and soon Sikorsky sold its first helicopter for commercial operations, which also turned out to be agriculture work. No matter where one looked around a new Bell helicopter, there was test and demonstration pilot Joe Mashman.

No matter where one looked around a new Sikorsky helicopter, there was test and demonstration pilot Les Morris.

With those two and others showing the way, the machine required the same ingredients as any other risky business: capital, know-how, equipment, and not-so-ordinary luck.

LIFE

SIKORSKY'S HELICOPTER

JUNE 21, 1943 **10** CENT

YEARLY SUBSCRIPTION $4.5

Most of all, it required transition of the dream into a hard-nosed business stance. Without that, the dream died. It was a bit like show business, where a great deal of money and hard work went into something that could be a smashing success or a one-night disaster.

On May 16, 1946, the musical "Annie Get Your Gun" opened on Broadway with Irving Berlin's songs and starred Ethel Merman.

New England Helicopter Service, Inc., based at the State Airport in Hillsgrove, Rhode Island, under the presidency of Leon W. Plympton, had been incorporated in January 1946. NEHS billed itself as the "Oldest Helicopter Service in the World."

In May 1946, Helicopter Air Transport (HAT) began operations as the Bell 47 was certificated for commercial service. HAT was among the early commercial helicopter operators and was near the head of the line for the new production units. Photos of Bell's first Model 47B production units rolling off an assembly line show them in HAT markings. According to Bell production records that covered test aircraft and others, HAT got units 5, 15, and 16 from the Bell plant.

NEHS received its first Bell 47 in January 1947 and opened the world's first commercial helicopter school at the same time. By June, the company had Veterans Administration approval for G.I. Bill flight training and eventually NEHS advertised that it had "More Helicopter Pilots Graduated Than All Other Schools Combined."

In other countries immediately after the war, corporations such as British European Airways (BEA) formed a helicopter unit to explore the possibilities of the new machine, and that unit eventually became British Airways Helicopters, now British International Helicopters. Individuals such as Carl Agar in Canada and Lennart Ostermans in Sweden got their first experience wearing many hats in order to start commercial operations.

On February 20, 1947, Lennart Ostermans flew the first helicopter in Sweden as his new firm, Ostermans Aero AB, became the first commercial helicopter operator outside the U.S. Even in 1946, Ostermans had seen the helicopter's potential and ordered three Bell 47B models. Very soon, the new machine was flying medical evacuation missions into the winter northland and finally breaking the total isolation of fishermen and farmers near the Arctic Circle. The Bell 47B provided mail, medicine, supplies, lighthouse maintenance, construction materials, and other necessities during seasons when nothing else could move.

Ostermans was not content with merely operating the helicopter; he also became a trainer, distributor, and maintenance facility for clients throughout Scandinavia. When the Norwegian Air Force got its first helicopter in 1952, Ostermans provided the training.

Among so many simultaneous entrepreneurs, as is always the case, the inexorable laws of economics decreed that some outlasted others.

BEA's offspring are still with us, as are Bristow, Ostermans, and Okanagan, but HAT left the scene in the late 1940s. Leon Plympton of NEHS acquired other firms, affiliated with international operators, and eventually sold the company to Vin Colicci, a long-time associate. Rick Helicopters, the largest commercial operator in the world for about five years, was overtaken by Petroleum Helicopters, Inc. (PHI) and Okanagan, then sold off its assets and finally was liquidated in 1985.

The "secret" ingredients used by successful pioneers were no more mysterious than sound business judgment, adequate capital, and a thorough knowledge of the machine that provided the service. Good fortune is still required for success, but the basics never change.

Did You Know?

45

Sometimes the spice in history is mystery.

The story goes that a Bell 47B was bought in March 1947 by Arizona Helicopter Service, which contracted with some people who wanted to go into the Superstition Mountains. According to the account, they were dropped off near the Lost Dutchman gold mine, with arrangements to be picked up a few days later.

When the helicopter returned for the pickup, the people had disappeared and were never seen again.

Civilian gasoline and engine oil were removed from the rationing lists within 24-hours after Japan surrendered in August 1945.

For The Record — 1948 - Velcro invented in Switzerland • State of Israel formed •

A good example is the initially successful Helicopter Air Transport. The Philadelphia businessmen who provided the capital for HAT were non-aviation types who knew a promising idea when they saw one. HAT also had the good sense to hire people who knew what they were doing. Norman Edgar, a former British Army captain who set up an aircraft dealership at Bristol, England, in 1919, was executive vice president of HAT, while its chief pilot, Frank Cashman, had been a U.S. Army Air Corps helicopter instructor at Wright Field, Ohio. HAT's sales manager was Peter Wright, Sr.

The commercial helicopter industry has always been a sling-load of contradictions, and this was borne out by early aviation magazine descriptions of HAT operations. While reporting that a single small helicopter cost more than the largest blackmarket automobile, the same aviation magazine reported that HAT, the largest fixed-base helicopter operator in the country, was started "with a few thousand dollars capital." The monetary amount was the same in both references, but the magazine's phraseology implied considerable contrast, making the same amount seem huge on one hand and small on the other.

HAT began operating S-51 helicopters from Central Airport in Camden, New Jersey, in May 1946. Its first flight was a charter from Bridgeport, Connecticut (most likely the Sikorsky plant there), to New York City. By the end of its first year of operations, it had flown 2,000 passengers and increased its capital to half a million dollars.

The abundance of work was illustrated by the fact that HAT acquired nine helicopters in its first year of operation. Four of these were the four-place S-51s and five were Bell 47 models with two seats. Other models were on order, and HAT was impatiently waiting their delivery. The company was also hoping to order a 10-passenger Piasecki Model HRP-2 when that became available. (Piasecki had elected to focus on military business, and won a navy contract in 1944 for large, tandem-twin-rotor HRP-1 models.) HAT also had modified a military surplus Platt Le Page lateral-twin-rotor helicopter for agricultural and utility work.

By the end of the 1940s, the general makeup of the helicopter industry was such that Bell and Hiller produced small helicopters while Sikorsky and Piasecki concentrated their efforts on larger models. This gave a balanced and competitive, if small, industry.

"Bell Helicopters really started the commercial helicopter activity in the world," said Dr. Carrol Voss, one of the industry's pioneers and an entomologist who had gotten his start with Leon Plympton at New England Helicopter Service. "Sikorsky had the first production machine for the military, [the] R-4, but went for the commercial market after Bell, as well as Stanley Hiller."

April 1947 was a month of beginnings and endings.

On April 11, Jackie Robinson made his major-league baseball debut, playing in an exhibition between the Brooklyn Dodgers and the New York Yankees.

On April 17, the Sikorsky S-51 received its commercial helicopter certification.

April 27 was "Babe Ruth Day" at Yankee Stadium as baseball fans honored the ailing star.

The S-51 was the first Sikorsky model certificated for commercial use, more than a year behind the Bell 47. The S-51 was developed from the military H-5 design, having four seats in anticipation of commuter, corporate, and sightseeing roles.

In 1946 dollars, a Sikorsky S-51 cost about $70,000 and a Bell 47B-3 about $25,000. The S-51 was described as carrying a 610-pound cargo load, and the Bell 47 about 240 pounds.

High overall costs relative to light airplanes caused HAT, for example, to set charges of $125/hour for the

1948 - NBC introduces "The Texaco Star Theater" starring "Uncle Miltie," Milton Berle •

S-51 and $75/hour for the Bell 47. The per-mile-one-way passenger rate was $0.35, which was doubled if there was no revenue return flight. HAT's profit at the time was described by "Flying" magazine as "meager."

For most flights, the passengers were fill-in revenue while the aircraft was doing a different kind of job. HAT was very aware of its ability to generate favorable publicity, but it carried sightseers or others only to gain maximum utilization during more mundane work. Publicity was always the icing on the cake.

Within a few months of its being founded, the pioneering operator was hired to provide a crowd-pleasing attraction by flying a Sikorsky S-51 into Washington, D.C.'s Griffith Stadium to promote a football game.

Indeed, advertising jobs, publicity "stunts" such as Santa Claus flights, and other high-profile operations were HAT's revenue mainstay during those early days when more mundane tasks for the helicopter were still being developed. Politicians particularly loved the helicopter for its crowd-attracting qualities, and voter psychology linked helicopters with a politician who was obviously farsighted. News value was a major plus.

Two ranking New Jersey political leaders — Senator H. Alexander Smith and Governor Alfred E. Driscoll — used the first-generation civil helicopters of Camden-based HAT for their 1946 campaigns. They skipped across the Garden State from Cape May to Princeton, Wildwood, Clarksboro, and other towns.

Both candidates won their election races. Whether or not he made the connection between the helicopter and winning, Lyndon B. Johnson was to be another early user of helicopters on the political campaign trail in 1948.

In 1946, a Hartford, Connecticut, department store chartered a HAT helicopter to deliver gifts marking the store's one hundredth anniversary to the mayors of 66 nearby towns. There is little doubt the gift made an impression.

While high-profile one-of-a-kind flights like these and the occasional air mail or high-priority freight trip got headlines in the early days, HAT's bread-and-butter work was in agricultural aviation, and for this the company used its Bell 47B-3 fleet with great effect. Delivering Santa Claus to a temporary heliport atop a department store roof won't carry an operator for an entire year, even when — as it did in 1946 — HAT dropped off at least six Santa Clauses.

As the familiar expression reminds us, the more things change, the more they remain the same.

One of the earliest uses of helicopters was to fly corporate executives from headquarters to outlying facilities. To this day it remains a mainstay of helicopter applications. Corporations among the first to avail themselves of helicopter convenience included Weirton Steel Company, Hercules Powder Company, Campbell Soup, RCA, and many others who found the convenience well worth the price.

To a great extent, pointed out "Flying" magazine, the helicopter operator of 1946 was in the same position as an airplane operator of 1920 immediately after World War I: the machine was a military variant that generated great curiosity, rapid development, and ad lib applications for whatever task happened to come along.

Nor were there enough pilots for the new aircraft. There had never been civil helicopters to attract civil pilots, and not all of the few military helicopter pilots wanted to do the same in civilian life. HAT therefore opened its own helicopter flight training school, with former major Frank Cashman as chief instructor. Class sizes were kept to 25 students. Each of the student pilots was required to have 500 hours solo in conventional airplanes to be eligible to train in the S-51, and at least 200 airplane hours to transition to the Bell 47. They also were required to have a commercial rating for the S-51, but could be qualified with only a private rating for the Bell 47.

Aviation writers themselves had not shifted gears to accommodate the new aircraft, referring to HAT's helicopter fleet as "planes."

After paying a $2,000 tuition fee, student pilots got 20 hours total dual and solo time in the S-51 before being rated. A $1,500 tuition fee for the Bell 47 paid for 20 hours of ground instruction and 25 dual and solo flight hours. A transition course from the Bell 47 to the S-51 cost $2,300.

HAT informed prospective students that it had "many hundred applications in hand" for the flight training and advised them not to delay applying for class slots.

Along with its pilot training course, the obviously progressive HAT management opened a helicopter mechanics school, with all HAT courses being certified by the CAA and the Veterans Administration under the G.I. Bill. HAT got students from all over the U.S., as well as France, whose government sent three Air Ministry pilots to HAT for training.

One of the pioneering pilots was Ann Shaw Carter, a former Women Air Force Service Pilot (WASP) during World War II who checked out in a Bell 47 in June 1947. She was the first woman commercial helicopter pilot in the U.S. and flew charters for Metropolitan Aviation Corp. in New York City for one of the earliest commercial services.

The appeal of helicopters for agricultural applications had several aspects, including the fact that the main-rotor downwash would drive pesticides and other chemicals into the foliage of plants rather than let them settle on the top layer. The estimated speed of the downwash was 25 mph, and the forward speed of the helicopter could be anywhere between zero and 90 mph, so both features allowed more precise application and tighter turns in confined areas. (Tug Gustafson learned the hard way in a potato field that a lot of downwash was too much of a good thing.)

*Bell 47 flown by Carrol "Doc" Voss
on agricultural application.*

About 150 acres could be treated by one Bell 47B-3 in an hour. Of that hour the helicopter was airborne for 42 minutes and refueled from trucks parked on the farmer's property. HAT said at the time that a comparable figure for agricultural airplanes was 17 minutes flight time for each hour because the airplane had to go to the nearest airport to refuel and lost more time in transit, on approaches, and making turns.

Not surprisingly, therefore, some of HAT's earliest long-term contracts called for the company to follow the planting seasons to treat potato, corn, and tomato crops. Other contracts covered the spraying of mosquito breeding areas and other pest control, while HAT also had its cap set for contracts to spot and control forest fires.

The early HAT applications of helicopters are with the industry today. In addition to agricultural, corporate, and high-priority cargo, the company pioneered powerline and pipeline patrol, aerial photography, and similar tasks.

Past success does not guarantee future success, however, and HAT eventually went into bankruptcy, with Bell Helicopter repossessing some of its equipment. Two of those helicopters were bought from Bell by Rick Helicopters.

Bell Helicopters received a visit in late 1946 at its relatively new Texas plant from Herman Poulin, a Yakima, Washington, undertaker who had aviation as a favorite sideline. Poulin's firm, Central Aircraft Company, had been formed by Poulin, A.L.

Baxter, and Joe Scaman in Yakima, Washington, to spray crops. The company ordered four Bell 47B-3 heli-copters for delivery in early 1947, and got units 11, 12, 26, and 27. There were now helicopters aggressively working on agricultural problems on both coasts.

Near Poulin's operation in the Yakima Valley, a young cropdusting pilot got out of a Stearman and became interested in the helicopter. His name was Carl Brady.

"I told them that I'd continue cropdusting for them in the Stearman if they'd sell me a course in the helicopter, which was $1,500 for 20 hours, and hire me the first time they had an opening.

An experimental Bell model 42 in 1944.

"They only had one pilot flying it at that time. I started flying and got my heli-copter license on July 4, 1947."

Central Aircraft was one of those early commercial helicopter operators that just seemed to fade away after pioneering a new industry.

"I don't know what happened to them. I left them that same year. Two other fellows and myself formed Economy Pest Control. We lease-purchased a couple of helicopters from two farmers in Walla Walla who had bought them. They were the B3 models for cropdusting and they didn't work out for the farmers. We began cropdusting with those in 1948, then I brought one of Central's helicopters to Alaska in 1948. I had it leased and I operated for the U.S. Geological Survey mapping. It wasn't all that much fun because the [47B-3] had wheels that castered on the front . . . no brakes . . . it was pretty tough landing on tundra or rocky mountain tops. It had an open cockpit . . . colder than hell when it was raining or cold — which it is in southeast Alaska quite a bit," said Brady.

Meanwhile, back in sunny California, Armstrong-Flint began operations with Bell 47 production units 20 and 21. The helicopters were used for movie work, putting crosses on steeples, fire fighting, external loads, and other innovative work. Knute Flint was the pilot who teamed up with a banker and made the venture work.

The first newspaper in the U.S. to use helicopters in newsgathering was the "Oregon Journal," which bought Bell 47, number 25 in March 1947, and had it flown by pilot Joe Stein. The paper nicknamed its aircraft "Dragonfly."

New ventures were getting under way in other fields at the same time.

On November 5, 1946, a gawky young navy veteran, Massachusetts Democrat John F. Kennedy, was elected to the U.S. House of Representatives for his first term.

At the National Aircraft Show in Cleveland in mid-November, about 163,000 people saw — for many of them — their first helicopter. Bell had put six of its models on display there: five Model 47s and the Model 42, a design that had a short life. Three of the Model 47s were flying demonstrations from a ramp adjacent to the exhibit hall. The two remaining Model 47s and the Model 42 were inside on static display.

The 92 flights carried 412 passengers from the exhibit hall to the downtown city hall and back (and some to Niagara Falls), as well as 5,112 pieces of mail from the airport to the roof of the main post office. Despite poor weather, demonstration landings were made at the Rainbow Hospital for Crippled Children and other facilities. It was a tour de force of what helicopters could do, just eight months after the first commercial helicopter had been certificated.

On December 19, 1946, war broke out in Indochina as troops under Ho Chi Minh launched widespread attacks against the colonial French. Ho had tried to get the U.S. to honor its anti-colonialist rhetoric and ally itself with him against the French, but the U.S. felt too strong a wartime bond with France to comply. Eventually, as millions of television watchers were to learn, it would be the greatest helicopter war in history.

But the late-1940s era of the commercial helicopter was not yet clouded by another war, except against far more ancient enemies of the insect world.

Argentina, having seen the benefits of the machine, ordered 11 Bell 47B-3 open-cockpit models and two Bell 47Bs with enclosed cabins. The 11 spray models were to combat locusts that caused huge crop losses annually. A single swarm of locusts was measured at 33 miles long during the campaign.

A Bell 47D on floats.

The efforts of the early helicopter operators solidified the helicopter's reputation for being able to do jobs no other aircraft could touch.

With them to train new pilots went Joe Mashman and Cloyce "Tip" Tippett, along with Wes Moore, Don Jergens, Len Lavassor, Elton Smith, D.F. McDowell, Hal Symes, Harlan Hosler, and Harry Windes.

The result? A letter from the government of Argentina to Tip Tippett after just two weeks:

"This is the first time the locust has been effectively stopped in Argentina."

by Elfan ap Rees

At the end of World War II, when Europe's airlines were still in chaos and trying to rebuild routes and business, the British government moved ahead with the development of two nationalized airlines: BOAC (British Overseas Airways Corporation) for the long-haul routes and BEA (British European Airways) for the domestic and West European business.

Early on, BEA determined that helicopters might play a role in the European passenger-carrying business. In mid-1947, pushed by BEA's Chief of Research and Long Term Development N.E. Rowe, the Board placed an order for two Bell 47B-3 and three Sikorsky S-51 helicopters at a total cost of £53,750 ($87,612).

At the same time, staff was recruited for a BEA Experimental Helicopter Unit, under the direction of Wing Commander RAC "Reggie" Brie, to be initially based at Yeovil in Somerset, England. Brie had been associated with helicopter development since the beginning of the 1940s as the British defense ministry representative in Washington. Prior to that, he had built up considerable rotary-wing experience with the Cierva Autogiro Co.

Supporting Brie in this fresh pioneering operation were several early ex-military helicopter pilots, including Eric Corbin, Gerald Ford, John Fay, and one John "Jock" Cameron, who had learned to fly Sikorsky R-4s with the Royal Air Force Anti-Submarine Warfare Development Unit only a year or so before.

Initially the new unit was unsure of its purpose. Scheduled passenger services, especially across short stretches of water such as Southampton-Isle of Wight or Bristol-Cardiff were considered but rejected as impractical at such an early stage of helicopter development. Then a possible operation did emerge, carrying mail between the rural towns and villages. This experiment began in January 1948 with two circuits based on Yeovil.

The shorter route covered 22 miles and five stops, using the Bell 47s. The daily flight took 23 minutes Mondays to Fridays, but no mail was actually carried since the aim was simply to build experience and test reliability.

The second route was operated by the larger S-51s, flying two daily circuits with 10 stops, but again not actually carrying real mail. In April 1948 the unit relocated to Peterborough and soon began the first commercial day and night mail service, using the S-51s over a 13-stop route around the Norfolk area. By the time this service finished, in April 1950, 95,000 pounds of mail had been carried, with a 77 percent reliability rate.

Meanwhile the unit had begun to seriously look at passenger-carrying services, initially on a route over the Welsh Mountains between Cardiff and Liverpool. Using the S-51s, this service was inaugurated on June 1, 1950, with an optional stop in a farmer's field at Wrexham introduced a month later. Even before the service began, BEA realized it was unlikely to be economically viable, but it would provide valuable experience and pave the way for new services with larger helicopters.

In 1951 the S-51s were switched to an equally uneconomic Birmingham-London service, which carried just over 1,000 passengers in a 10-month operation funded by an £80,000 government grant.

In April 1952, the BEA Experimental Helicopter Unit relocated once again, to a new base at what was to become Gatwick Airport.

Soon afterward, it ordered new equipment in the shape of three five-seat Bristol Sycamores. These were delivered in 1953, with the S-51s being sold overseas. The Sycamores continued the route experiments, connecting Southampton with London Airport for example, but still failing to make any money. In 1954, two S-55s were added to the fleet and Waterloo-Heathrow and Birmingham-Leicester-Nottingham services were tried.

However, the simple fact was that none of the five routes tried over a six-year period proved profitable, and in late 1956, the unit finally abandoned the idea of scheduled passenger operations until larger and more economic helicopters might become available.

A driving force in this decision was the withdrawal of government subsidies for the helicopter unit, now running at £100,000 per year, and BEA's ruling that, if the helicopter operation were to continue, it would have to stand on its own feet.

Reggie Brie moved on to head up development of the Westland London Heliport at Battersea, and Captain "Jock" Cameron stepped into the manager's shoes — with strict instructions to turn the finances from red into black.

Initially Cameron concentrated on charter operations, which were netting about £20,000 per year in 1957 when he took control. Nevertheless, despite a slow and steady increase, this revenue was not sufficient, and it was clear that the unit could not continue without re-organization and more profitable helicopters.

Both Brie and Cameron had already been pushing the industry to develop more suitable machines. Both had put their weight behind the 13-passenger Bristol Model 173 tandem-rotor design in the early 1950s, and the even more innovative Fairey Rotodyne compound helicopter that was tested later in the 1950s.

Neither type, however, was to enter production, and eventually Cameron turned to Sikorsky to encourage development of a stretched passenger-carrying version of the S-61 Sea King. Cameron also had a scheduled route in mind for the new helicopter: the service between Lands End at the tip of Cornwall and St. Marys in the Scilly Isles.

A fixed-wing service, using pre-war Rapide biplanes, had been operating this route since 1946. By the early 1960s the Rapides were clearly overdue for replacement. However, the airfield on St. Marys was too small for any fixed-wing airliner replacement of the period, and amphibious S-61s were an obvious answer.

Cameron's Scottish tenacity ensured that Sikorsky progressed with development and the BEA Board placed an order for two aircraft in 1963. Along with the new equipment came a further reorganization, with BEA forming a new subsidiary, BEA Helicopters Ltd., under the continued management of Cameron and his team.

In 1964, with delivery of the S-61Ns, the new company had 96 employees and an annual turnover of £43,000. A year later, the S-61N service was carrying 54,000 passengers annually and growing, and was finally moving toward the black.

So far as the Scilly service is concerned, the rest is, as they say, history. Year after year the passenger numbers rose, along with the reliability of the S-61N, such that the operation was largely able to be conducted with just a single aircraft day in and day out, thus maximizing the profitability. Studies for other new scheduled service, however, still demonstrated uneconomic returns.

Meanwhile the discovery of oil in the North Sea offered Jock Cameron a completely new business opportunity. Drilling began in the southern North Sea in 1964 and over the next six years slowly moved north. BEA Helicopters moved with it, initially winning contracts with Shell in a joint venture with Okanagan Helicopters and subsequently, when that partnership broke up, going it alone and opening a base at Aberdeen (Dyce) Airport.

In 1971, with the demise of the BEA parent, the helicopter division underwent another name change to British Airways Helicopters (BAH), still under Cameron's leadership. Initially the S-61N remained the fleet mainstay, with more than 20 in service by early 1978. Later that year Cameron added the first Bell 212s and then, in the early 1980s, purchased four Sikorsky S-76s (including one G-BZAC registered in the name of his dog!).

Still sold on the idea of big helicopters — unlike his contemporary and arch-rival Alan Bristow — Cameron had been looking at both the S-65 and the Chinook for future operations. At the beginning of the 1970s, Cameron thought a 44-seat S-65 would prove suitable for new inter-city services between London, Paris, Amsterdam, and Brussels, as well as the Channel Islands, Scottish Highlands, and Islands routes.

The ideas collapsed when Sikorsky decided not to go ahead with a civil variant of the S-65. Cameron now switched his attention to the Chinook, looking especially at the potentially lucrative and time-saving London-Paris route. Thus, in February 1981, the first of six commercial Chinooks entered service, albeit for offshore support work based at Aberdeen and not the long-dreamed-of inter-city services.

Jock Cameron retired as managing director that same year, although he remained on the BAH Board until 1984 and continues to take a very active interest in scheduled helicopter services to this day. Arguably, with his retirement, the company also reached its historical zenith.

A subsequent sell-off to Robert Maxwell and the financial disaster that followed should be no part of this chronicle. Nevertheless from the ashes of the Maxwell empire arose a new British International Helicopters, which today continues to be a major player in the North Sea — and the Scilly Isles service goes on!

S-61 in use for passenger transport.

> *"... Art Fornoff of Bell. He was the one who really set [the new helicopter association] up . . . he was the guy who had the idea in 1948 and we elected me president, but Art was the spark plug."*
>
> Jim Ricklefs

The next stop for some of the team was Brazil, under the auspices of the Rockefeller Foundation, to control insects that were ruining the coffee crop.

Those efforts, along with similar successes in the U.S., England, and other countries, solidified at the very outset the helicopter's reputation for being able to do jobs no other aircraft could touch. With all the constantly increasing activity, however, there was still not quite enough substance to call the new enterprises an "industry." That was soon to change as helicopter operations' momentum picked up in a world churning with political change.

The years 1946 and 1947 brought many new developments as farsighted entrepreneurs in several nations saw the promise of the machine. The new efforts were so numerous that they seem tumbled into the pages of contemporary publications like international alphabet soup, some surviving to this day. In 1946 Ostermans Aero in Sweden was founded and ordered three Bell 47B models, becoming the first commercial operator outside the U.S. The company got production unit 10 in January 1947, and it was flown often by the company's Nels Seifert. The following year saw the founding of Okanagan Air Services in Canada's British Columbia province. The company later became Okanagan Helicopters and is now part of Canadian Helicopters with operations around the world.

On November 2, 1947, Howard Hughes personally piloted his eight-engine wooden transport airplane on its only flight . . . over Long Beach Harbor in California. Even though the airplane's principal material was birch, the mellifluous term "Spruce Goose" caught the media's attention and it stuck.

Flying overhead during the one-minute flight was a Bell 47B in the markings of AF Helicopters, one of the firms that would later form a helicopter association to represent commercial operators. In fact, examination of many photos of the flight leads to the conclusion that only helicopters could have provided an appropriate platform for the dozens of photographers who assembled there.

On April 3, 1948, President Harry Truman signed the Marshall Plan, which allocated more than $5 billion in aid for 16 European nations.

That same month of April 1948, Bell Aircraft president Larry Bell wrote to the New York City Police Department (NYPD), congratulating the aviation aide there on his accumulation of four-and-a-half hours flight instruction in a Bell 47D. Bell urged the NYPD to consider helicopters for search and rescue missions, as well as other police tasks. NYPD had acquired its first Bell 47, under the command of Captain Gus Crawford, and pilots were trained at the Niagara Falls, New York, site. It was the first police helicopter in the world and the start of a long, productive relationship between law enforcement and helicopters.

On June 24, 1948, Communist forces cut off all land and water routes between West Germany and West Berlin, prompting the United States to begin a massive airlift of supplies into the city's western sector to counter the blockade.

On the domestic front, the Ed Sullivan variety show premiered on television and Bell Laboratories announced development of the transistor. Other inventions cascading onto the civil marketplace included the Polaroid Land Camera, long-playing records, and a remarkable game called Scrabble. New York City's new international airport — inaugurated as Idlewild, then changed to Kennedy International — opened on July 1, 1948, while in that same summer Bernard Baruch coined the term "Cold War."

Skids became favored over whee

1951 - New York Yankees win the World Series over Giants

In the United States at the time, more operators launched commercial helicopter services, leaning heavily on Bell 47 models as the workhorse of the fleet. The Bell 47D-1, introduced in 1950 with skids instead of wheels and a more powerful engine, was the most recognized helicopter in the world for decades.

As the 1940s dwindled away, a salesman for Hiller Aircraft spent his time in Saigon and surrounding Indochinese areas, demonstrating the humanitarian capabilities of the Hiller 360 on the French colonial battlefield and elsewhere. His name was J. Alan Bristow and he created a sensation by landing in a Saigon street to demonstrate the aircraft to His Majesty Bao Dai and the French High Commissioner.

Other demonstrations were going on throughout the world as a new industry consisting of helicopter manufacturers and the commercial operators of their products tried to show what the machine could do.

It was not the technicalities or capabilities of machines, however, that spurred the formation of an organization of commercial helicopter operators.

The uncharted, ad hoc business climate, in which many entrepreneurs found themselves in the latter half of the forties, prompted them to band together for collective benefit. The initial name was the "Helicopter Council" and the war had been over for barely three years. The first controllable helicopter had been flown by Igor Sikorsky less than a decade earlier and there were now hundreds of early technology machines at work throughout the world in all manner of jobs.

On December 13, 1948, a handful of operators and Art Fornoff, a representative from Bell Helicopter, met in Burbank, California, at the offices of AF Helicopters to form an association. There were so few they could almost have met in a Sikorsky S-55 or a Piasecki HRP-1, typical of the largest and newest machines of the day.

Present at that historic first meeting were:

Knute Flint, Harry Armstrong, Fred Bowen, and James Newcomb of AF Helicopters, Inc.;
Joe Seward and Roy Falconer of Rotor-Aids;
James L. Ricklefs and Arni L. Sumarlidason of Rick Helicopters, Inc.;
Elynor Rudnick and Bob Facer of Kern Copters, Inc.;
Fred Blymyer and Bob Boughton of Helicopter Service, Inc.;
James I. "Tommy" Thomas, Ed Eskridge, and Phil Johnson of Sky Farming, Inc.; and
Art Fornoff of Bell Helicopter.

According to Jim Ricklefs, "one person who hasn't gotten as much credit as he should have gotten is Art Fornoff of Bell. He was the fourth or fifth person to be hired by Bell. He was the one who really set [the new helicopter association] up. . . . He was the guy who had the idea in 1948 and we elected me president, but Art was the spark plug."

Jim Ricklefs was indeed elected the first president of the new group, with Joseph Seward as secretary and Elynor Rudnick as treasurer. Demonstrated to the new organization was a Hiller 360, a very stable machine that closely resembled the Bell 47 in concept and had been developed with Bell's help in providing main rotor blades.

ASSESSMENT FOR DUES (1952)
ship in Helicopter Association of America
s for 1952——————————$10.00
e make check payable to Helicopter
ciation of America and mail to—
. Falconer
. Box 1850
tura, Calif.
Yours very truly,
R K Falconer
Helicopter Assoc. of America
R.K. Falconer, Treas.
PAID

Did You Know?

Carl Brady describes the first helicopter skids . . .

"In 1948, my first year up here [in Alaska], I was with Joe Beebe, an ex-Bell mechanic, and . . . when I leased the helicopter [from Central Aircraft] he came with it. He was a hell of a fine mechanic and the two of us [found that in] the soft areas where we had to land in the valleys, or the rocky mountain tops, or slopes . . . the wheels [of the Bell 47B-3] would caster on you and try to run you downhill — if you didn't have somebody to chock them with a rock. If you were by yourself you couldn't do that, of course.

"Anyway, we had a sawmill on the island cut us two two-by-fours out of hardwood, long enough to tie them with clothesline wire to the front and back wheel on each side. That was the first set of skid gear I ever saw. It kept the wheels from castering and we could land on rocks with the wheels still in the air, if we had to. We tried to avoid that, in case a two-by-four would break, but it didn't although I had to land that way a few times. Primarily it really helped on soft ground, like tundra.

"There was no law in Pelican, Alaska, 80 miles west of Juneau on an island! There were no FAA people around or I'd probably have gotten in trouble. But it worked. We had no STC [supplemental type certificate] for the two-by-fours. We just flew it, then took them off before we went back to town."

An astonished Joe Mashman asked why he had helped their competition and Larry Bell replied, "If you guys are as good as I think you are, competition is going to make you even better."

Larry Bell may or may not have had his tongue in his cheek when replying to Mashman, but the fact remains that it was a remarkably generous act.

Not only was the Bell team very good, as Larry Bell had anticipated, but the young commercial operators who pioneered this new industry matched them point for point. Ricklefs, an aeronautical engineer who began flying helicopters with the Landgraf Helicopter Company in 1944, eventually started his own firm with a pair of Bell 47B models in 1948. The company grew to be, at one time, the largest commercial operator in the world. Rick Helicopters had 35 of the rotary-winged newcomers to aviation and grossed more revenue than any one of the major passenger airlines in New York, Chicago, or Los Angeles.

"The first machines we got from Bell were $25,000 and Bell was so apologetic about that. They said: 'This is a terribly high price, we realize that, but as soon as we get into production the prices are going to come down.' Of course, that never happened and the small machine we bought for $25,000 is now $500,000."

Rick also owned Alaska Helicopters and Rick Helicopter Maintenance Company in San Francisco and Los Angeles, California. His various operations did pioneering work on sling loads and on cold weather operations throughout the late 1940s and '50s.

Pretty fair work in a new industry based on a machine less than 10 years old!

Jim Ricklefs, President and owner, Rick Helicopters, Inc.

On January 5, 1949, in his State of the Union address, President Harry Truman labeled his newly elected administration the "Fair Deal."

Within weeks, Arthur Miller's play "Death of a Salesman" opened at Broadway's Morosco Theater.

Aviation news was made on March 2, 1949, when an American B-50 Superfortress, the Lucky Lady 2, landed at Fort Worth, Texas, after completing the first non-stop flight around the world.

At the January 1949 meeting of the Helicopter Council, the name California Helicopter Association (CHA) was chosen, with membership open to any helicopter operator in California for an annual dues payment of $10.

The new group was growing just as helicopter use was growing. At the February meeting the first new member was admitted, Helicopter Services of California. And there were others.

"I'll never forget it," said Ricklefs, "I got a letter in 1949 from a guy who said he was considering getting into the helicopter business and asked if I could give him any pointers. His name was Suggs, and afterwards I never let him forget it!"

It was in 1949 that Robert L. Suggs and Maurice Bayon launched Petroleum Helicopters, Inc., eventually to become one of the industry giants. By 1954, PHI was spraying bananas in Colombia, then took geophysical crews into the interior of South America.

The early days were not a time of guaranteed growth, however, for the new industry or the new association. The CHA leadership decided at one point that monthly meetings would be unnecessary, that future meetings would be held as necessary instead of on a regular schedule. (By 1951, CHA was renamed the Helicopter Association of America (HAA), which it would remain until January 1981, when it became the Helicopter Association International.)

Sabena Belgian Airlines completed its first year of air mail service by carrying 4.6 million pieces with a pair of Bell 47D-1s. Sabena linked nine Belgian cities in a 268-mile route that took less than five hours to complete. Reliability of the service, even at that early developmental stage, was 91.2 percent.

Hiller XROE-1
Experimental helicopter

In the United States, Helicopter Air Service, a Chicago commercial operator, was honored by its insurance broker in 1951 for completing two accident-free years. In an operation similar to Sabena's, HAS linked 40 suburban communities around Chicago with air mail service, also carrying mail to the downtown Loop district and Midway Airport with six Bell 47s. They carried six million pounds of mail and flew 704,046 miles during the same period.

There was no doubt about it, the Bell 47 dominated the early days of commercial helicopter operations, simply by being the first on the scene, with the best-capitalized production and marketing organization behind it. The Sikorsky Division of United Aircraft had not exploited the early renown of Igor Sikorsky by vigorously pursuing the civil market with commercial versions of its R-4 and R-6. The company got commercial certification for the S-51 only a year after Bell, and many of the early applications for commercial helicopters did not require the larger machine.

The issues of concern to the helicopter community in those years included workmen's compensation rates, service fees, and a bill in the state legislature — remarkable, considering the helicopter's success — that would prohibit aerial dusting or spraying. There were also issues concerning the U.S. Forest Service, spare parts availability, flight regulations, a group insurance plan, efforts to get a student pilot training program approved under the G.I. Bill, and contributions to Bell's new manual on pest control from the air.

At the California Helicopter Association meeting in May 1949, Joe Mashman was introduced as "one of Bell's most experienced pilots." He had been flying helicopters since about April 1945, and his four-year career represented the entire history of the commercial helicopter industry!

Model 30 carries seven people in demonstration. Mashman at controls with Arthur Young standing on far side, facing camera.

Mashman — who often seemed to be everywhere at once — had turned up to explain the features of the just-introduced Bell 47D-1 with its new three-person bench seat and other improvements. He also had scheduled visits to all the association's members to demonstrate and check out their pilots on low-altitude auto rotations.

The knowledge would come in handy the next year.

As is often the job of associations, one of the critical tasks facing the helicopter group was to debunk myths. Local politicians believed that a helicopter would crash if it had an engine failure in a 10- to 300-foot altitude range. In September 1950, association pilots gathered at the Rick Helicopters heliport on Central Avenue in Los Angeles and demonstrated autorotation techniques for a number of political observers. They even took some for short flights that ended in an autorotation to a fixed spot. The aircraft's safety was clearly demonstrated.

It was just as well that the political leaders hadn't seen the first autorotation test by Stan Hiller in his new XH-44 design. At a small private airstrip in the Sacramento Valley, he took off and — instead of autorotating to a fixed altitude, as in normal practice — he elected to autorotate to the ground. Not having done an autorotation before, Hiller inadvertently began his test under the worst possible conditions in what is known as the height-velocity curve.

Halfway through the maneuver, the aircraft began to twist wildly, and when Hiller tried to correct with the opposite rudder the rotation increased. Dangerously near a crash, he desperately reversed the rudder and to his amazement the spinning stopped and he landed just short of a disaster.

In June 1949, a labor strike at the Bell plant resulted in a field shortage of 100-hour bearings. This, on top of recurring problems with carburetor icing, gave a commercial operator's maintenance department an abundance of challenges.

Agricultural work occupied much of the available capacity of commercial operators, but they were also busy with mapping, geological surveys, geodetic surveys, powerline patrol, seeding and baiting, dam inspections, and other work, as well as with rental for flight training and proficiency checks.

By 1950 the association was engaged in its first lobbying efforts to gain more favorable legislation and regulation for the industry.

Elsewhere in the world, North Korean forces poured across the 38th Parallel in Korea to invade the south on June 25 and begin a three-year war.

Helicopters were used extensively for resupply and medevac missions in the conflict. An army officer at the time derided five days of resupply flights by a single Bell H-13 helicopter to a strategic hill, saying it amounted to using a sedan to do a truck's work. The passage of years showed the great significance of that early "sedan," which was a glimpse into the future.

At the beginning of 1951 the CHA leadership polled its members, who voted to admit to membership any helicopter operator in the U.S. and its territories. The membership move was the subject of the association's second press release, and dues were still $10 a year.

That $10 had already bought a lot for the operators of the day. In November 1950, the association had won its first legal battle for the membership when a court ruled that insurance companies could not use the findings of state agricultural hearing boards as grounds for invalidating insurance coverage. USAIG (United States Aviation Insurance Group) and Lloyds of London removed the relevant clauses from their policies.

At the CHA annual meeting in January 1951, Elmer "Pete" Schlesinger of U.S. Helicopters was elected the association's second president, while Knute Flint of AF Helicopters became secretary, and Vaughn Krug of Pacific Helicopters became treasurer. There were eight regular members and two associate members at the meeting.

In January 1951, a small newspaper in California's San Joaquin Valley reported that Helicopter Services of California (later U.S. Helicopter Inc.), a commercial helicopter operator, had engaged in seeding tests under the auspices of the Forestry Service. The government wanted a seed density of 21 seeds per square foot, but would accept anywhere from 16 to 31 seeds.

A Bell 47 flown by Carrol Voss did the test flights. When a grid was laid on the ground and the government did the counting, it was found that the average seed density was 21 seeds per square foot. The helicopter permanently impressed many government officials and skeptical farmers with that test.

One 80-year-old farm wife was invited to fly in the helicopter and accepted, having previously refused to get into an airplane. She later was asked what made the difference.

"This isn't like flying, it's just like sitting in a rocking chair on the front porch while the ground moves by under you."

Bell 47s

By February 1951, the California Helicopter Association revamped its statement of purpose to broaden and detail the original mission statement, then sent the new document to 43 prospective members around the U.S. This was the association's first recruiting drive and made it abundantly clear that a name change would be necessary to reflect the broader geographic spread of an enlarged membership.

Association President Pete Schlesinger, in a classic understatement, said in March 1951 that the three major uses of helicopters were forest control, agriculture, and utilities.

In May 1951, CHA membership consisted of 17 commercial operators and two associate members: Bell and Hiller. By August, Sikorsky joined to make a third associate member. The total association fleet numbered more than 50 helicopters.

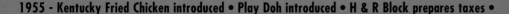

by Elfan ap Rees

When a young Royal Navy lieutenant was put in charge of a flight of Sikorsky R-4 helicopters at Hatson in the Orkney Islands (off the northeast coast of Scotland) in 1945, even he could never have imagined that, more than 50 years later, his name would still be inscribed on helicopters flying daily on offshore support routes all over the North Sea.

Yet Lt. Alan Bristow, and the company that later bore his name, didn't immediately find success when he decided to leave the navy in 1946. His first move was to Westland Aircraft as a test pilot, a career that ended three years later when he allegedly punched a very senior director on the nose!

Bristow moved on to Helicop Air in Paris. This company represented Hiller and was especially involved in marketing the early Model 360 throughout Europe and further afield. Helicop Air introduced the young Bristow to the commercial helicopter operating business the hard way. He was technical manager, chief pilot, instructor, and engineer, assembling the first Helicop Air Hiller 360 with the maintenance manual in one hand and the wrench in the other, before loading it onto a trailer and driving 500 km (310 miles) to Strasbourg, France, to meet a contract deadline.

During this same period the French military was heavily involved in a colonial war in Indochina, where Alan eventually found himself demonstrating the virtues of the Hiller 360 under fire. He did such a good job evacuating the wounded that he was awarded the Croix de Guerre for his bravery.

In 1950, however, the French Air Ministry decided that, unless he took out French citizenship, his job at Helicop Air would be forfeited, since there were French citizens now capable of doing the work. Bristow resigned but, through his contacts at Hiller, was introduced to Aristotle Onassis who was planning to use a Model 360 for whale-spotting on his first Antarctic whaling expedition in early 1951. Bristow was engaged as the helicopter pilot.

At this period in history the whaling fleets plying the waters of Antarctica and the south Atlantic still relied mainly on mast-top lookouts to spot the breaching whales that were the source of the sperm oil used in the edible fats industry. In the post war years, occasional experiments were carried out with fixed-wing amphibians, but sea states and launch/recovery problems made such spotting options quite impractical.

The Onassis initiative immediately led to Bristow forming his own company, Air Whaling Ltd., to promote and develop the use of helicopters for not only whale-spotting but actually hunting them with a specially developed harpoon. This followed on from primitive tests in 1950, with a Portuguese company, when it was determined that more success could be obtained by striking the whale on the head with the nosewheel of the Westland-Sikorsky WS-51 being used for the trials!

Air Whaling's 1951 trials with the Hiller 360 showed that this small helicopter lacked the necessary endurance and performance. For the following season, a lease was taken on another WS-51 for further trials in conjunction with a Norwegian whaling company, Melsom and Melsom. These were more successful, but power and performance were still marginal, especially when flying over waters where the freezing conditions would measure survival in minutes rather than hours.

The WS-51 was retained through both the 1952 and 1953 whaling seasons, but only while the company was waiting for the still larger and more powerful Westland-Sikorsky S-55 to become available. Four were ordered in conjunction with Christian Salvensen for delivery in mid-1954 to the Air Whaling base at Henstridge, near Yeovil. These entered service in time for the 1954 whaling season, although only one was to survive the next two years. During this period, development of the harpoon continued and, by 1956, was nearing perfection. At this point the International Whaling Commission recognized the threat and banned the use of helicopters for killing whales. By the mid-1950s, the whale population was already being depleted and there was clearly no long-term future in the business.

Bristow had already recognized this fact and in 1954, between whaling seasons, had begun to look at alternatives, trying to identify markets that could provide his company with a sound foundation for the future. He soon realized that, to survive, the company would have to adopt an international outlook, that there was little future in scheduled services, and that, to be truly successful, collaboration with overseas partners would be more profitable in the long term than trying to compete.

Meanwhile, by the spring of 1955, the Air Whaling operations were winning Bristow a favorable reputation. He found himself invited to the London offices of Shell Oil to meet the managing director of Shell Aircraft Ltd., one Group Captain Douglas Bader. As a result of this meeting, Bristow and his team were given the chance to become a helicopter contractor to the new oil industry.

The two-year agreement arranged for Shell to provide the helicopters, support equipment, and base installations, with Bristow providing the crews and management know-how to set up and run the seven-days-per-week operation.

Although 1955 marked the end of Air Whaling, it also marked the launch of Bristow Helicopters Ltd. A new era had begun.

Initially the company continued operating the WS-55, with two new machines for Shell delivered first to the Henstridge base and then flown out to Bahrain in an eight-day, 3,700-mile flight to a rig 50 miles offshore in the Persian Gulf. (The first WS-55 used by Bristow for offshore support in 1955 is preserved at the International Helicopter Museum in the United Kingdom.)

The many lessons learned and procedures introduced on this first offshore support contract were to form the basis of numerous similar contracts in the years to come. After a quiet 1956, Bristow, with headquarters now located at Redhill in Surrey, England, secured a contract with British Petroleum in 1957 to operate two Westland Widgeons from Das Island offshore from Qatar. A contract with Standard Oil to use three Bell 47G-2 helicopters to support geological surveys in Bolivia followed.

By 1960 Bristow Helicopters was well established and growing. That year the company absorbed the Fison-Airwork helicopter fleet and flew over 13,000 revenue hours, moving 40,321 passengers and 2,127,000 pounds of freight with eight different types of helicopter! Bristow began to declare "open-season" on his main British competitor, the state-owned BEA Helicopters. He campaigned against its subsidies and what he saw as unfair competition, the "creative accounting" and import duty exemptions enjoyed by BEA when buying U.S. helicopters. He also openly criticized manufacturers who, in his eyes, failed to live up to delivery promises and product reliability.

He was especially annoyed when BEA Helicopters was able to use its financial benefits in the mid-1960s not only to introduce the S-61N into the U.K. market, but to match the charter rate being offered by Bristow on the smaller and less expensive Wessex 60. Despite this competition, by early 1968 Bristow Helicopters and its associated companies were operating a mixed fleet of more than 80 helicopters, which in terms of asset value, if not actual numbers, made it the largest commercial helicopter operator in the world.

Over the next 10 years the growth continued with but one notable exception: an attempt to enter the Gulf of Mexico market at the end of the 1970s. Market saturation, intense competition, and resulting losses forced a pull-out in mid-1981. Nevertheless, that same year the company placed the largest commercial helicopter order in history when it contracted with Aerospatiale to purchase 35 customized AS.332L Super Pumas at a total value of some $200 million. In the following year Bristow bought a 49 percent share of Canada's biggest helicopter operation, Okanagan, and sold its Malaysian operation to a new, domestically owned company, Malaysian Helicopter Services.

Alan Bristow continued at the helm of his company until 1985, by which time it had diversified into military pilot training, search and rescue contracts, and other missions as well as major oil support operations in Australia, Indonesia, Malaysia, Nigeria, and, of course, the North Sea. At his retirement, the company operated 144 helicopters in eight countries, employed 1,800 staff, and was valued at around £125 million.

Today Alan Bristow clearly enjoys his retirement and is rarely seen at helicopter gatherings. His views on the metamorphosis of Okanagan into Canadian Helicopters and its emergence as a major competitor, and the buy-in by a former competitor, Offshore Logistics, of 49 percent of today's Bristow Helicopters, are unknown.

Given his reputation over the years, that may be just as well.

The WS-51 Dragonfly, subject of the original agreement with Sikorsky in 1947, from which Westland evolved as a helicopter manufacturer.

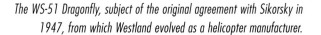

On April 11, 1951, President Truman fired General Douglas MacArthur in a small concrete building on Wake Island.

The Korean War came home to most commercial operators in the form of a letter from Bell in May 1951, advising that there would be minimum availability of maintenance and spare parts for commercial operators due to commitments to the armed forces.

An internal memo of May 26, 1951, announced that members had voted to change the name of the California Helicopter Association to the Helicopter Association of America (HAA), but new articles of incorporation were not filed until November 1954, leading to some confusion about when the changeover occurred.

(Letters on file show an internal memo on typed letterhead from "California Helicopter Association" dated May 5, 1951, and a typed letterhead from "Helicopter Association of America" dated June 11, 1951. Both showed an address at One Montgomery Street, San Francisco, California.)

Hiller Model 12-B

On June 25, 1951, the first commercial color TV program was broadcast to four cities, and on November 10, 1951, direct-dial coast-to-coast telephone service began in the U.S.

For The Record   1956 - Andrea Doria sinks off coast of Nantucket • Grace Kelly becomes Princess of Monaco •

Dwight David Eisenhower was elected President of the United States in November 1952 on a pledge to go to Korea to try ending that war.

The Korean War ended in July 1953, after three years and one month, at the cost of more than 50,000 American lives and countless lives of allies and others. The human loss would have been greater had it not been for the launch of helicopter medevac flights.

The decade of the 1950s was a time when young people were called "The Silent Generation," a term that might well describe the calm before the storms of the 1960s.

In 1953, Jean Ross Howard, then a staffer at the Helicopter Council of the Aircraft Industries Association, approached Larry Bell at a dinner and suggested he arrange for her to learn to fly one of these marvelous machines she was writing about. He did so, and the following year she got her helicopter pilot's license . . . then launched an international organization of women helicopter pilots called the "Whirly-Girls." Its members now operate helicopters in every sector of the industry.

Throughout the mid- and late-1950s, when the national and world political scenes were ominous but relatively stable, the business of the industry was conducted with little fanfare, and technical developments slowed with the decline in military work after the Korean War.

While drilling for offshore oil actually began before the turn of the century from piers extended off the California coast, it was the Eisenhower Administration that gave true offshore oil and gas exploration the boost that propelled the industry into what we know today.

Helicopter support of offshore rigs is one of the most critical elements in the economic viability of offshore exploration and production, and in turn, offshore operations are a major contributor to commercial helicopter operations.

Not to be outdone by offshore hospitality for helicopters, the Western Hills Hotel in Fort Worth, Texas, supported the home team of Bell Helicopters by opening the world's first official hotel heliport in 1953, in conjunction with the annual meeting of the Aviation Writers Association.

There were certainly enough local products to keep the heliport busy. Bell had rolled the one-thousandth Model 47 out the door just weeks before the hotel heliport opened, and seven years after the aircraft had received the world's first commercial certification.

Carl Brady of Economy Helicopters had been elected the third HAA president in 1952, succeeded in 1954 by Joe Seward of Rotor-Aids. Seward at the time was the only helicopter pilot in the world to carry a membership card in the Screen Actors Guild; he had appeared in at least 25 Hollywood productions as a pilot.

Bell Helicopters also hosted the January 1954 annual HAA convention at its plant in Hurst, Texas, where 75 attendees from the U.S., Canada, France, Italy, Japan, and Sweden heard presentations on lowering insurance costs, new air-cooled engines, overhaul costs, and the use of fuel additives. The world's largest commercial helicopter operator was still Rick Helicopters.

Helicopter pioneers may have struggled, improvised, and scratched their heads a lot, but they occasionally had their tongues in their cheeks.

Carrol Voss distributed the following "advertisement" to prospective clients long after turbines had entered the agricultural aviation marketplace:

"Enjoy the thrill of having your crop dusted by an open cockpit antique Bell 47 helicopter as it sputters over your fields applying materials the organic natural way as in the early years before the invention of chemicals.

"This fast disappearing breed of reciprocating engine helicopter flown by senior citizen pilots is available to our customers who would appreciate this nostalgia. This minority group should warrant special consideration on contracts.

"Don't give in to the temptation to use one of those new fangled screaming turbine types that complete your job too rapidly. The barking rumble of the piston engine helicopter definitely has a more romantic sound as they slowly traverse the terrain. They spend three times as much time to finish the job for your continued enjoyment. The bugs even stop eating in respect as we fly over.

"Remember when dust clouds would drift across the country and wipe out all the bugs over broad areas? We didn't have the insect problems that we have now. Current materials are restricted to the field being treated and we are being overrun by insects from the untreated areas.

"Don't forget the 47s and the senior citizen operators."

1956 - Yankee pitcher Don Larsen pitches first, and only perfect World Series game •

Carl and Carol Brady, and Joe and Jean Seward
(1957). Both Carl and Joe served as HAA presidents.

The world outside Texas continued to boil and bubble with good news and bad.

On March 1, 1954, Puerto Rican nationalists opened fire from the gallery of the U.S. House of Representatives, wounding five congressmen.

On March 9, 1954, CBS newsman Edward R. Murrow set the nation buzzing when he criticized Wisconsin Senator Joseph R. McCarthy's anti-communism campaign on television.

May 6, 1954, was the day that medical student Roger Bannister broke the four-minute mile at a track meet in Oxford, England, in 3 minutes, 59.4 seconds.

On May 7, 1954, the 55-day Battle of Dien Bien Phu in Vietnam ended with Communist insurgents overrunning French forces. The stage was set for France's withdrawal.

In the autumn of 1954, new articles of incorporation for HAA declared that the association's additional focus would include increasing membership, building a film library, becoming a clearing house for pilot and mechanic applications, printing a monthly newsletter, and various other tasks.

For the commercial helicopter industry and its association, there were a number of inevitable firsts in this early period. In 1955, Elynor Rudnick of Kern Copters, Inc., was elected president of HAA, the first woman to hold the post.

The January 1955 annual meeting was held at the Piasecki plant in Morton, Pennsylvania, where the press reported that flying cranes capable of lifting as much as 15 tons were possible.

The late 1950s were a period of steady growth and development for the entire industry. In the absence of a major hot war, but with the military stimulus of the Cold War, American industry improved the machine, and commercial operators improved their application of the machine to all sorts of challenges, both old and new.

Humble Oil sent several representatives to the 1955 helicopter association meeting and made arrangements with Rotor-Aids for offshore support work. The going rate at the time for pilots on a year-round basis was $700/month in Louisiana, with 750 hours flight time required per pilot per year.

In 1955, Elynor Rudnick of Kern Copters was elected president of HAA, the first woman to hold the post.

Piasecki HRP

For The Record

1957 - The Frisbee is introduced • American Bandstand debuts •

65

On July 11, 1955, the new U.S. Air Force Academy was dedicated at Lowry Air Force Base in Colorado.

On July 17, Disneyland opened in Anaheim, California.

At the 1956 annual convention at San Francisco in January, Rick Helicopters had several Piasecki models flying demonstrations. The company had at least one HRP-2 and a pair of HRP-1s. These machines were apparently bought as surplus from the U.S. Navy, one for $5,000, and two others at $3,000 each. Civil Defense officials were interested that year in renting commercial helicopters for disaster relief work, and discussed the possibility with several operators. The federal agency said it would pay half the cost of the helicopters.

European helicopter developments were picking up speed along with U.S. progress, and the French Djinn helicopter was gaining favorable comments from those who used it in Latin America and elsewhere.

*Sikorsky VS-300
Piloted by Les Morris*

Best wishes to Vin Colicci

Les Morris (Pilot)

HAA President Elynor Rudnick was succeeded in 1956 by Carl Agar of Okanagan Helicopters, the first non-U.S. president. A priority for the coming year was a survey to determine the size and shape of the industry in order that promotion of helicopters would be on a sound statistical basis.

The industry had done remarkably well in its 10 years.

Less than a decade after the Bell 47 certification, the industry had 11 different models in production, 14 were in prototype stage, and nine were in the design phase. The manufacturing industry employed 15,000 people and sales averaged $150 million annually. The backlog of orders had reached half a billion dollars in 1954.

Nowhere was the contribution and the remarkable growth of the industry more clearly summed up than in a 1956 address by Civil Aeronautics Board (CAB) Executive Director Raymond Sawyer, who noted that in six years of scheduled helicopter passenger transportation in Europe and the United States, not a single life had been lost to an accident. Sawyer further told the January 1956 HAA convention attendees:

"One of the major accident hazards of fixed-wing flying is engine failure, [but] our records show that there has never been a fatal accident, due solely to engine failure, in any kind of civilian helicopter operation scheduled or non-scheduled, commercial or private."

It would be difficult to find a more remarkable record of aircraft safety — not only for a new model — but for an entirely new type of flying machine having so many more moving parts than an airplane.

The federal government, through CAB, was subsidizing scheduled helicopter passenger airlines at the time in New York, Chicago, and Los Angeles for a total of about $3 million annually.

The Civil Aeronautics Board, in fact, had been astonishingly prescient, considering its reputation as a stodgy government bureaucracy. The Board had scheduled hearings in April 1944 on an application to provide helicopter services in Los Angeles. This was less than five years since the first practical helicopter had been demonstrated, and three years before the Bell 47 — hardly a high-capacity aircraft — had been certificated for commercial service.

CAB decided, even at that early time in the industry's development, not to reject the idea merely because there was a war on and there were no aircraft capable of providing the service. The hearing was postponed, and

eventually, with the support of the U.S. Post Office, CAB awarded a certificate to Los Angeles Airways (LAA) to operate a scheduled mail service in May 1947, two months after the Bell 47 certification.

In awarding a scheduled operating certificate for a fledgling aircraft type in 1947, the Board said in an opinion marked by foresight, "We do not believe that its present high cost of operation alone should deter the experiment since a more economical helicopter may be anticipated just as more economical conventional aircraft have been developed."

The Board continued: "The potential of the helicopter in commercial air transport is unknown and whether the service proposed can be maintained on an economically sound basis with substantial public benefit is a matter that can be established only by experience."

LAA was later certificated to carry passengers. Then in 1948 Chicago's Helicopter Air Service was certificated to carry mail in a contested case that brought out a huge cost disparity but did not deter CAB. Mail could have been carried to and from airports by trucks for $75,000, but CAB awarded the service to the commercial helicopter service, along with a subsidy for $437,000.

Addressing the opposing view, CAB was just as visionary as in its earlier opinion. "It is, of course, clear that the operation of trucks could be conducted at a substantially lower cost to the government than the helicopter service. However, there are, we believe, considerations of broad national interest that justify the inauguration of the proposed helicopter service on an experimental basis. Moreover, further development of the helicopter and the experience to be gained from the operation are desirable in the interest of the national defense."

1958 - Hula Hoop, Sweet 'N' Low, and the American Express Card are introduced •

"Experience to be gained." The phrase was easily skimmed over but had profound implications. There was more experience than CAB or Raymond Sawyer had in mind. According to the association's first president, James Ricklefs, "We tried everything. We hauled Santa Claus to department stores. We performed at air shows. We made a number of rescues. We hunted coyotes. We chased bandits. We herded cattle, elk, and wild horses. We sprayed wheat in eastern Washington. We reseeded forests in Washington and Oregon. We helped map remote areas of Alaska. It was a life of constant challenges and new experiences."

Bell 47

Two years after CAB pointed out the military benefits to be gained from government subsidies for commercial helicopters, the Korean War erupted. Sawyer's subsequent 1956 presentation to the HAA reflected the Board's satisfaction that its faith in rotary-wing aircraft had been justified by evacuation of 22,000 Korean War casualties via helicopter, and by later rescue work during U.S. natural disasters.

Whereas conventional wisdom has developments of any technology flowing from the military to civilian sectors, Sawyer pointed out the opposite at that 1956 meeting: "A surprising amount of the military progress of the helicopter is due directly to the rigorous experimental laboratory provided by the civilian commercial heli-

1959 - Panty hose and nonstick pan introduced • Phone-booth packing craze started •

copter operator. The military testified at great length at Board hearings this past year [1955] to many specific examples of new learning from the experience of civilian operators.

"One of the most dramatic was the ungrounding of a large part of the military at the height of the fighting in the Korean War. The service life of the tail-rotor gear box on the H-13 had been listed at 300 hours. The fleet was grounded for lack of replacement gear boxes. Based on the experience of one of the civilian helicopter operators in using these gear boxes 600 hours, the Army was able to double their service life by a simple field order."

Sawyer went on to describe commercial helicopter experience being applied to military problems on total engine time, main rotor blade time (which the army then doubled), spark plug fouling, fuel consumption, time-limited parts, maintenance procedures, and man-hours involved in removal/inspection operations.

The world at large, however, was not captivated at the time by national security contributions of commercial helicopter operators, but by high-profile cultural events.

> *On April 18, 1956, actress Grace Kelly married Prince Rainier of Monaco; on September 9, Elvis Presley made the first of three appearances on the Ed Sullivan television show; and on October 8, Don Larsen pitched the only perfect game ever in a World Series as the New York Yankees beat the Brooklyn Dodgers, 2-0.*

Not all the news that year was cultural, and much of it had definite impact on the helicopter industry as rapid-fire simultaneous world events again reminded the industry that its bread-winning machine had clear military obligations.

> *On October 23, 1956, an anti-Stalinist revolt began in Hungary and less than a week later, Israel invaded Egypt's Sinai Peninsula.*

> *Soviet troops moved in to crush the Hungarian Revolution by November 4, and the very next day, Britain and France sent troops to Egypt to seize the Suez Canal.*

> *The U.S., while harshly criticizing the Soviet action, felt undercut by the actions of its own allies and pressured them to withdraw. On December 5, 1956, British and French forces withdrew from Egypt amid much anger at Washington.*

Carl Brady repeated as HAA president in 1957, the first to do so. By now the association was actively pushing for construction of more public-use heliports in each city. The topic of group insurance coverage was also rising in HAA meetings, for personnel as well as for aircraft.

Consolidation and mergers in the industry were typified by the acquisition in February 1957 of Cleveland Air Taxi — operating five Bell 47s — by Louisiana-based Petroleum Helicopters, Inc.

In June 1957, helicopters made different news along the Gulf Coast as more than 500 people were killed when Hurricane Audrey ripped through coastal Louisiana and Texas, and helicopters provided much emergency relief.

> *Historic news streaked across the skies on October 4 when the Soviet Union launched Sputnik, the first artificial satellite to orbit around the Earth.*

In 1958, HAA elected Richard D. Eccles of Calicopters as its president. It was the year Bell produced its two-thousandth Model 47, 700 of which were in commercial service. The ribbon on the two-thousandth unit was ceremonially snipped by Texas Senator Lyndon Johnson.

In 1948, NYPD acquired its first Bell 47. It was the first police helicopter in the world and the start of a long, productive relationship between law enforcement and helicopters.

1959 - Guggenheim Museum (designed by Frank Lloyd Wright) opens in New York •

San Francisco Mayor George Christopher, pilot Rick Eccles in a Bell
model 47D1 N21H. Eccles served as HAA President in 1958.

J. Cullen Weadock of Chesapeake & Potomac Airways took the association helm in 1959. His tenure as president closed out the decade. For the first time in 10 years, HAA raised its membership dues from $10 to $50.

On July 15, 1958, President Eisenhower ordered U.S. Marines to Lebanon at the request of that country's president, Camille Chamoun, to face a threat by Muslim rebels.

In aviation, it was a banner time. On October 4, 1958, trans-Atlantic passenger jetliner service began with British Overseas Airways Corporation flights between London and New York. On October 26, Pan American Airways flew its first Boeing 707 jetliner from New York to Paris in eight hours and 41 minutes. In December, the first domestic passenger jet flight in the U.S. saw a National Airlines Boeing 707 fly 111 passengers from New York to Miami in about two and a half hours.

As the decade neared its end, HAA leaders focused on three main issues: ethics, association publications, and a meaningful awards program for those deserving recognition. The major operating concern was an unfilled need for public-use heliports, an issue that gained momentum as time passed.

PHI's Robert Suggs sounded a battle cry at the January 1959 convention when he challenged helicopter manufacturers to stop competing with their own best customers, the commercial operators.

Manufacturers, he said, competed against the operators in various ways and made life difficult for them in other ways. Suggs said the manufacturers conducted their own flight operations in the marketing territory served by commercial operators and performed maintenance and other services in competition with their own customers.

Suggs, speaking for the operator industry, said the manufacturers routinely over-rated their equipment, leaving the operator with the task of explaining to the customer why the machine wasn't doing what the customer had been led to believe it could do. He added that the manufacturers were encouraging prospective operators to get into the business in order to sell those operators new helicopters, while established operators were having a hard time surviving.

One manufacturer, Suggs said, made more money one year in flight operations than it did as a manufacturer of helicopters.

With a newly established five-member Board of Directors, HAA faced the 1960s leading an industry generating an estimated $30-40 million in annual gross revenues, depending on whose figures were most acceptable. Some put the gross significantly higher. The Board had decided in January 1959 to delay establishment of a trade show until 1960. Prior annual meetings of HAA had not included industry exhibits, but that was about to change as manufacturers sought to reach an increasing clientele.

President Cully Weadock proposed an HAA committee to develop criteria for various kinds of external load operations, and that resulted eventually in the FAA's Part 133 regulations.

New-technology machines using vertical lift entered the picture. A hovercraft made its first crossing of the English Channel from Dover to Calais on July 25, 1959.

As the 1950s ended, Helicopter Airlift's Hal Conners recommended to Weadock that the Helicopter Association of America consider a name change "to better reflect the international aspects of the association."

A name change was not to occur for many more years, but nevertheless, merely considering a name that reflected worldwide involvement was not a bad way to close out 11 years that began as a one-state helicopter council with only eight members.

Bell model 47 helicopter at work

The 1960s saw many innovative leaders in the helicopter industry. Pictured is Carl Brady with a Hiller 12E.

THE SIXTIES

*"History is always repeating itself,
but each time the price goes up."*

Anonymous

Robert L. "Bob" Suggs of Petroleum Helicopters, Inc. (PHI), was elected president of the Helicopter Association of America (HAA) in January 1960 at the convention in Anaheim, California.

It was also at HAA's 1960 convention that the Federal Aviation Agency (FAA), which it was still called at the time, described its Project Humming Bird plan to "take a newer and broader interest" in the development of the entire helicopter industry.

Immediately following the FAA's Humming Bird presentation was a panel discussion on external load operations. The FAA official on the panel provided few concrete answers to questions about FAA regulations concerning external loads and where commercial operators fit into that legal picture.

Bell 206 III

Industry leaders understandably took a dim view of the murky external load discussion.

"Bob Suggs, after listening for some time, got down to the meat of the matter and asked just where he, as an operator, stood; whether he could legally fly with an external load the following day." The FAA panelist told Suggs to consult his lawyer.

Someone also apparently forgot to pass word of the FAA's benevolent Humming Bird mindset along to the New York Port Authority, whose director, Austin Tobin, told the "Newark Evening News" that helicopters would not be providing service to the new airport proposed at Newark because they were not "feasible," and he added that helicopters were "unreliable" and "not sufficiently developed to warrant serious consideration."

While the New York Port Authority was declining to seriously consider helicopter passenger services, Los Angeles Airways, a scheduled helicopter airline, routinely reminded those arriving for the 1960 HAA convention that interline bookings could be made straight through to Anaheim by using the helicopter service. One-way fare from Los Angeles International Airport to Disneyland was seven dollars. The seven dollars included all taxes, and few thought the idea of completing the trip by helicopter wasn't feasible.

By then, Carl Brady had left the three-way partnership in Economy Helicopters ("We started as Economy Pest Control but changed it because if you walk into an oil company office with a business card that says 'Economy Pest Control,' they throw you out.") and he moved from the state of Washington to Alaska, where he formed a joint venture with Rotor-Aids. The initials of Economy and Rotor-Aids were combined to name the new venture

Era Helicopters, owned by Brady, Joe Seward, and Roy Falconer. It was soon a very big commercial operator of the 1960s and beyond.

Cessna promoted its CH-1 four-place Skyhook light helicopter to the market, after the November 1960 introduction, saying its 400 worldwide dealers would sell the machine at less than $80,000. Expectations were high enough that 50 helicopters were scheduled for production the first year.

The Brantly helicopter, built in Oklahoma, had a jump in sales and increased production from four aircraft a month to two each week. The two-place helicopter sold for less than $20,000.

Aerospace Industries Association reported in 1960 that commercial helicopter operators in the U.S. totaled 160 in 1959, and the fleet total was 635 helicopters. The numbers represented an increase of 62 percent in the number of operators and 35 percent in the number of helicopters since 1957.

Appropriately, that news was accompanied by an announcement that brandy-carrying St. Bernard rescue dogs in the Alps had been replaced by helicopters and walkie-talkies.

It was also a year of musical names. Vertol Aircraft Corp. (formerly Piasecki Helicopter Corp.) agreed to be acquired by the Boeing Company. Frank Piasecki formed another enterprise called Piasecki Aircraft Corp., because in 1955 he had been replaced as chairman of the original company bearing his name by those who had provided the capital. He continued to develop new-design helicopters, as did Vertol, which used Piasecki's existing tandem-rotor designs.

On February 29, 1960, the first Playboy Club, featuring waitresses in "bunny" outfits, opened in Chicago. The last of the clubs closed in 1986.

In May, Jim Ricklefs — who had served as the association's first president and devoted a remarkable amount of time and energy to the industry group — proposed to current-president Bob Suggs that HAA members be polled to determine their preferences for convention programs.

Ricklefs chaired the Program Committee that year and wanted to be sure the membership was getting what it needed and wanted. Suggs concurred and the survey went out.

Members indicated strong preference for more forums on maintenance, piloting, insurance, Civil Aeronautics Board (CAB) certificates, accident analysis, and construction. There was less enthusiasm for more financial tutoring, nationally known speakers, civil defense, manufacturers' presentations, flight demonstrations, and many other topics. Interest in night club tours was virtually zero.

In July 1960, New York Airways submitted an application to the CAB to provide scheduled helicopter passenger service between Dulles International Airport and downtown Washington, D.C. The proposed service would operate every 20 minutes, using twin-engine Vertol 107 tandem-rotor helicopters carrying 25 passengers.

Also in July, PHI bought an amphibious Sikorsky S-62 single-turbine helicopter to serve offshore rigs in the Gulf of Mexico. The S-62 was the first turbine helicopter to be certificated for commercial service by the FAA.

Offshore activity in the Gulf of Mexico was rapidly expanding in those years. The 600-mile stretch of Texas and Louisiana coastline had hundreds of offshore rigs supported by hundreds of helicopters.

On August 13, 1960, the first two-way phone conversation via satellite took place.

On August 18, 1960, the first birth control pill was sold in Skokie, Illinois.

On August 29, 1960, Jordan Prime Minister Hazza El-Majali and 10 others were assassinated by a bomb.

1961 - Commander Alan Shepard is first American in space • The Peace Corps is formed •

On January 20, 1961, President John F. Kennedy (JFK) stood coatless in a vicious January wind at the U.S. Capitol. There were more words in his 1,347-word inaugural address than there would be days of his presidency.

Though the 1950s had seen steady but modest growth in commercial helicopter operations, the 1960s were to see a sudden mushrooming of that industry for reasons that did not seem related at the time.

International tensions that would profoundly affect the industry were rising even before Kennedy took office. On January 3, 1961, the Eisenhower Administration had severed diplomatic relations with Cuba, and a secret invasion was being prepared by the Central Intelligence Agency (CIA) and parts of the Defense Department.

Agreeing to go along with that plan was "the most un-intelligent thing that Kennedy did . . . but if he had been smart enough not to inherit a covert operation that had been created by Eisenhower, he would have not been dropped into this problem," said his former press secretary, Pierre Salinger.

On April 17, 1961, that not-so-secret invasion created a major military and political disaster for the 90-day-old Kennedy Administration. Fifteen-hundred CIA-trained Cuban exiles launched the "Bay of Pigs" invasion of Cuba, in a poorly planned and worse-executed attempt to overthrow Fidel Castro.

After that, the Kennedy Administration tried to keep a lower profile in international military adventures. Kennedy's faith in his own judgment had been seriously shaken. He had assumed that the famous general preceding him in the Oval Office, and many experienced advisors, had more military savvy than himself, so he deferred to their judgment. Worse yet, the Kennedy Administration had failed to follow his predecessor's plan. A major mistake was withholding, at the last minute, the close air support so critical to the invasion.

No sooner had the Bay of Pigs storm subsided than another major spike occurred in the international temperature. Berlin was divided on August 13, 1961, by East Germany, which sealed the border between the city's eastern and western sectors in order to halt the flight of refugees.

Two days later, work began on the Berlin Wall, which stood for 30 years, until 1991.

There was no escaping the succession of global crises.

The decade of the 1960s thus made military and commercial helicopter developments unavoidably intertwined, largely due to the war in Southeast Asia. Just as in the science and art of medicine, other technologies make major advances during periods of national military action. Helicopters have been no exception.

Shortly before Kennedy's election, on August 9, 1960, a coup had been staged in Laos, a small country most Americans never knew existed. That event and other indicators convinced JFK, as it had President Eisenhower, that the Communist push in the former Indochina was inexorably long-term, despite treaties that purported to show better intentions. Eisenhower warned Kennedy that Laos was "the cork in the bottle" of Southeast Asia.

One of JFK's major initial decisions, therefore, was to increase the small number of military advisors that Eisenhower had sent to Southeast Asia — and to add helicopters for support — hopefully stemming the Communist guerrilla war. On December 11, 1961, a U.S. aircraft carrier loaded with Army helicopters arrived in Vietnam — the first direct American military support for South Vietnam.

Vietnam was not the first real helicopter war — though it was certainly the biggest and most publicized. WWII saw the introduction of helicopters for some logistical tasks, and helicopters were successfully used in Korea for troop movement and for medical evacuation of wounded. It was the back-to-back French military efforts in Indochina and Algeria during the late 1940s, 1950s, and into the early 1960s that saw helicopters greatly expand their battlefield role to include heliborne assault, armed attack, and other missions.

Since December 19, 1946, after the U.S. rejected Ho Chi Minh's request for help, war in Indochina had pitted troops under Ho against the French until May 7, 1954, when the 55-day Battle of Dien Bien Phu ended as the Viet Minh overran French forces. That seven-and-a-half year war ended in August 1954.

No sooner had France wrapped up its bloody struggle in Indochina than rebels in the French colony of Algeria began fighting on November 1, 1954, having seen what happened to the French in Indochina. The Algerian guerrilla war lasted almost another seven years and resulted in independence in July 1962.

It was the 15-year-long French experience in Indochina and Algeria, therefore, that other global powers watched with interest for tactical military helicopter developments.

In addition to direct military applications, there was intense research and development in generic helicopter technology to improve reliability, maintainability, payload, crashworthiness, and other features. Much of this new technology benefitted the commercial helicopter industry, reversing the earlier flow from civil to military uses that CAB's Raymond Sawyer had described in 1956 at HAA's eighth annual convention.

By this point in his presidency, John F. Kennedy had more confidence in his own assessments of what was militarily possible. He was not blinded by the developments of technology, but used different arithmetic to reach a conclusion.

One of JFK's last decisions, days before his death on November 22, 1963, was to order many U.S. personnel — and specifically the helicopters — withdrawn in preparation for a complete pullout after his anticipated re-election in November 1964. For domestic political reasons after the October 1962 Cuban Missile Crisis, he didn't want to seem soft on communism in an election year.

JFK was convinced by then that the Southeast Asia war could not be won without a huge American effort, including combat forces, and that the South Vietnamese could not defend themselves without U.S. help. The French, hardly a minor military power, had demonstrated the hazards of deep involvement. JFK, therefore, was unwilling to go down a road that had no visible end, heeding the widely quoted maxim by General Douglas MacArthur that the U.S. should never become involved in an Asian land war.

Chatting with "The Washington Post" editor Ben Bradlee during a dinner at Bradlee's home soon after taking office, Kennedy said he had learned a new and discouraging math.

"One guerrilla can pin down 12 conventional soldiers, and we've got nothing equivalent." That math was to spur JFK's decision to bolster U.S. Special Forces and de-emphasize conventional forces for such wars.

JFK's order to withdraw from Vietnam was canceled by President Lyndon Johnson while John Kennedy's body was still in the Capitol Rotunda.

The following 10 years not only cost 55,000 American and countless Asian lives, but also had a profound impact on the commercial helicopter industry around the world as new technology, new capabilities, and newly trained personnel flowed from military applications into the commercial sector.

America's Southeast Asia war was on, and the helicopter would never be the same, either in technology or application.

All that, however, was still to come during the long bloody decade of the sixties.

Reporting for USAF duty, Sikorsky twin-turbine CH-3C transport helicopter

In the Pacific Northwest, a Hiller 12E placed 40 poles up a mountainside in less than four hours, then laid two manila "sock lines" along a three-mile right-of-way in 12 minutes.

On the French Riviera, more and more celebrities were using helicopters to drop in on friends, allowing them to attend several beach parties in one afternoon.

Autumn of 1960 was presidential election time, and it nearly brought a significant problem to commercial helicopter operators, apparently through no intent by any of the parties directly involved. The Tennessee state legislature hastily considered and passed — during its final days in session — a bill allowing any city, town, or municipality to regulate the operation of helicopters. Only a last-minute appeal by the state aeronautics commissioner caused the governor to veto the bill.

HAA discovered that trouble could originate from anonymous places. During that fall election campaign in Tennessee, there had been two complaints made about low-flying helicopters near crowds that had gathered to hear Senator John F. Kennedy speak. No one from the Kennedy campaign staff or local political party had filed any complaints, but HAA nonetheless warned members to avoid low flight near all crowds lest local interests become angry over noise.

The presidential election of 1960 came and went.

The climate for helicopter commercial business was assessed in that transition period by L. Welch Pogue, of the Pogue & Neal law firm, counsel to the Helicopter Council of the Aerospace Industries Association. He reported his comprehensive survey findings to the HAA convention of January 1961.

Commercial operators who responded, said Pogue, "listed 57 different types of services rendered for hire in the 12 months ended September 30, 1960. As a commentary upon the versatility of this 'iron mule,' note that of the 57 types of services reported, 42 either could not or would not normally be performed by fixed-wing aircraft."

Pogue noted that Los Angeles Airways, New York Airways, and Chicago Helicopter Airways together had carried 475,000 passengers in that year, a 45 percent increase over the prior year. He said he had conservatively calculated, allowing various adjustments, that the 14-year-old commercial helicopter operating industry did about $50 million in business from September 1959 to September 1960, excluding the three helicopter airlines.

It was not all peaches and cream that Pogue served up to the operators, however. He noted that their own comments returned with his survey form complained that "increased costs are absorbing increased income," "the industry is distressingly competitive," "too many contracts are too short," "too many restrictions are imposed by insurance underwriters," and "premium rates are far too high."

Pogue reviewed the Civil Aeronautics Board's actions concerning a scheduled helicopter airline for the three-airport Washington, D.C., area and concluded that the prospects were very good for such a service in the foreseeable future.

At a board meeting that same day, the Helicopter Association of America had considered the name change suggested by Hal Conners, who was now president. It would be another 20 years, however, before the fundamental change would be voted upon and passed.

On another issue, the association had long been concerned about the ethics of the rough-and-tumble commercial helicopter marketplace. Everything from noise abatement to marketing tactics and safety were on the ethics table.

Six weeks after President John F. Kennedy's inauguration at the Capitol and two miles away, HAA opened its new headquarters on March 1, 1961, in the Landmark Building at 1343 H Street, N.W., under newly appointed Executive Secretary John T. Pennewell, formerly with Keystone Helicopter Corp.

Meanwhile, commercial helicopters quietly went about their work.

For The Record

Hiller 12E rescues crew of the Alaska Cedar Lumber vessel off Oregon coast on December 4, 1962. Pilot Klotz of Evergreen Helicopters saved all 24 crew members.

In the Pacific Northwest, a Hiller 12E placed 40 poles up a mountainside in less than four hours, then laid two manila "sock lines" along a three-mile right-of-way in 12 minutes.

On July 2, 1961, a chronically depressed Ernest Hemingway shot himself to death at his home in Ketchum, Idaho.

At its March 1961 meeting, the Board had received a proposal from Rick Eccles on "Suggested Ethics and Standards" for agricultural work. By November 1961, the groundwork had been done and Robert Facer of Utility Helicopters was appointed chairman of an Ethics and Standards Committee. The committee wasted little time in producing a draft of industry ethics and standards. It was ready for member comments in January 1962.

The issue of low altitude flight did not end with the Tennessee effort. HAA learned of a similarly restrictive bill introduced into the U.S. Congress in the spring of 1961 by a congressman from California. When queried, he said he knew little about the bill and had dropped it into the congressional hopper at the request of some constituents. Of such mindless actions are laws made. He withdrew support for it after helicopter industry representatives explained the ramifications.

With the Eisenhower Administration's strong promotion of offshore oil exploration and drilling during the 1950s, the need for offshore-support helicopters increased steadily through the 1960s.

Tragedy struck the commercial helicopter industry on August 4, 1961, when HAA vice-president Bob Trimble of Aetna Helicopters was killed when he autorotated into a ravine and the helicopter rolled over.

The U.S. Forest Service in mid-1961 started the purchasing process for a new four-place utility helicopter, immediately alarming commercial operators that perhaps an entire government-owned fleet was in the offing. Discussions between industry representatives and Forest Service officials completely reassured the industry that the government had a well-thought-out plan concerning the government-owned helicopter, and that it made a great deal of sense.

On October 30, 1961, the Soviet Party Congress unanimously approved a resolution ordering the removal of Josef Stalin's body from Lenin's tomb in Red Square. It signaled neither a rise nor fall in the international temperature, but did create a stir.

By the first week of January 1962 the first draft of a Code of Ethics was presented for adoption by the Board of the Helicopter Association of America.

It was also the occasion when Enstrom introduced its F-28, a three-place, piston-powered model using a drive belt between the engine and rotor shaft. The price was given as $25,000 for 1963 deliveries.

The Insurance Forum held at HAA's 1962 Dallas meeting also brought to light the fact that insurance costs resulted in more lost helicopter sales than did maintenance costs. A 25 to 30 percent premium was not uncommon for hull coverage, and often had various deductibles or restricted-use clauses tacked on.

In the following month, February 20, 1962, astronaut and Marine Colonel John Glenn became the first American to orbit Earth after blasting off aboard the Friendship 7 Mercury capsule.

In March 1962, HAA moved its headquarters to the Dupont Circle Building in Washington, D.C., and at about the same time (but with no connection), publication of "Up Collective" magazine was suspended. The magazine had been a joint venture of HAA and a commercial publisher, but HAA had no financial interest or editorial control.

For The Record   1963 - John F. Kennedy assassinated in Dallas, Texas • Touch Tone telephone introduced •

Hughes 500
lifting a VW "Bug"

The helicopter had long become a fixture not only of American life but of global efforts to support offshore operations, evacuate casualties from war zones, save victims of disasters, and move executives and high-priority cargo; and now it also became a partisan symbol of progress in national politics.

On May 8, 1962, President Kennedy told United Auto Workers union leaders at the convention hall in Atlantic City, New Jersey, "On a whole variety of ways employment, education, the fight for equality of opportunity for all Americans, regardless of their race and their color — these are the things for which America stands, and for which this union stands. And that is why I flew longer — and this will go down in the history books — that is why I flew longer in a helicopter than any President of the United States to come here today. That is the kind of forward-looking administration we have."

On July 3, 1962, Algeria became independent after 132 years of French rule. The Algerian war had cost an estimated $20 billion and 250,000 lives.

The ending of just one life a month later, August 5, 1962, got even more world attention when actress Marilyn Monroe, 36, was found dead in her bedroom.

On October 22, 1962, President Kennedy ordered U.S. forces to quarantine Cuba following discovery of Soviet strategic missile bases there. "Quarantine" was the chosen term in order to avoid "blockade," which, under international law, is an act of war.

Aviation of all kinds continued making major strides in the U.S., and on November 17, 1962, Dulles International Airport outside Washington, D.C., was dedicated.

Sikorsky S64 SkyCrane
with utility pod attached.

After 10 years and various prototypes, Cessna Aircraft announced just before Christmas 1962 that it had dropped out of the helicopter market. The Kansas firm had its four-place Skyhook design of 1956 as an entry in the light personal helicopter field, but finally gave up the effort.

Cessna bought back the 23 helicopters it sold for $80,000 each, scrapped all of them, and got out of the business.

By January 1963, the HAA regular membership had climbed to 73 commercial operators, 31 associate members, and 18 government agencies that operated heli- copters. Cully Weadock was re-elected president, succeeding Donald A. Larson.

Though commercial helicopter operators grew and prospered, 1963 was generally a bad year for the nation and the world, despite symbolic advances.

Cully Weadock

On April 10, 1963, the submarine USS Thresher failed to surface off Cape Cod, Massachusetts, in a disaster that claimed 129 lives.

At a three-day annual meeting of the Aviation/Space Writers Association in Dallas, Texas, the meeting chairman, George Haddaway, posed a hypothetical question intended to get the attention of news media. The question in this case was: "Could a grandmother [learn to] solo a helicopter in three days?"

Picked to provide the answer was Doris Renninger, whose husband, Henry Renninger, was a founder of Seaboard World Airlines. Doris had set records in all types of jet and prop aircraft and for these she had won a bundle of awards. Helicopters were not among the aircraft she had flown, but when the Whirly-Girls interna- tional organization of women helicopter pilots asked her to take the challenge, she did.

Bell Helicopter agreed to go along with the idea only if she actually flew the helicopter and didn't simply hover close to the ground.

On May 23, 1963, Doris Renninger soloed a Bell 47G after seven hours of instruction.

At a Helicopter Roundtable discussion in May, Cully Weadock of Chesapeake & Potomac Helicopter Airways, asked Bell's Bud Orpen how the manufacturer arrives at its overhaul and cost figures. The question had been bedeviling operators for years with no satisfactory response.

Orpen gave a detailed response complete with numbers, hours, calculation bases, and Bell's maintenance philosophy.

1964 - Arnold Palmer wins 4th Master's Golf Tournament • Acrylic paint introduced •

Did You Know?

Mid-1960s Statistics

In the mid-1960s, the Helicopter Association of America compiled data in preparation for its first directory of commercial operators. Some data were clearly limited by the division of the world into "free world" and "Communist bloc" nations, which distorted some of the information. Nevertheless, summarized data showed that the world's largest commercial operators were Petroleum Helicopters, Inc. (PHI), with 96 aircraft; Bristow with 73; and Okanagan with 68.

There were 1,937 commercial helicopters of all types in the "free world," operated by 588 commercial helicopter operators, of which 236 operated three or more aircraft. U.S. operators totaled 439, accounting for 1,236 helicopters, and 176 of these oper- ators had three or more aircraft. Book value of all U.S. helicopters was estimated at $68 million.

Canadian helicopters were the most active per unit, with 45 operators flying 296 helicopters. In Canada, 21 operators had three or more aircraft.

Most active areas for commercial helicopters included Alaska, the western U.S., and western Canada. Fastest-growing helicopter activity in the mid-1960s was for offshore oil-gas exploration in Louisiana, Texas, the western U.S., and Alaska.

PHI's Bob Suggs was unimpressed, as many operators had been before and since: "In a corporate fleet, it all depends on your operational philosophy. You can overhaul an engine every 100 hours. You may think you have the finest fleet in the world, but I'm not so sure that an engine overhauled every 100 hours is a good engine. On the other hand, you might be an operator out in the bush and run an engine to the bitter end. When you compare, you have to compare what type of operation you run. . . . The thing you want to say is, be very careful how you accept manufacturers' figures. They are not all-inclusive — they purposely paint a very good picture. I don't blame them; they have a product to sell."

At mid-year, 1963 took a decidedly downward turn:

On June 12, 1963, U.S. civil rights leader Medgar Evers was assassinated.

On November 2, 1963, South Vietnam President Ngo Dihn Diem was assassinated.

On November 22, 1963, President John F. Kennedy was assassinated.

The November 1963 HAA newsletter announced a near-future startup date for helicopter instrument flight rules (IFR) operations in the New York area after agreement was reached by FAA and New York Airways, a scheduled passenger carrier.

There was never any guarantee that industry growth would be steadily upward. At the outset of 1964, Walter Attebery of Condor Helicopters & Aviation succeeded Cully Weadock as president of the association. The makeup and size of the membership shifted in that year. Whereas there were 82 commercial operator, 32 associate (mostly manufacturers), and 27 government agency members in mid-June 1963; by January 1964 there were 67 commercial operator, 26 associate, and 28 government agency members. Membership was down by 20, 15 of which were commercial operators.

Yet another FAA review of all rotorcraft regulations was set for mid-February 1964. At the same time, the agency said it was considering registration fees for all aircraft, which would be in addition to fees charged by individual states.

It was in 1964 that the Geneva Continental Shelf Convention was ratified, portioning out the floor of the North Sea for mineral exploration by surrounding nations.

Typical of the special tasks that only helicopters could perform at the time was support for demolition of a Cold War artifact known as the Texas Towers about 30 miles off the northeast coast of the U.S.

An Atlantic Ocean storm had toppled one of the early warning radar towers into the sea, killing the entire crew. The Air Force, reviewing its need for the 100-foot-tall steel-and-concrete towers, decided to demolish the remaining two towers. Copters Unlimited Inc. of Warwick, Rhode Island, flew demolition personnel to the towers and removed the last worker several months later, just minutes before explosive charges severed the three legs of the towers. The platforms were towed to a salvage yard by tugboats.

The Code of Ethics proposal of March 1961 by Rick Eccles of Calicopters was now presented to the HAA Board for approval, which it received. It was submitted to the regular membership at the January 1965 annual meeting, where it got "enthusiastic and unanimous approval" and was printed in the first edition of the association's directory. It covered flight operations, maintenance, personnel and equipment, insurance, sales and advertising, and general business practices.

H.C. "Pete" Brown was elected HAA president at that January session. At the meeting, several important regulatory developments occurred, including an announcement by FAA that it was amending Part 133 to allow simultaneous internal carrying of personnel necessary to work a project, along with an external load of materials.

It was also the era when FAA proposed special recurrency flight checks for pilots of "complex" airplanes and small helicopters. The proposal ran into such opposition that it was dropped, along with FAA's proposal that it more actively regulate agricultural aviation.

The helicopter may have evolved over a quarter of a century by this time, but much FAA thinking had not changed since the earliest days. Part of the agency's regulatory stance was that helicopters over 12,500 pounds maximum gross weight (MGW) must be limited to only three types of operations: scheduled or charter passenger service, external load carriage, or special purpose operations.

"What is totally lacking," said HAA at the time, "is broader operating authority for the many other diversified commercial industrial operations of the type now being performed by small helicopters."

There was, of course, no comparably restrictive FAA attitude regarding large airplanes.

In the spring of 1965, the association launched a major effort to get a public-use heliport opened in Washington, D.C. The industry considered this a major priority of public image and national precedent for all large cities. New York Airways sent a Boeing Vertol 107 to land near the Capitol and bring the issue to the public's attention.

Whatever constitutes that elusive blend of public, political, and private support needed for public heliport efforts to succeed, it was not found. Later attempts focused on sites along the Potomac or Anacostia Rivers, the roof of Union Station, and other locations.

Never was the magic combination found, and to this day the "versatile, go-anywhere"

Piasecki Workhorse, N10109, aids in the construction of power line.

helicopter must fly to National Airport like the biggest jets so the helicopter's passengers can ride in an automobile back to the same Capitol where the federal government used a commercial helicopter to remove and replace the Statue of Freedom on the dome.

Not only did the helicopter industry's effort to get a public-use heliport in Washington, D.C., fail to gain support, but in the first quarter of 1965, the Congress discontinued federal subsidies for helicopter passenger airlines. There was strong opposition from the industry, which pointed out that congressionally approved federal subsidies averaging more than $5 million each continued to be paid to more than a dozen local service airlines that operated airplanes.

The industry's disappointment in the subsidy cutoff was fueled by knowledge that New York Airways alone had increased its capacity by 93 percent in two and a half years, and that the four operating helicopter airlines (New York, Chicago, Los Angeles, and San Francisco) had substantially cut their seat-mile costs. Both New York Airways and Los Angeles Airways had recently been authorized to operate IFR flights (greatly improving completion rates), and other internally generated efficiencies had further cut costs. HAA believed the four airlines would be in the financial black within five years.

It was not to be. Congress eliminated the subsidy for small helicopter airlines while continuing subsidies for small airplane airlines.

Population of commercial helicopters and operators in the U.S. and Canada was tallied in mid-1965 by the Aerospace Industries Association (AIA), which announced a 21 percent increase in commercial operators over the prior year. The new total of 760 operators accounted for a 16 percent increase in the number of helicopters, said AIA, to a North American total of 2,053 aircraft. The number of helicopter flight schools jumped from 121 to 156 in a year, said the manufacturers' association, noting that as recently as 1960 there had been only 50 helicopter flight schools in the U.S. and Canada.

By the spring of 1965, Bell Helicopter was increasingly concerned about its civil customer relations. Teams of representatives were sent on a six-month tour to visit all commercial customers to "review any maintenance and flight operations problems the customer may have and try to assist in their solution. Overall aim of the program is to improve customer relations."

History repeated itself as the U.S. replaced the French in what had been called Indochina and was now Vietnam. The changed name did not change the outcome.

On the front page of the June 1965 issue of Bell Helicopter's "Rotor Breeze" newsletter was a photo of South Vietnamese soldiers jumping from Bell UH-1B troop-carriers into a firefight. U.S. involvement was slowly increasing, but full-scale war was still beyond the visible horizon. Meanwhile, helicopters had a more conspicuous public profile as the technology of communications kept pace with advances in helicopter technology and made nightly television news a family affair.

John Pennewell resigned as Executive Secretary of HAA October 1965, and was succeeded in January 1966 by John Ryan, whose title became Executive Director later in 1966 when he signed a contract for the position. As a condition of that contract, association headquarters offices were moved to Stratford, Connecticut. Bob Richardson of Chicago's Helicopter Air Lift, Inc. was elected president.

It was the 20th anniversary of the certification of the Bell 47, and by the time March 8 arrived, Bell had produced 1,600 commercial helicopters, more than all other makers combined. There was, however, competition for U.S. makers coming down the line from Europe, and it arrived in North America at the end of the 1960s for those who wanted it. As Ann Davis and Bob Richardson noted, "European technological creativity has been

For The Record

1966 - Fiber-optic telephone cables introduced • Fuel injection for autos introduced •

demonstrated repeatedly. With the Alouette II came the gas turbine powerplant, which marked a turning point in the history of rotorcraft. This was followed by glass fiber/resin composite blades, standard equipment on the Gazelle and the BO-105. Modern hubs have been installed in the Lynx and the BO-105, eliminating conventional hinges. The Aerospatiale Star Flex hub belongs to this generation of equipment. The shrouded tail rotor, which is standard equipment on the Gazelle and Dauphin, represents a safety advance through elimination of accidents caused by contact with tail rotor blades."

"European industry selects its market slots carefully," said the U.S. industry's organization. "Political factors have also stimulated commerce. There are preferential ties with certain countries. The most important single factor was unquestionably the inception, in 1967, of the Gazelle, Puma, and Lynx Anglo-French cooperative programs."

"The technology's been great in the past few years," said Era's Carl Brady. "The innovation of jet engines in helicopters took away a lot of problems. In Alaska, on the North Slope particularly, you had to take the battery to bed with you, and heat the oil in the morning, and heat the engine for a couple hours before you could start it. All those problems were with the old piston engines in cold weather."

Pilots of that pre-turbine era often carried a crayon or wax candle in their pockets. When the piston engine began running roughly and split the needles, he'd land and touch the crayon or candle to each exhaust manifold. When the crayon or candle didn't melt, the pilot knew that spark plug needed replacement.

Time and again, U.S. operators asked U.S. manufacturers why improved technology often arrived first in Europe. The dialogue seemed an echo of that between U.S. automobile buyers and the Detroit giants regarding Japanese cars.

The helicopter's primary commercial market, offshore oil/gas support, continued to boom throughout the 1960s, especially in the North Sea after ratification of the 1964 Geneva Convention.

Between 1965 and 1967, geologists identified five major fields under the North Sea in British waters. The search for oil/gas in waters of the Netherlands and Germany was somewhat discouraging, but luck favored Norway, where a 1969 discovery was named the Ekofisk field. In 1970, waters off Aberdeen, Scotland, yielded data on the Forties field. More than half the aircraft movements at Aberdeen Airport — the third busiest in the U.K. — soon consisted of helicopters.

In March the first edition of a new newsletter titled "Our Rotor News" was issued by HAA to replace the "Confidential" publication of prior years. The organization also announced plans to publish "the world's most accurate directory of commercial helicopter operators." In a development familiar to anyone who has ever tried to administer a survey, however, the project was stymied by a return of only 10 data sheets of the 115 it sent to members. HAA membership grew in the first two months of 1966 from 74 to 89 regular members, from 22 to 27 associates, and from 29 to 36 government members for a total of 152.

Bell JetRanger on Police mission

Hiller 12E delivers concrete for a helicopter landing pad on Mile Rock Lighthouse.

New-generation helicopters sought by the industry included anything productive that would cut maintenance costs, always far higher for helicopters than for airplanes.

The industry saw part of its economics and public perception problems in a light described well by Jock Cameron of British Airways Helicopters, who said a helicopter airline could make money only when new-generation aircraft became available with far better economics than current equipment. As he noted with considerable irony: "Ground movement by airlines at London's Heathrow and Paris' Charles DeGaulle Airport almost equals the flight time between the two cities."

The issue of available and suitable transport category helicopters with sufficiently good economics for scheduled passenger airline service has always been a thorn for that sector of the industry. Once a helicopter airline launches service in any market area with helicopters that are only marginally suitable for the task, and the company fails to survive, later attempts are at a serious psychological and political disadvantage. Even if economics turn in favor of the operator because of the introduction of new and more efficient equipment, the reaction of politicians and other opinion-makers at regulatory-hearing time is likely to be "No, no . . . we tried that once and it didn't work."

Tug Gustafson, veteran Sikorsky salesman, said the world's first scheduled helicopter passenger airline got under way in Boston in 1947, using Sikorsky S-51s. As he described it, "We believed our own sales pitch. We started a service flying from the roof of a downtown parking garage to Logan Airport. We had three three-seat S-51s and charged $3.50 for the 72-second flight. We made 168 flights a day. Arithmetic was against us. Each trip cost us $20 plus 42 cents ticket tax. No way we could make any money, yet we were thinking of Los Angeles, Chicago, New York, and San Francisco! At that, the service lasted four months; and it was the noise we made, not the losses, that drove us to the wall."

Later, scheduled passenger services were launched by British European Airways and by New York Airways, both in 1952. All the pioneers had the same lament as subsequent efforts: Give us better technology and quieter helicopters.

New-generation helicopters sought by the industry included anything productive that would cut maintenance costs, always far higher for helicopters than for airplanes. Lockheed's new Model 286 rigid-rotor system was finally out of the Skunk Works (a special design shop within Lockheed). Noted aviatrix Jacqueline Cochrane was allowed to fly the 4,700 pound Model 286, and the aircraft did set a speed record of 206 mph in a shallow dive, but eventually the project simply faded away.

Kaman, another industry pioneer, said it was considering entering the commercial field after many years of military work, but that, too, came to naught until decades later. The firm told stockholders it was interested in the 12,000 to 14,000-lb. multi-engine transport category, for which the firm acknowledged there was a need.

Sikorsky disappointed the commercial helicopter industry in subsequent years by deciding not to produce the 44-seat S-65. Thus, the most promising large transport model available for some time was the Vertol H-47 Chinook, which was not the most cost-effective helicopter for the role but was eventually bought by British Airways Helicopters for offshore oil/gas support. No other commercial passenger operator followed suit. Passenger services continued to be provided mostly by the Sikorsky S-61 class, which was not the new-technology example that industry sought.

With successful FAA certification of the Lockheed rigid-rotor 286 design on July 25, 1966, it appeared that the industry's search for new technology was about to bring welcome results. Lockheed had taken its speedy 286 on a three-month, 7,000-mile demonstration tour of U.S. commercial

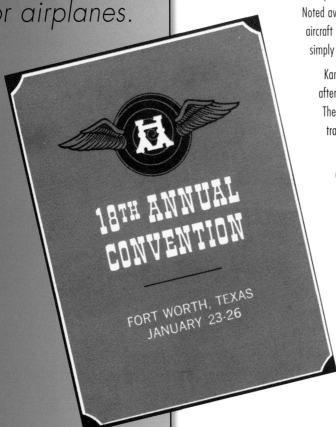

18TH ANNUAL CONVENTION

FORT WORTH, TEXAS
JANUARY 23-26

operators, during which it totaled 250 flight hours and had a 99 percent reliability record for availability. The 286 carried 2,640 passengers, of whom more than a thousand actually flew the aircraft. The Model 286 demonstrator was also flown at the 1967 HAA show.

Despite that, Lockheed made no comment on commercial production plans, and no civil aircraft ever emerged from the program.

Fairchild-Hiller introduced its new FH-1100 at the Paris Air Show in 1965. Later it announced that it would market a commercial version of the OH-5A prototype, which had been developed to meet the U.S. Army light observation helicopter (LOH) competition. But that was a four-place machine, not a transport-category aircraft. The FH-1100 was widely praised for technical innovations and low-maintenance features. Fairchild-Hiller set the price for the army version at $29,415 per aircraft.

Hughes Tool Company said in March 1966 that its own four-place LOH entry (the OH-6, ancestor of the aircraft that evolved into the MD-500) also would be sold as a commercial model.

Then followed a lesson for the industry and the nation in government economics.

Hughes won the government contract over Fairchild-Hiller largely on the basis of price, saying it would sell each OH-6 to the army for $19,860. Commercial operators were stunned. The price to a commercial operator for the same Hughes model was initially $69,000, which quickly jumped to $78,800. Then the army agreed to pay the "civil price" for the OH-6 of nearly four times the official contract price (and two-and-half times the Fairchild-Hiller bid), "in order to speed up production."

Congress asked some very pointed questions about the pricing arrangements.

Army Chief of Staff General Harold Johnson replied, "When a contract is set up, a company agrees to commit a certain portion of its line to military deliveries [and] the remaining portion goes to civilian sales, if they are able to sell this machine. We are buying the civil portion of the line during this particular time and paying the higher civil price."

It would be hard to find a better example of a big company "buying into" a military market by underpricing the product and having commercial operators make up the difference. There was no explanation for the fourfold price increase to commercial operators.

FAA spent much of 1966 evaluating markers for high-tension powerlines, pylons, and tall towers. Collisions with these structures caused at least 150 aviation accidents yearly, and Columbia Helicopters had lost an aircraft and a pilot to such an encounter. Livingston Helicopters reported many unmarked trams operating in Alaska. Most of the deadly obstructions were near local airports or in mountain canyons.

It was in that year of increasing conflict in Southeast Asia that Bell received the largest contract in the history of helicopters. The U.S. Army awarded the firm $250 million for 2,115 Bell UH-1B and UH-1D models, with delivery to be completed by the end of 1967. Kaman reported that its helicopters had rescued more than 250 military personnel during the year.

In its September 1966 newsletter, the industry association published a lengthy article titled "Nation's Capital Discovers — Almost Too Late — That It Must Have Downtown Helicopter Service." The saga of public heliport efforts was laid out in detail.

Development of the Federal Aviation Administration

The Air Commerce Act of May 20, 1926, the government's first step in regulating aviation, charged the Secretary of Commerce with fostering air commerce, issuing and enforcing air traffic rules, and certifying aircraft. In 1938, the Civil Aeronautics Act transferred the government's civil aviation role from the Commerce Department to the Civil Aeronautics Authority (CAA). In 1940, President Franklin Roosevelt split the Authority into two agencies, the Civil Aeronautics Board (CAB) and the CAA.

In 1958, the Federal Aviation Act transferred the CAA's functions to a new independent body, the Federal Aviation Agency, which had broader authority to combat the increasing number of aviation hazards. The Act took safety rulemaking from the Civil Aeronautics Board (CAB) and gave the Agency sole responsibility for developing and maintaining a common civil-military system of air navigation and air traffic control.

In 1966, President Lyndon B. Johnson sought legislative authority for a new cabinet department that would combine all major federal transportation responsibilities. The move reflected a growing belief that such an organization could best meet the nation's need for integrated systems and policies to facilitate the transport of goods and people. The result was the Department of Transportation (DOT), which began operations on April 1, 1967. The Federal Aviation Agency was renamed the Federal Aviation Administration.

The FAA gradually assumed responsibilities not originally contemplated by the Federal Aviation Act. The hijacking epidemic of the 1960s involved the agency in the field of aviation security. In 1968, Congress vested in the FAA Administrator the power to prescribe aircraft noise standards. These changes were the first of many for the FAA.

21st ANNUAL MEETING
AND
HELICOPTER SHOWCASE
at
Florida's Fabulous
Diplomat Hotel & Country Club
Hollywood, Florida

**Advertising, Exhibit & Sales Managers
Information Kit and
Application Form**

JANUARY 8–11, 1969

HELICOPTER ASSOCIATION
of America

Hangar D • Westchester County Airport • White Plains • N.Y. 10604   914 949-1600

Everything, it seems, is in the eye of the beholder, including a definition of "too late." As the 20th century closed, the nation's capital still had no downtown helicopter service.

By the time the 1967 January HAA convention rolled around in Palm Springs, California, the helicopter world was agog with new technology developments. Some were driven by military requirements, some were not. Hughes had announced research into hot-cycle systems for commercial models that would greatly reduce rotating machinery and eliminate the tail rotor, gearboxes, and other major maintenance items. Lockheed demonstrated its Model 286 rigid-rotor system, and the latest turbine-powered helicopters such as the Fairchild-Hiller FH-1100 and newest Bell JetRanger models (Price: $85,000) were in Palm Springs.

HAA had record-breaking attendance of 1,132 — three times the prior year's record. Membership was then at 417, up from the 1966 total of 119, while exhibits stood at 60 compared with only 20 in 1966.

That 1967 convention also featured a tragedy, when an Alouette II crashed at the 7,500-foot level in nearby mountains during a demonstration flight, killing two of the three people aboard.

Nevertheless, the helicopter as an executive transport was now getting more serious attention than it previously had, especially since the 1967 show brought out three new turbine helicopter models.

Even in 1967, however, "Business & Commercial Aviation" magazine editor James Holahan could describe the helicopter as an "airplane" and decry its ride characteristics as he wrote about "that normal helicopter feeling that you are riding in a pendulum swinging from beneath the rotor." The description was a comparison with the Lockheed Model 286 rigid-rotor design flown at the meeting.

Holahan noted with some frustration, "What was difficult to understand was Lockheed's big push to 'sell' the rigid-rotor concept . . . then confess it had no plans to make the aircraft available commercially. None of the company's marketing or flight test people could explain why."

That, continued Holahan, "was not the only enigma at the convention. Another was the wide communications gap between helicopter manufacturers and operators and corporate aviation." The summing up of a corporate aviation panel discussion was that the helicopter was not yet ready for corporate aviation because its reliability and IFR operations were not yet acceptable. Three of four panelists said they would insist on two engines, while the fourth said he was not so much concerned about the engines as about other failure-prone parts like transmissions, clutches, and rotating assemblies.

The debate about helicopter technology continued through the 1960s, with operators seeking higher productivity and lower maintenance, while manufacturers responded that they were doing the best they could do.

(The author once interviewed a manufacturer of accessory equipment for aircraft. In the course of discussions, the firm's chief engineer said they had equipment designs in the company vault that were far superior to those currently being sold. When asked why the newer-and-better designs were not being produced and sold, the chief engineer said the current design, though not as good, had not yet returned the investment the firm had put into it. Thus, the new design would be held in a vault until the old design returned its investment. It is, he explained, a reality of economics. He's right; and there is, of course, no way of telling how many other new-technology designs are being held in vaults until old designs are fully amortized.)

The industry's unrelenting quest for simple, inexpensive, low-maintenance technology seemed to appear at that 1967 helicopter association convention, and just as quickly disappeared. Filper Research Corp. of San Ramon, California, announced it would soon bring to the marketplace a six-place, turbine-powered helicopter called the Beta 300. Filper, basically a food-machinery manufacturer that had entered the helicopter design field, also had plans for a low-cost, piston-powered light helicopter called the Beta 200. The aircraft had tandem rigid "Gyroflex" rotors and was intended to sell for less than $20,000. The Beta 200 carried two people (and had a jump seat); featured retractable gear, speeds above 150 mph, and a range of 400 miles; and was due to be sold to law enforcement, utility firms, foresters, corporations, and private pilots. The engine was a 210-hp Continental. In flight, the aircraft looked "like a flying Jaguar XKE."

Filper Research said its certification program for the Beta 200 piston-powered design was proceeding and that the firm had hired experimental test pilot Zeke Hopkins to direct the effort. Filper and Lockheed appeared to be ahead of the pack on new technology.

But the Filper designs did not advance to production status and Lockheed dropped from the arena. The helicopter industry continued seeking that elusive new technology.

In a renewed effort to establish a voice for the industry, HAA and PJS Publications, of Peoria, Illinois, joined forces to produce a new magazine called "Rotor & Wing," which began as a semi-monthly and became a monthly. PJS Publications also published "Peoria Journal-Star" daily newspaper.

Bob Richardson was succeeded as president in 1967 by Roy Falconer, and the Board voted to admit short takeoff and landing (STOL) and vertical/short takeoff and landing (V/STOL) manufacturers as associate members.

In a setback for internationalists, however, the Board tabled a motion to change the name of the association to "International Helicopter Association." That change eventually would take place with different terminology 14 years later.

Out in the field, Alaska Helicopters was operating from its Anchorage base and surveying the Prudhoe Bay area by using a Bell 206B JetRanger and a 330-lb. Litton Auto-Surveyor system. In a scant 10 days in 1967, the operator surveyed an area the size of Indiana.

Walter Attebery of Arctic Air Service took the first FH-1100 up to Alaska for commercial work in 1967.

That was about the time that Era was bought by Rowan Drilling, now called the Rowan Companies. Carl Brady, former cropduster pilot, sat on the Rowan Board for 25 years while the company's stock was traded on the New York Stock Exchange. Then he retired and became chairman of the executive committee of subsidiary Era Helicopters.

The top 10 commercial operators (and their helicopter fleet size) in 1967 were PHI, Lafayette, Louisiana (76); Air America, Washington, D.C. (41); Francha Enterprises, Long Beach, California (28); American Investments, Lakewood, California (20); Orlando Helicopter Airways, Orlando, Florida (19); Panhandle Aviation, Omaha, Nebraska (19); Columbia Helicopters, Portland, Oregon (16); Era Helicopters of Alaska, Anchorage, Alaska (16); National Helicopter Service, Van Nuys, California (16); and World Wide Helicopters, White Plains, New York (15).

In a major development toward safety improvement, the Flight Safety Foundation announced in November 1967 that it would begin working with HAA to perform aviation safety surveys of commercial helicopter operators, with one stated goal being the lowering of insurance rates.

In January 1968 the annual convention was held in Las Vegas, Nevada. Godfrey Rockefeller of Chesapeake & Potomac Airways was elected president at a gathering that drew 1,300 registrants for the first time. At the flying display, a Sikorsky SkyCrane hauled trucks around, while the flight line also featured a pair of Pilatus Porter STOL airplanes.

By 1968 it also was apparent that the association was outgrowing its Stratford, Connecticut, offices, so HAA moved to Westchester County Airport in White Plains, New York. The association also arranged to have its annual directory published as an issue of "Rotor & Wing" magazine.

In 1969 HAA met in Hollywood, Florida. Okanagan's Glenn McPherson was elected president and served through 1971. At the same time, Bell Helicopter's James Atkins was seated on the HAA Board as the first ex officio representative of a manufacturer.

In September of 1969, Gates Learjet took the wraps off its Twinjet helicopter mockup, a beautifully sleek, dreamlike machine. Unlike some predecessors, it was solid with engineering, proven hardware and systems,

"Victim" is lifted from a life raft onto the rescue platform of a Sikorsky S-61A helicopter.

tooling, investment capital, and all the other vital elements of a sound program. If the commercial helicopter operating industry wanted new technology and new thinking, here it was from Wichita, Kansas. The 6,000-lb. MGW Gates Twinjet seemed on paper to answer the dreams of many operators. And the paper was backed by the output of one hundred full-time engineers who had come from all the big helicopter makers.

The Twinjet was designed to cruise at 180 mph with eight to 12 passengers over a 400-mile range with power from two Garrett 474 shaft horsepower (shp) turboshaft engines. It had a four-blade, 40-ft-diameter main rotor on a 42-ft-long fuselage made of high-strength, lightweight materials.

With four million dollars of Gates money invested, master tooling and production facilities nearly complete, and even the final price range — $400,000 to $450,000 — established, the Twinjet appeared to be as solid as it could possibly be. First flight was due in 1971 and FAA certification was expected in 1972.

The 1970-71 recession caused Gates to agonize over the project and finally drop it. The Twinjet was "10 years and one recession ahead of its time." A shaky economy and fears of oil shortages caused the plans of many enterprises to change.

The Southeast Asia war, too, changed many things, and the decade ended with a massive change in helicopter technology, as well as future commercial services inextricably linked to helicopters. While most development has been historically aided by military funding, commercial operators often see the potential of the machine first. That changed in Southeast Asia, where a military that had been reluctant to use the vulnerable and expensive machine began the war with older helicopters like the H-13, H-23, H-19, H-34, and H-21 models, then evolved to much more advanced aircraft like the UH-1 series, OH-6, OH-58, CH-3, CH-46, and CH-47, and finally finished the long war with end-stage models like AH-1, CH-53, and CH-54.

1968 - Robert F. Kennedy assassinated • Water beds introduced • Laugh-In debuts on television •

Emergency medical services blossomed after the Southeast Asia War, exploiting the lessons of that war. In contrast to the wartime setting, this time the services were commercial.

It was said at the time that the U.S. spent $40,000 to kill each enemy soldier in Southeast Asia. (We call it the Vietnam War, they call it the American War.) We found that it cost much less to bring wounded Americans to medical treatment.

If it had cost a hundred times more, it would have been worth it. In World War II, the wounded typically waited eight hours to get full medical treatment, and 10 percent of all wounded died. Transportation was by stretcher, road, or airplane.

In terms of helicopter rescues, the first case was almost a worst-case.

On April 4, 1944, Captain James Green, U.S. Tenth Air Force, crashed in northern Burma's jungle on a reconnaissance flight. He was three minutes flying time from his base at Shinbwiyang.

It took a medical team nearly two days to reach him on foot, and they found that Green had spinal injuries and could not be moved back through the jungle on a stretcher. A new type of aircraft called a helicopter was summoned, but to clear a landing pad, the rescue operation required a unit of combat engineers, a special Air Transport Command rescue team, and an assortment of volunteers from Green's unit.

It took two weeks for the composite group to clear a spot in the dense jungle, then the Sikorsky R-4B routinely landed. Green was taken from his temporary tent in the jungle, put aboard the helicopter and the R-4B took off.

Flying time to the base hospital was five minutes.

In Korea, the wait for medical treatment was about three hours. In Southeast Asia, wounded were treated at a rear hospital less than two hours after being hit, and only one percent died.

Those numbers percolated in the heads of medical professionals, and as the war decelerated for Americans, its lessons accelerated for them. From the blood of Southeast Asia, a new set of initials was painted across the American landscape.

Those initials were EMS.

Emergency medical services blossomed after the Southeast Asia War, exploiting the lessons of that war. In contrast to the wartime setting, this time the services were commercial.

By 1972, half a dozen U.S. hospitals were operating helicopters — either through an in-house department or under contract — and the death rate from massive trauma dropped all over the nation. The number of EMS programs grew quickly as their human value was realized. Other countries took the same lessons and applied them.

Countless lives were saved in Vietnam by military helicopters, and it triggered a new phenomenon called EMS, which was made possible for the rest of us only by the civil helicopter.

It was one of the best things to come out of the Traumatic Sixties.

Early HAA Logo

1969 - Neil Armstrong stepped down from the Apollo 11 landing craft and onto the moon •

Bell 47 places cross on church

HELICOPTER PROFILES

The author, editor, and publisher
are truly grateful to the following profile
companies whose financial support
helped to make this book possible.

AGUSTA

Agusta: The Science of Vertical Flight

Agusta belongs to the exclusive group of helicopter companies that are leaders at world level, both for the complete range of products and services it offers and for its technological know-how strengthened by a tradition that goes back to the origins of aviation.

Its founder, Giovanni Agusta, flew his first airplane in 1907, and from 1923 onward the company was active in the design, production, and maintenance of fixed-wing aircraft. Agusta entered the world of vertical flight in 1952 after signing an agreement with Bell to produce its helicopters under license. Similar accords were reached in the 1960s with other major U.S. producers: Sikorsky, Boeing, and McDonnell Douglas.

Agusta did not limit itself to production under license. Starting from this experience, and in a relatively short time, independent research and development capacity was created. The numerous projects and the experimental work carried out at the end of the 1950s led to the construction of no less than nine prototypes, all flight-tested with success. The innovations associated with two of these models, the A101G and the A106, allowed Agusta to enter, as a full member, the select club of companies able to produce independent helicopter designs.

Agusta's place among the leaders in vertical flight was secured in 1971 with the first flight of the A109 twin-turbine helicopter, a design with innovative features and high performance that was realized entirely at Cascina Costa. Newer versions of the A109 are still in production; many hundreds of its civil, military, and public utility variants have been

manufactured. The universal reputation it enjoys is a demonstration of Agusta's command of helicopter technological know-how.

A fundamental stage in Agusta's development of helicopter technology was reached in 1983 with the first flight of the A129 Mangusta anti-tank helicopter, the first attack helicopter to be designed and produced wholly in Europe, which demonstrated Agusta's capacity to satisfy the most complex technical requirements.

The success of these models opened up for Agusta the road of cooperation with other European helicopter manufacturers in jointly defined projects. In 1981 the design of the EH-101 was initiated in collaboration with Westland of the U.K., in line with the requirements of the Italian and British navies. In 1985 in collaboration with the aeronautic industries of France, Germany, and the Netherlands, Agusta launched a program for the development of the NH90, a twin-engine multi-role helicopter of nine tons that will meet the medium helicopter requirements of these countries' armed forces. In 1994 Agusta's own product range was widened with the introduction of the single-turbine A119 Koala and the twin-turbine A109 Power, products that open a new chapter in the company's history.

Agusta is a patrimony of technology and of human resources in a story that started 90 years ago and that will continue beyond the year 2000.

Agusta A102

A119 Koala

AIR LOGISTICS

Air Logistics Bell 214 ST

Air Logistics was founded in 1972 to serve the offshore oil and gas indus- try. After 25 years, the focus of the company has remained consistent — to provide the most reliable and efficient helicopter transportation of personnel and equipment in support of offshore, energy-related operations.

The parent company of Air Logistics, Offshore Logistics, Inc., was incorporated in 1969 as a marine transportation company. As production in the Gulf of Mexico and around the world moved further offshore, the leaders of this Lafayette, Louisiana — based company realized that the future of offshore transportation would rely on helicopter service.

Air Logistics was formed just in time to ride the upswing in the oil and gas industry. The years from 1974 to 1982 took Air Logistics from a fledgling subsidiary to a major provider in the Gulf of Mexico, Alaska, and overseas. By 1983, Air Logistics owned 191 helicopters and had established successful joint ventures in Central and South America, Mexico, and Egypt.

Air Logistics was able to weather the difficult years between 1982 and 1987 because of its ability to stay focused on the oil and gas service industry. After limited efforts in diversification, Air Logistics remained stable by simplifying and concentrating all efforts on its strengths — qualified personnel, a strong emphasis on safety and the development of a modern helicopter fleet.

The stabilization of the oil and gas industry began in late 1987 and allowed Air Logistics to expand its operations with the acquisition of Pumpkin Air in 1987 and of the off - shore operations of Omni Flight in 1989. In 1993, the company acquired 100 percent of their joint venture company, Heli-Lift, Inc., to become Air Logistics of Alaska, Inc., providing complete service to the Aleyeska Pipeline.

Bristow Eurocopter Super-Puma

In 1996, Offshore Logistics made a significant investment in Bristow Helicopter Group Limited of the United Kingdom, thereby creating a partnership that covers the world. Bristow, founded in 1953, was one of the very first civil helicopter companies. Although best known for their offshore operations in the North Sea, Bristow has operated across both hemispheres — from the Caribbean and the South China Sea to West Africa, Asia, and Australia. The company is a major contractor to government agencies worldwide and is the pioneer and sole supplier of civil search and rescue helicopters in the U.K.

This alliance provides customers with a large, diverse fleet of over 300 premium aircraft with operational experience in approximately 100 countries. Bristow and Air Logistics employ 2,600 people with outstanding records of safety, reliability, and efficiency. Together, they offer the total transportation package at the highest level of service, expertise, and technical ability.

ALLISON ENGINE COMPANY

Allison Engine Company was founded in 1915 by James A. Allison to provide engineering support to racing teams competing at the nearby Indianapolis Motor Speedway. The outbreak of World War I shifted the company's focus to aircraft engines, beginning with the V-12 "Liberty." World War II would establish Allison's wartime legacy as its V-1710 engine powered the legendary P-38 "Lightning" and P-40 "Warhawk" fighter planes.

The post-war era saw Allison develop the first of many gas turbine-powered engines, including its first turboshaft helicopter engine, the T63, which established the groundwork for today's modern, FADEC-controlled Model 250s. Through the years Allison has produced over 26,000 Model 250 engines, which have accumulated more than 110 million flight hours, and the company continues to lead the industry in providing gas turbine engine power for light helicopters for both commercial and military applications around the world.

Today, Allison Engine Company designs, manufactures, markets, and supports gas turbine engines and components for aviation, marine, and industrial applications, with over 140,000 engines produced. Allison employs approximately 4,300 people at its research, engineering, and manufacturing facilities in Indianapolis, Indiana, and three satellite operations. These include the Single Crystal Operation, located in Indianapolis, which is dedicated to the development and fabrication of advanced single crystal engine parts and components for Allison Engine Company and other customers; the Allison Engine Repair Operation (AERO) facility, also located in Indianapolis and dedicated to developing engine overhaul and repair methods supporting field operators; and the Allison Evansville Operation, located in Evansville, Indiana, which is dedicated to the development and fabrication of advanced sheet metal products for engines and exhaust systems.

Allison's current Model 250 engine (above) and its predecessor, the Model T63 (bottom - shown in its turboprop configuration).

Allison operated as part of General Motors Corporation from 1929 until December 1993 when it separated from GM to become an independent company. Allison was acquired by Rolls-Royce plc, a world-leading power systems company, in March 1995 and operates as a member of the Rolls-Royce Aerospace Group.

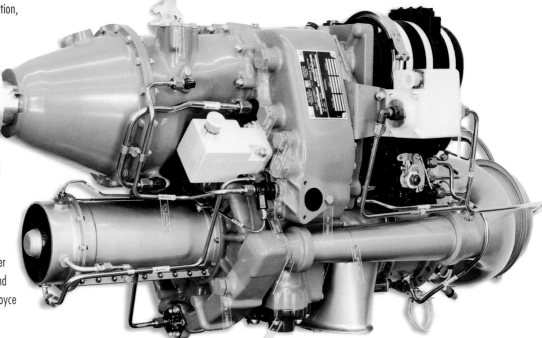

BELL HELICOPTER TEXTRON, INC.

Bell Helicopter Textron, Inc. is the world's leading producer of vertical flight aircraft for commercial and military customers. Since 1946, when the Bell 47 was certificated as the world's first commercial helicopter, Bell Helicopter has been the industry leader with every major advancement of rotorcraft development.

Bell Helicopter was originally founded as the helicopter division of the former Bell Aircraft Company of Buffalo, New York, the manufacturer of the P-39 and P-63 WWII fighter planes as well as America's first jet-powered airplane, the P-59, and the Bell X-1A, the first plane to break the sound barrier.

Bell 430

Headquartered in Fort Worth, Texas, Bell Helicopter has built more than 34,000 helicopters. The Bell 47 was the first to be successfully produced in large numbers and placed in service around the globe. During the Korean War, the Bell 47 demonstrated the value of the helicopter as an air ambulance. Bell's commanding leadership of the rotorcraft industry continued during the 1950s and 1960s when the company developed and produced in large numbers the first successful turbine-powered helicopter, the UH-1, better known as the Huey, as well as the AH-1 Cobra, the world's first dedicated attack helicopter.

With its continued advanced technology design engineering and high-quality manufacturing, Bell aircraft are still acknowledged to be the most reliable helicopters in the world. Bell aircraft can be found flying in over 120 nations, accumulating fleet time at a rate in excess of 10 flight hours every minute of the day.

Current production commercial helicopters include the turbine-powered, five-place Bell 206B JetRanger-III, the seven-place 206L LongRanger-IV, and the Bell 407, which is a new light single with an advanced four-blade main rotor system. Bell's twin engine fleet includes the 6- to 10-place Bell 430, which holds the around-the-world helicopter speed record, the 12- to 15-place Bell 212, and the 412EP, a four-blade variant of the 212.

Bell and Samsung Aerospace Industries, Ltd., of Korea have formed a collaborative agreement to design and build a new light twin-engine helicopter called the Bell 427. It is 13 inches longer than the Bell 407 and will meet anticipated

ICAO and JAR twin-engine requirements. Certification is scheduled for late 1998 with first deliveries in early 1999.

Teamed with Boeing, Bell is producing the V-22 Osprey tiltrotor for the U.S. Marine Corps and Special Operations Command. A truly revolutionary development in vertical flight development, the tiltrotor can take off, hover, and land like a helicopter and fly forward with the range and speed of a high-speed turboprop airplane.

With Boeing, Bell is also developing a nine-passenger commercial tilt-rotor called the Bell Boeing 609. The first flight is scheduled for 1999, with certification in 2000 and first deliveries in 2001. U.S. military helicopters currently being manufactured by Bell include the AH-1W SuperCobra for the U.S. Marine Corps; and the armed OH-58D Kiowa Warrior for the U.S. Army. In 1996, Bell completed delivery of a 137-aircraft order for the TH-67 Creek new training helicopter for the U.S. Army. For the Canadian Forces' utility tactical helicopter program, Bell is under contract to manufacture 100 CH-146 Griffon helicopters, which are highly modified versions of the 412EP. Most recently, Bell delivered nine Bell 412EP helicopters to the British Defence Helicopter Flying School for use as advanced crew training aircraft. In keeping with its reputation as the helicopter company most responsive to its customers, Bell has representatives in over 50 countries. In addition, Bell maintains an extensive spare parts distribution network that ensures spare parts shipment to customers anywhere in the world within 24 hours.

Over the years, Bell has participated in a number of co-production programs to assemble helicopters in different nations, including Japan, Norway, Turkey, and Indonesia. The company operates 10 plants with over three million square feet of manufacturing floor space; Bell Helicopter Textron employs about 8,000 people worldwide. Bell's commercial helicopters are assembled at the company's plant in Mirabel, Quebec.

Bell Helicopter Textron can be found on the World Wide Web at www.bellhelicopter.textron.com. Bell is a subsidiary of Textron Inc. (NYSE: TXT), a global multi-industry company with market-leading operations in five business segments: Aircraft, Automotive, Industrial, Systems and Components, and Finance.

CARRAWAY METHODIST HEALTH SYSTEMS

Health care would be radically different in Alabama without the Life Saver program at Carraway Methodist Health Systems. With three helicopters, nine pilots, 11 nurses, four physicians, and six dispatchers, this service makes approximately 1,500 flights a year, transporting critically ill or injured patients. In fact, since 1981, this program has transported almost 25,000 patients.

Life Saver lands at small community hospitals — and occasionally along busy highways or rural lanes — then rushes back to major medical centers in Birmingham. The fate of their patients often depends upon the crew's skill and the remarkable array of medical equipment tucked inside this flying intensive care unit.

"Time and again, Life Saver has made a critical difference in the transport of patients. I'm very proud of this program and its contributions to health care in our state," says Dr. Robert P. Carraway, founder of the program and chairman of the Board/CEO of Carraway Methodist Health Systems.

Almost 20 years ago, Dr. Carraway and an emergency medicine physician at Carraway Methodist Medical Center were discussing a magazine article about a critically injured accident victim rescued by a helicopter. The two men talked about the tremendous potential of aeromedical programs to save lives. When the conversation ended, Dr. Carraway was determined to explore the subject.

Dr. Carraway became convinced that a well-run program would be a tremendous benefit for the people of Alabama. But to fulfill its mission, he realized, Life Saver would have to be totally dedicated to safety and quality care. To ensure that commitment, Carraway Methodist Health Systems owns and operates the entire program which includes three Bell 206 LongRangers.

This insistence on safety is reflected in every aspect of the program and is a key factor in its success, according to Brooks Wall, who has served as director of Life Saver since it began. "To have operated almost 17 years accident-free is really phenomenal. What this record speaks to is the hospital's commitment to excellence and safety. You just can't be that lucky," Wall says. "Our safety record is a tribute to the expertise of our pilots and mechanics and to the support of the hospital."

Another important element in this success is the presence on every flight of a physician trained in emergency medicine and a highly qualified nurse, according to Dr. Carraway. "That's certainly a key factor in Life Saver's success."

An outstanding medical team, exceptional pilots and maintenance people, a solid administrative staff, and a tenacious commitment to safety and quality patient care — these have been the hallmarks of Carraway's Life Saver. They are the foundation upon which this program will continue to serve the people of Alabama.

Dedication ceremony and ribbon cutting: November 17, 1980. Pictured (L-R) Dr. Benjamin Carraway, DOB/CEO; Perry Cox, Administrator; Will Wakefield, CFO; and Dr. Robert Carraway, Executive Director.

Present facility of Carraway Life Saver

COLUMBIA HELICOPTERS, INC.

It all started by selling helicopter rides at county fairs.

Looking back over 40 years, it is interesting to realize that one of the world's largest heavy-lift helicopter companies had such a humble beginning.

Columbia Helicopters, Inc. was founded by Wes Lematta in April 1957. Following service in WW II, Wes used the GI Bill to complete flight training. With the assistance of his brother Eddie, Wes purchased a used Hiller 12B, and the fledgling company came to life. Today, Columbia Helicopters has expanded to include a worldwide fleet of over 30 aircraft and approximately 800 employees.

In 1958, Wes gained national recognition when he rescued 17 seamen from a sinking dredge off Coos Bay, Oregon. Maneuvering close to the foundering vessel, Wes was able to save all hands.

Columbia's fleet began to expand in 1959 with the purchase of a second helicopter, a new Bell 47-G2. The addition of a third aircraft, a new Hiller 12E, followed in 1960. During this year, the company received a contract to place wood poles for power lines. This job provided an opportunity for Wes to try out a new method of external load placement — using a long attachment line and leaning out of the left side of the helicopter to look directly at the load and placement site. This technique, the Direct Visual Operational Control (or DVOC), proved successful and has become the accepted method of safe, precision cargo placement by operators worldwide.

Columbia Helicopters continued to grow during the 1960s, buying larger helicopters such as the Sikorsky S-58 and S-61. However, the greatest change to the company came in 1969 with the purchase of three Boeing Vertol 107-IIs from Pan Am. These aircraft immediately went to work on construction projects and on oil exploration support in Alaska's North Slope oil fields.

The addition of these aircraft was the basis for Columbia's development of helicopter logging. Wes had proved heli-logging

was feasible using a Sikorsky S-61 in 1971, and began logging with Vertols in 1972. Columbia has since become the world leader in heli-logging, annually yarding more timber than any other company.

Columbia's role in fighting wildfires is well known across the United States. Strategically located in various timberland sites throughout the West, the company's aircraft are called upon regularly to drop water or retardant on summer wildfires.

Columbia's petroleum exploration support work in Papua New Guinea has continued as the company developed expertise in moving oil drilling rigs in remote areas. The company recently completed its 131st rig move. Columbia has conducted petroleum support work in Burma, Indonesia, Papua New Guinea, Peru, Sudan, and the United States. Currently, operations continue in Indonesia, Papua New Guinea, and Peru.

Today, Columbia's fleet of Vertols, Boeing 234 Chinooks, Sikorsky CH-54s, and assorted support aircraft continue to work on a global basis. With an expansive spare parts system, highly trained mechanics, and highly experienced long-line precision placement pilots, Columbia provides safe, efficient, cost-effective, heavy-lift helicopter services anywhere, anytime.

From construction and logging to forest fire fighting and petroleum exploration, Columbia Helicopters, Inc., has certainly come a long way from the county fair.

Columbia Helicopters, Inc., Founder and Chairman Wes Lematta (left) and President Roy Simmons with a model of a Boeing Vertol 107-II.

DALLAS AIRMOTIVE

A Rich Tradition of Service Excellence.

Dallas Airmotive was born more than 65 years ago. It was one of the first to witness the beginning of the modern helicopter industry. Back then, service meant a quick, direct, and personal response to a customer's needs. The skills and pride of workmanship an individual brought to the job were as important as the technology. A simple handshake cemented business relationships.

At Dallas Airmotive, that tradition of providing helicopter customers with high-quality, personalized, responsive service continues today. In fact, they have a name for it: "Humaneering". . . a delicate blend of advanced technology, experience, dedication, and commitment to quality workmanship that they give all their customers.

Through the years, Dallas Airmotive has worked hard to establish its world-class reputation for providing "Five Star" service to helicopter operators. Its hallmark is helping customers lower direct operating costs with support that keeps their aircraft operational and producing revenue for as long as possible. When Allison 250 engine service is necessary, they keep downtime to an absolute minimum, as they have done for more than 30 years.

Back in 1967, Dallas Airmotive was the world's first authorized independent distributor of the Allison 250. Later, in 1977, they were the first to develop a mini-turbine overhaul, which established a new service benchmark — further maximizing engine performance as well as minimizing downtime and repair costs. Because of their SFAR 36 authorization, they have developed several hundred approved engine repairs over the past three decades.

Today, they are the world's largest independently owned, Allison-Authorized Maintenance Center. With extensive in-house and on-site service capabilities, they overhaul, repair, and test every variant of the Allison 250 — the world's most popular helicopter engine.

Their highly trained engine professionals are specialists in the latest repair technology and have broad, hands-on experience — nearly 20 years per technician. "Humaneering" is much more than technological expertise; it's the added touch of experience and commitment to quality. "Humaneering" is the fine line between trusting completely the marvels of advanced technology and knowing when to rely on the lessons learned from experience.

It's this experience and commitment to service excellence that makes Dallas Airmotive a different kind of company. . . one that's totally committed to the helicopter market and highly flexible in the services they provide. Dallas Airmotive's commitment to interacting with customers individually, and adapting support programs to meet their particular needs makes the company unique. It is, after all, this rich heritage that serves as the cornerstone for success in the rotor-wing community.

From their first shop on Cedar Springs Road in Dallas, Texas, Dallas Airmotive has grown to become the world's largest, independently-owned business aircraft and regional airline turbine engine overhaul and repair facility — employing more than 750 people and encompassing over 500,000 square feet of shop space.

Background photo: Utilizing state-of-the-art facilities and techniques, Dallas Airmotive's "Humaneers" overhaul and repair more than 300 helicopter engines per year.

ERA AVIATION, INC.

Fifty years ago, Carl F. Brady, an early member of the Helicopter Association of America, flew the first commercial helicopter in Alaska to work on a mapping contract for the U.S. government. In a state that covers 367 million acres and has few roads, Brady saw the potential of serving various ventures around the state.

 **Era Aviation, Inc.**

He continued to work with mapping and government contracts until oil was discovered in Cook Inlet. This new market opportunity necessitated the expansion of Brady's small company, then Economy Helicopters, Inc. The company also began to provide helicopter support for mineral exploration, the construction industry, and topographical studies.

Brady merged Economy Helicopters with Rotor-Aids, Inc. in 1958 and the company became Era Helicopters, Inc., taking its name from the first letters of Economy and Rotor-Aids. After five decades of operation, today Era is the world's oldest continuously operating helicopter company, and one of the largest civil aviation operators, with over 2 million company flight hours and a fleet of more than 100 helicopters and 21 fixed-wing aircraft.

For the past 50 years, HAI has advanced the civil helicopter industry worldwide by promoting the safety and efficiency of helicopter transportation. Era Helicopters strengthened these efforts by developing and manufacturing many innovative products now used by military and civilian fleets around the world.

Era brought the first turbine-powered and twin-engine helicopters to Alaska and marked the first domestic commercial use of the Eurocopter Super Puma

and the 44-passenger Boeing Vertol 234. As oil industry needs evolved, Era pioneered IFR helicopter service and later developed techniques for IFR external sling loads on the North Slope. Other Era innovations include helicopter modifications to provide more reliable performance in extremely cold climates. Era performs extensive IFR and VFR operations in some of the most remote locations in the world, ranging from the Arctic Circle to equatorial deserts. Era's FAA-approved auxiliary fuel tank systems have played a crucial role in increasing helicopter flight range and payload capabilities.

In the Gulf of Mexico, Era developed and perfected sophisticated offshore operations and was the first company to receive approval for airborne radar approaches. Because of unpredictable weather, Era established supplementary aviation weather reporting stations (SAWRS) and helped to introduce TCOM/GPS navigation equipment to the gulf.

Above, Carl Brady with his Bell 47B

Top, Charles W. Johnson and Carl F. Brady

Era's corporate headquarters are based in Anchorage, Alaska, the state's transportation hub and "Air Crossroads of the World." Era's fixed-wing division is Alaska's largest regional carrier, with scheduled air service between Anchorage and rural communities. Convair 580s, de Havilland Dash 8s, and Twin Otters carry both passengers and cargo. Services range from business flights to tourism charters, oil exploration crew changes, smoke jumping, and whale surveying. During the winter months, Era's Convair 580s shuttle college sports teams across the continental United States.

Era was the first commercial helicopter company to be allowed to operate on Sakhalin Island in the former Soviet Union and has also conducted operations in the People's Republic of China, Argentina, Africa, the Netherlands, Canada, Thailand, Greece, and Italy. In the former Yugoslavia, Era provided helicopter support to United Nations peace-keeping missions.

Era is a leader in providing fire fighting services throughout the United States. In conjunction with federal and state forestry departments, Era developed new fire fighting methods and equipment. Era's expert pilots transport initial attack crews and use precision water-bombing techniques, while maintenance teams and fuel trucks provide essential support from below.

Era offers spectacular flightseeing adventures in various areas of Alaska. Passengers can enjoy the grandeur of Mt. McKinley and Denali National Park, Juneau's ice fields, pristine Prince William Sound, and a panoramic view of the Anchorage area. Heli-hiking packages are also available in the Valdez and Denali National Park areas.

Era is proud to note that the Helicopter Association International has operated under the presidency of a member of Era's management team for 9 of its 50 years.

From 1948 to 1998, Era Aviation has combined talent with technology, to grow as a rotary-wing service and product provider, and a leader in the helicopter industry worldwide. With Brady's pioneer spirit, which established Era 50 years ago, and a management philosophy of professionalism, reliability, and innovation, Era Aviation will prosper far into the next century.

ERICKSON AIR-CRANE CO.

From the first time you see it, it is clear that the Erickson Air-Crane Company is no ordinary helicopter operator. In fact, the Sikorsky S-64 Air-Crane was the only helicopter ever designed specifically to perform precision external load operations. Founded in 1971, Erickson Air-Crane became the first company to successfully harvest timber using the Air-Crane. With the initial success of the logging operations, other applications were soon to follow, including fire fighting and electrical transmission line construction equipment.

The Air-Crane is the only helicopter with an aft (rear)-facing pilot that allows an unrestricted view of the load during placement. With a 25,000-pound lifting capacity and Erickson's patented Cargo Handling System, the Air-Crane can perform like no other helicopter. This capability was demonstrated in 1993 as Erickson Air-Crane removed and replaced the Statue of Freedom that sits on top of the U.S. Capitol in Washington, D.C.

In 1991, Erickson Air-Crane developed the most effective fire fighting system available. The Erickson Air-Crane Helitanker combines the capacity of a fixed-wing airtanker with the precision and quick refilling of a helicopter. The Helitanker system delivers a higher volume of water or retardant per hour at a lower cost per gallon than any other delivery system available today.

Erickson Air-Crane currently operates a fleet of 15 Air-Cranes throughout the United States, Canada, and Malaysia. With the acquisition of the Aircraft Type Certificate from Sikorsky in 1992, Erickson secured the capability to overhaul all of the aircraft's components and manufacture new airframes. Erickson Air-Crane plans to increase the size of the fleet, allowing continued expansion in domestic and international markets.

Air-Crane demonstrates water drop.

Air-Crane lifts Freedom statue.

P R O F I L E

EUROCOPTER

Eurocopter: A history of responding to the needs of an ever-evolving marketplace.

Eurocopter has been responding to the diverse needs of helicopter operators for some time. In fact, they were one of the first on the scene in the beginning of the modern helicopter industry and are still an integral part of this dynamic movement today.

Their earliest roots in the helicopter industry can be traced back to 1955 with the development of the Alouette II by SNCASE, which later became Aerospatiale.

Alouette III

Two months after the first flight on June 6, 1955, the Alouette II broke the international altitude record for all helicopter categories. The first production Alouette II was built in April 1956 and continued to be manufactured until 1975 — totaling 1,305 in number. The Alouette II program's success served as the cornerstone for the entire helicopter industry in France.

During the same time period, development was under way to engineer a light observation helicopter with a jet rotor driven by ram-jet engines at the blade tips. This led to the development of the Djinn, and in July 1956, 150 of these jet-tip aircraft were already in production for the French army. The French certificate of airworthiness was granted on May 2, 1957. The Djinn was the first French helicopter and only jet helicopter in the world to have reached the certification and industrial production stages during this time.

The corporation's heritage was further strengthened by MBB/Deutsche Aerospace's creation of the BO105 — the world's first light twin-engine helicopter — in February 1967. Known for its low initial, maintenance and direct operating costs, the BO105 quickly established itself as a reliable,

heavy-duty helicopter capable of handling a wide range of demanding missions. Proof of its durability is evident by the fact that many of these aircraft are still in service.

In January 1992, the helicopter divisions of Aerospatiale and MBB/Deutsche Aerospace (now Daimler-Benz Aerospace) joined forces to form Eurocopter. All with the promise of delivering new ideas, bold new products, and a new spirit of service and support for customers worldwide. With more than 9,000 helicopters in service internationally, Eurocopter is the world's leading producer of civil helicopters. Furthermore, they offer the broadest line of commercial helicopters to serve the emergency medical services, business, utility, offshore, search and rescue, and law enforcement markets.

Today, Eurocopter continues to aggressively push the envelope — branching into new frontiers of research and development. A sterling example of their commitment to developing new technology can be seen in the EC135, EC120, Tiger, and NH-90. Even as we speak, more projects are on the drawing board and moving rapidly into their growing product line. And they are currently well into development of more advanced helicopters with design emphasis on reducing external sound levels, simplifying maintenance, and lowering direct operating costs.

At Eurocopter, they are responding to operators' unique requirements with the latest technologies, new product developments, and ongoing product improvements — all in an effort to better support the diverse missions operators fly in an ever-changing marketplace.

EC120

GKN WESTLAND HELICOPTERS

The manufacture of aircraft has been undertaken at Yeovil, England, under the name of Westland for over 80 years. Westland Helicopters grew from the well-established aircraft company, Westland Aircraft Limited, when the management made a policy decision in 1946 to specialize in the design and manufacture of helicopters.

Westland pursued a different approach than any other British company entering the helicopter field, in that it arranged a license agreement with Sikorsky, USA, to build the S-51 helicopter, so it could market the aircraft worldwide outside North America.

The Helicopter Division was formed under the leadership of O.L.L. Fitzwilliams and proceeded to manufacture and market the S-51, built to a British standard, under the name Dragonfly. The aircraft was used to promote helicopter operations, including a helicopter night mail service between Norwich and Peterborough, England, and can also be claimed as the "the world's first scheduled helicopter passenger service," operating between London and Birmingham during the British Industries Fair in 1950. Dragonflies were also used for a number of spectacular flood relief operations in Europe and for lighthouse relief trials.

Westland also demonstrated its faith in the future of helicopter operations by opening a heliport at Battersea in 1959. Since that time, over 300,000 movements have been recorded and the Battersea site remains London's only commercial heliport, situated in the heart of the London capital.

The company continued its association with Sikorsky to produce the Whirlwind, based on the S-55, and the Wessex, developed from the S-58. It was Westland policy to introduce modifications to the basic aircraft, and in the case of both Whirlwind and Wessex, this included the installation of turbines. The Wessex 60 played an important part in the establishment of helicopter operations in the harsh environments experienced in the North Sea.

The company achieved significant market success. So by 1960, when the British industry was reduced to two major aircraft and one helicopter manufacturer, Westland acquired the helicopter interests of Bristol, Fairey, and Saunders-Roe to form Westland Helicopters Ltd.

The reorganized company was in a strong position to start production of a range of helicopters. The Scout and Wasp were manufactured at the Fairey company's factory in Hayes, England, while production of the Wessex was undertaken at Yeovil. The company produced over 200 Bell 47G Sioux helicopters

through a sub-license arrangement with the Italian company Agusta SpA.

In 1966, the license with Sikorsky was extended to build the SH-3D Sea King. Like all the previous agreements with Sikorsky, Westland was allowed to market its version of the aircraft worldwide. The Westland-built aircraft contained several unique features and when production ceased in 1996, a total of 330 had been built.

At the same time, work was started to satisfy a British requirement for army utility and naval small ship helicopters with one aircraft, WG-13, which was later to become the Lynx. The design incorporated an all-titanium semi-rigid rotor, which set new standards of maneuverability and control response. Lynx achieved success in the world's markets and continues to be in demand with over 380 built to date.

The EH101 Heliliner, seen here flying into the Battersea heliport, offers airliner comfort for 30 passengers and incorporates many advanced features including BERP blades, active vibration control, and health usage monitoring.

Westland composite rotor blade technology was dramatically demonstrated when a Lynx helicopter, fitted with BERP (British Experimental Rotor Program) blades claimed the helicopter world speed record in 1986. At a speed of 249.10 mph (400.87 kph), the record has remained unbeaten for over 10 years.

The French company Aerospatiale was working on two helicopters, the Puma and the Gazelle, to satisfy requirements for support and light helicopters, both of which were suitable to meet British needs. It was at this point that Britain joined the European Community. With the support of the two governments, the Anglo-French Helicopter Package Deal was struck, involving the two French aircraft and the Lynx. The deal included collaborative involvement in both development and production for all the aircraft, requiring the production of over 200 helicopters for the British requirement alone. This heralded a period of unprecedented prosperity for Westland throughout the 1970s.

Westland began design studies to utilize the proven Lynx dynamic system as the basis of a larger helicopter for the civil market. This became the Westland 30, a private venture that had a larger cabin capable of carrying 17 passengers. The prototype flew for the first time in 1979 and achieved certification during the two years of development. A total of 40 were built and operated in Europe, the U.S., and Asia, on airport/city links, and with the oil industry.

By 1985, Westland had established facilities for the manufacture of composite main rotor blades, producing a new blade for the Sea King. This led to a new project: The British Experimental Rotor Program (BERP). The blade was designed to take full advantage of all the benefits to be gained from composite construction, to optimize the aerodynamics of the blade, and to accurately manufacture the complex profile necessary for the section of blade subject to high Mach numbers

at the tip. The BERP was test flown on a Lynx in August 1986 and captured the world absolute speed record at an average speed of 249.10 mph (400.87 kph). This record has now stood for over 10 years.

In 1980 European Helicopter Industries (E.H. Industries) was formed by Westland Helicopters Ltd. and Agusta SpA to produce a large helicopter for both the civil and military markets. The result was the EH101, a joint program undertaken in the U.K. and Italy for a three-engine helicopter of 32,000 pounds for military and civil operation. The aircraft achieved simultaneous CAA (U.K.), RAI (Italy), and FAA (U.S.) type certification in 1994. The EH101 civil version can carry 30 passengers in airline comfort, incorporating many new features including BERP blades, active control of structural response, and integrated health usage monitoring.

The international engineering company GKN acquired full control of Westland Helicopters Ltd. in 1994 and the company's name changed to GKN Westland in 1996.

GKN Westland views its association with the international helicopter industry with pride in the knowledge that, while the HAI celebrates its 50th anniversary, it is also 50 years since Westland took the first step into the helicopter business, through its license agreement with Sikorsky in 1947, a decision that has since led to the production of over 2,500 Westland helicopters.

HELI-EXPO exhibit hall static display

Helicopter
Association
International

HELICOPTER ASSOCIATION INTERNATIONAL

Helicopter professionals, almost without exception, can be recognized as "rugged individualists," persons who have a strong and independent nature, coupled with the ability to survive against challenging odds. It's only natural that these traits flourish within the helicopter industry, where we work with very capable yet complex machines in environments that are often less than ideal.

Yet even rugged individualists know there are times and situations where teamwork counts the most, where the task is too big or the goals too vast and complicated for one person to effectively go it alone, where dedicated men and women working together is the only way to really accomplish the job. It was in this spirit that the Helicopter Association International, the HAI, was formed in 1948. And it is in this same spirit today that HAI continues to grow, prosper, and represent its membership around the globe, serving as the pulse for the civil helicopter industry worldwide.

It is impossible in these few pages to name and discuss each of the many persons responsible for the growth of HAI and its many accomplishments. In reality, each and every organization and individual who has ever paid dues or volunteered has contributed to HAI's successful history. Many of the events, issues, and decisions that have shaped this industry and HAI are discussed in the chapters in this book. For example, each of HAI's top elected leaders, initially referred to as president and later as chairman, is named in the main text. These leaders, and many others too numerous to mention, have been true helicopter pioneers and their accomplishments are truly appreciated.

Fifty years ago a small group of early helicopter pioneers, recognizing the need to work together to achieve their common goals, established what they called the Helicopter Council, changing the name just six weeks later to the California Helicopter Association. In 1951, as the organization's membership expanded around the country, the name was changed to the Helicopter Association of America (HAA), and stayed that way for the next 30 years. Finally in 1981, the organization became the Helicopter Association International, or HAI, in recognition of its truly international status.

Think about the situation that prevailed, as the initial efforts were being made to establish a helicopter organization. It was only three years after World War II had ended, and the transition from global war to a more peaceful world was not yet complete. The helicopters of that day were very rudimentary, particularly when judged by today's very high standards of safety and performance. The operational potential of helicopters had not been explored, nor had their commercial viability. Only a small number of helicopters was available, and a relative few of these had been placed into operation. There were extremely few guidelines or precedents, and very little applicable experience upon which to draw.

In reviewing documents and minutes from meetings in those early days, it's interesting to note how many of the subjects and concerns addressed back then are still relevant to today's operators: the sharing of information on helicopter safety; the availability of parts; insurance coverage costs; international operations; government contracting; aerial applications; and fire suppression, just to name a few. What's also apparent over the five decades since the association got its start is just how many of the actions taken on behalf of helicopter operators have benefitted the entire industry, from manufacturers to suppliers to everyone in between. Additionally, many of HAI's initiatives undertaken in the United States have had a direct and positive impact on helicopter activities around the world.

History & Organization

On December 13, 1948, at 8 p.m. a group of helicopter operators held a meeting at the offices of AF Helicopters, Inc., 2945 Hollywood Way (on the Burbank Airport), Burbank, California. Joe Seward served as temporary chairman to conduct the organizational proceedings. The founding companies and their representatives were:

AF Helicopters, Inc., represented by Knute Flint, Harry Armstrong, Fred Bowen, and James Newcomb.

Rotor-Aids, represented by Joe Seward and Roy Falconer

Rick Helicopters, Inc., represented by James L. Ricklefs and Arni L. Sumarlidason

Kern Copters, Inc., represented by Elynor Rudnick and Bob Facer

Helicopter Service, Inc., represented by Fred Blymyer and Bob Boughton

Sky Farming, Inc., represented by James I. "Tommy" Thomas, Ed Eskridge and Phil Johnson

Bell Aircraft Corp., represented by Art Fornoff

The meeting ended with the following resolutions in place:

"BE IT RESOLVED that the group gathered here form a helicopter operators' council for the purpose of promoting the interests of helicopter operators, for the mutual cooperation and aid and for other purposes not specifically mentioned.

"RESOLVED FURTHER, that each operator attending this meeting . . . be entitled to cast one vote on each question and be considered a charter member of the group.

"RESOLVED FURTHER, that rules of parliamentary procedure shall govern the conduct of the business of the organization."

Doing business at HELI-EXPO

For the first 13 years of existence, the association continued to grow. The first professional manager, John L. Pennewell, was hired as HAA executive secretary in March 1961. He established the association's headquarters in Washington, D.C., and continued to serve until his resignation in October 1965. He was succeeded by John E. Ryan who served as executive secretary/director from January 1966 to February 1971, during which time the association's headquarters was in Stratford, Connecticut.

Robert A. Richardson, who had already served as HAA's elected president, became executive director in April 1971 and returned the headquarters to Washington, D.C. He served as executive director for almost 11 years. The association advanced considerably in size and importance. Under Richardson's leadership, the staff grew to 11 persons, and the office was relocated from 15th & M Streets, N.W., to another lease-hold at 1110 Vermont Avenue, N.W., in Washington, D.C. Frank L. Jensen, Jr. followed Richardson as executive director, starting in March 1982. His title was changed in 1985 to president; he is still serving in that capacity at the time of this writing. During his tenure, HAI has purchased two headquarters buildings, the staff has increased to 29 persons, and HAI's membership, productivity, and importance have continued to grow.

Frank L. Jensen, Jr., President

HAI has been present at events at the White House on an average of at least once a year, for the past 15 years. The association has testified before committees and sub-committees of the U.S. Congress several times a year; has maintained close contact with senior officials of a number of federal agencies, including members of the Cabinet and sub-Cabinet, on a wide range of matters involving both aviation and small business; and has written letters, and made personal appearances, to authorities around the world to represent the civil

helicopter industry. Such actions on behalf of the industry have continued to be a major priority for HAI.

Success, as we all know, is often the result of hard work and careful planning. And for any organization — particularly one that's non-profit — strict attention must be paid to the bottom line to ensure that the organization is able to sustain a strong and viable presence on behalf of its membership. In this regard, HAI handles its fiscal responsibilities conservatively, believing that in order to champion the interests of the civil helicopter industry in the most forceful and effective ways possible, it must operate from a position of strength.

"ROTOR" magazine,
"Operations Update"
"Maintenance Update"
and the "Helicopter Annual"
are some of HAI's publications.

Such was the mindset that caused HAI's leadership to purchase, rather than continue to rent, headquarters space. A small office building was purchased at 1619 Duke Street in Alexandria, Virginia, and the HAI staff moved in over the weekend of August 10, 1985, with virtually no interruption of operations. By reducing out-of-pocket expenses and providing more space than previously had been available at its lease-hold headquarters on Vermont Avenue in Washington, D.C., the entire organization immediately benefitted from a collective feeling of permanence and the resulting pride of ownership. Yet this was only a first step.

The accelerating tempo of HAI activities, including the growth in size and importance of HELI-EXPO, the creation of "ROTOR" magazine, the development of the Maintenance Malfunction Information Reporting program, the initiation of the "Operations Update" and "Maintenance Update" newsletters, the increase in HAI's professional education and training programs, the computerized HAI Hot Line, and the publishing of the "Helicopter Annual," all combined to create the need for more office space far sooner than anyone could have expected.

Committees

The HAI Board of Directors, reacting positively to the rapid growth of organizational needs, once again approved the search for a new building, preferably close to the site on Duke Street. After some negotiation, HAI's leadership purchased an unfinished building with 16,000 square feet of space only two blocks away from the Duke Street office. It was completed according to HAI's specifications in April 1994. The new building, at 1635 Prince Street in Alexandria, is ideal in space, location, and price, and should serve HAI's needs extremely well for many, many years to come.

A combination of careful budgeting, prudent professional management practices, and conservative financial planning have yielded a steadily increasing net worth of which the association members can be proud. The hard work is indeed paying off.

Much of HAI's accomplishments are the result of the excellent work done by its 21 committees, all of whose participants are volunteers working without compensation toward the advancement of the helicopter industry. In fact, the entire 50 years of HAI's existence could not have been possible without the dedicated, generous, and sustained efforts of those who have volunteered their time, their services, and their expertise: every member of the Board, every committee participant, and the countless others who have made significant contributions to HAI's progress over the years, often at personal expense. This is particularly true in the case of volunteers from small companies, whose absence from their workplace often affected the bottom line.

HAI headquarters at 1635 Prince Street, Alexandria, Virginia

Particularly valued over the years have been the contributions made by HAI's special advisors, who have remained on the Board far longer than most of its elected leaders. Joe Mashman, HAI's first special advisor, served from 1973 until his death in 1996. Ted Dumont, who was for many years the chairman of HAI's Regulations Committee, became a special advisor in 1979 and served until 1987, when he retired. Ted was recalled to active duty as special advisor emeritus and continues to serve in that capacity today. Dr. Walter Comeaux served as a special advisor from 1985

Joe Mashman   *Dr. Walter Comeaux*   *Ted Dumont*

until February 1998, having also served for a number of years on the Safety Committee, including one term as committee chair. Matt Zuccaro, a past chairman of HAI, also served as a special advisor from 1990 to 1997. And Larry Mattiello served first as Insurance Representative from 1986 to 1992, and then as Special Advisor until 1996, at which time he was again chosen by his insurance industry peers to represent them on the HAI Board. Other advisors to HAI's board as this is written include Timothy M. Biddle, Esq.; Christine Eberhard, Public Relations; and Paul Smith, Safety. Edwin Birtwell is Engine Representative and Paul Schweizer is Airframe Representative.

The list could go on and on. Suffice it to say that HAI, and the entire helicopter industry, owes an enormous debt of gratitude to all who have volunteered on behalf of the industry, and we thank them for everything they have done for the organization and its activities.

For 37 years now, HAI has recognized outstanding achievements in the civil helicopter industry, covering a wide range of industry accomplishments. HAI's Salute to Excellence Award winners are recognized at an annual banquet held during HELI-EXPO. In a true expression of esprit de corps, the awards ceremony has become the most prestigious event at each year's convention as it acknowledges the exceptional merit of the winners and encourages the continued attainment of the highest standards of professionalism in the civil helicopter industry.

HAI's Salute to Excellence Awards

The first HAA industry award was the Pilot of the Year Award given to Don Carson of Petroleum Helicopters, Inc., for achievements during 1960. The Robert E. Trimble Memorial Award became HAA's second award, presented for the first time in 1962. This award was named after Bob Trimble, an early pioneer in helicopter high altitude operations.

The Max Schumacher Memorial Award was presented for the first time in 1967. Named for an early-day helicopter pilot/radio announcer, this award recognized exemplary service to the helicopter industry through the use of helicopters in urban areas. This award has since been renamed the Community Service Award.

It is important to note that HAI's leadership has continued to take very seriously the establishment and administration of its professional awards. On the one hand, they have sought to have suitable awards for most aspects of helicopter activities. On the other hand, they have been mindful of the need to limit the number of awards, so as to preserve their value and significance.

HAI's Salute to Excellence Awards now number 13.

The awards program is administered by the HAI staff, which announces each year's awards cycle, receives the nominations and other correspondence, and prepares selection packages for the Awards Committee. This committee, again all volunteers, takes its responsibilities most seriously. And the award recipients, by their words and actions, reflect true appreciation for this recognition by their peers.

HAI's "Salute to Excellence" Awards

Aviation Repair Specialist Award

Aviation Maintenance Technician Award

Igor I. Sikorsky Award for Humanitarian Service

Joe Mashman Safety Award

Outstanding Certified Flight Instructor Award

Community Service Award

American Eurocopter Golden Hour Award

Excellence in Communications Award

Helicopter Maintenance Award

McDonnell Douglas Law Enforcement Award

Lawrence D. Bell Memorial Award

Robert E. Trimble Memorial Award

Pilot of the Year Award

For its first two decades, HAA held annual meetings which were quite small, reflecting the size of the fledgling industry and its trade association. In 1954 the annual convention was held in the Bell Aircraft Corporation's Hurst plant cafeteria in Fort Worth, Texas. Approximately 75 attendees were present with international guests from Canada, France, Italy, Japan, and Sweden.

Thirteen years later, the 1967 "Annual Meeting, Convention and Industry Showcase" housed 44 exhibitors in 61 booths. By 1980, the show had grown to the point that it was held in the Las Vegas Convention Center rather than being "self-contained" in a hotel.

Clearly the association's trade show was a most important event for the entire industry; it brought manufacturers and others with products or services to sell together with operators who would be the purchasers.

But the annual association meeting became much more than a trade show. It also facilitated meetings of the general membership, the Board, and Committees, as well as educational activities.

These meetings were the magnets that pulled together the entire industry.

Even though the industry experienced a severe slump in the early 1980s, due in large measure to the oil glut, the association's show continued on a generally upward trend, which accelerated in the late 1980s.

1988 HELI-EXPO Opening Ceremony; Steve Sullivan, Arlene Feldman, Vernon Albert, Ernest Borgnine, Tova Borgnine, Jeanna Yeager, and Frank L. Jensen, Jr.

Welcome

Clint Eastwood, actor and helicopter pilot visits HAI's HELI-EXPO

3,500 persons and saw the participation of most of the CEOs of the airframe and engine manufacturers.

Today HELI-EXPO is HAI's most visible activity, attracting some 13,000 or more professional registrants. Four-hundred-fifty exhibiting companies utilize 1,200 exhibit booths, with 65 to 70 helicopters on display inside the exhibit hall. Listed among the top 200 trade shows in the U.S., HELI-EXPO has earned a place of importance among helicopter professionals around the world.

HAI has grown in many other ways as well. Early publications such as the "ROTORnews" newsletter led the way to the highly effective multiple communication resources available to HAI members today. The "Helicopter Annual" (16 years), "ROTOR" magazine (10 years), "Operations Update" (10 years), "Maintenance Update" (8 years), "HAI Insider's Report" (15 years), and numerous special-purpose publications such as the "Fly Neighborly Guides" and "HAI Safety Manual" are all highly effective publications and all truly "by the industry and for the industry."

HAI has a professional staff of 29 persons, including several experienced helicopter pilots. This highly skilled and motivated staff utilizes top-of-the-line office equipment, including a very capable

By 1989, registration was consistently above 10,000, and there were regularly 60 or more helicopters on display inside the exhibit hall. The name HELI-EXPO was adopted for the 1990 show as being more suitable for this major worldwide helicopter event.

The professional education opportunities offered during the week before HELI-EXPO continued to grow in importance and number; by 1997 there were almost 500 helicopter professionals enrolled in 11 course offerings.

Dozens of ancillary events, many of which were highly important in their own right, were and still are held in conjunction with HELI-EXPO. For example, the Rotorcraft

Boeing 520N

fifth-generation local area network (LAN), designed and fabricated in-house. HAI has remained in the leading edge of computer technology with its first LAN installed in 1986, "Helicopter Hotline" installed in 1987, and its own Internet web-site at www.rotor.com in November 1995. Unlike many web-sites, HAI's web-site

Roundtable, started in 1983, has regularly attracted almost 200 helicopter professionals, regulators, legislators, and others from around the world, for a four-hour open discussion on topics of mutual interest.

Helicopter Foundation International (HFI), the history affiliate of HAI, conducts its Extravaganza, a fund-raising gala, on the middle night of HELI-EXPO. Started in 1990, the very first Extravaganza was a chili cook-off that attracted more than

is constantly being updated and also hosts some 81 other home pages.

At this writing, HAI has a total of 2,653 members, including 623 Regular members (i.e., commercial, corporate, or government organizations that operate helicopters). These members operate 4,000 helicopters, safely flying more than 2,000,000 hours annually. HAI's 683 Associate members include manufacturers of airframes, engines, avionics, components, and accessories, plus repair stations, insurance companies, financial firms, brokers, consultants, and all others that support the civil helicopter industry. In addition, HAI has 1,281 Individual members.

the opportunity to exchange views and discuss matters of mutual interest with each other and with HAI's Board, committees, and staff. That meeting is known as the Rotorcraft Roundtable, held just before HELI-EXPO. The relationship between HAI and the Affiliate members is healthy and synergistic. It facilitates

Rotorcraft Roundtable facilitates direct communications among helicopter interest groups from around the world.

Nearly 20 percent of HAI's total membership is based in over 65 countries other than the United States. Also, HAI has 72 Affiliate members in 14 countries. These Affiliate members are non-profit entities having interests and goals compatible with those of HAI.

Communications between HAI headquarters and the Affiliate members is fairly regular. There is at least one meeting each year where these organizations have

direct communications among helicopter interest groups from around the world, representing all facets of this small but diverse and dynamic industry.

HAI's leadership clearly understands the traditional functions, roles, and limitations of a trade association. To enable HAI to best accomplish its principal missions, and still ensure that certain other functions are covered adequately, HAI took legal action in 1983 to incorporate another non-profit entity: the

HELI-EXPO attracts more
than 13,000 registrants

Helicopter Foundation International (HFI), which is recognized by the Internal Revenue Service as a 501(c)(3) tax-exempt organization. HFI's primary mission is the preservation of the history of the rotorcraft industry. It has an autonomous Board of Directors, and owns the world's largest collection of scale-model helicopters.

In 1996, in conjunction with the European Helicopter Association and others, HAI activated the International Federation of Helicopter Associations (IFHA), also non-profit. IFHA's goal is to bring together helicopter interests from around the world in a common forum, to focus on international regulations, and, in time, to obtain accreditation at the International Civil Aviation Organization (ICAO).

A truly member-governed organization, HAI is led by a Board of Directors, elected by the members from among their ranks. The Board has nine operator voting members, including five commercial, three corporate, and one government. In addition, there are representatives of engine and airframe manufacturers; insurance, safety, and public relations advisors; and two special advisors. HAI's president and corporate secretary are ex officio members of the Board. Officers are elected by and from among the directors, including a chairman, vice chairman, treasurer, and assistant treasurer. Appointed officers are the president and corporate secretary, both of whom are on the HAI staff.

HAI Board of Directors

Front row: Peter Wright, Jr., Treasurer (Keystone Helicopter Corporation); Rod Kvamme, Immediate Past Chairman (Heli-Jet Corporation); Frank L. Jensen, Jr., President, HAI; Neill Osborne, Chairman (Air Logistics); James T. Cheatham, Vice Chairman (Verticare); Elling Halvorson, Director (Papillon Grand Canyon Helicopters); Second row: Christine L. Eberhard, Public Relations Advisor (CommuniQuest, Inc.); Edwin P. Birtwell, Engine Representative (GE Aircraft Engines); Timothy M. Biddle, Esq., HAI Special Advisor (Crowell & Moring); Ardis T. Ashton, Jr., Director (The Bonneville Power Administration); James A. Church, Director (United Technologies Corp.); Bill Griffiths, Director (Portland General Electric Company); Elizabeth W. Meade, Executive Vice President, HAI; Third row: Lawrence S. Mattiello, HAI Special Advisor (Willis Coroon Aerospace); Dr. Walter B. Comeaux, Jr., Special Advisor; Merrick W. Hellyar, Airframe Representative (Sikorsky Aircraft Corp.) (since replaced by Paul Schweizer); Arden E. Davis, Director (Weyerhaeuser Co.); Theodore E. Dumont, HAI Special Advisor. Not pictured: Paul H. Schweizer, Airframe Representative (Schweizer Aircraft Corporation); Paul M. Smith, Safety Advisor (National Helicopter Corp.).

It was only 50 years ago when a small group of dedicated helicopter pioneers gathered in California to establish what has since become the Helicopter Association International. While the time seems to have flown by for many of us, the memories of the achievements of the industry, of the organization, and of the many fine men and women who contributed so much remain fresh in the minds of us all. This sense of living history, and the obligation to continue the good work of all those who have come before us, drives our commitment to the industry and to the dedicated and loyal membership of HAI around the world.

The past 50 years have seen the helicopter advance from infancy to adolescence to full-fledged adulthood, evolving from a relatively unsophisticated machine into a high-tech, highly sophisticated rotorcraft that safely and consistently makes significant contributions to virtually every aspect of military and civilian life. The helicopter has earned its rightful place in the annals of 20th-century history, and all those responsible in any way — whether in manufacturing, research and development, pilot operations, instruction, maintenance, regulatory oversight or organizational support (such as the HAI) — have

every reason to be proud of the job they have done and the industry they have served so well.

But there is still much work to be done as we enter the next 50 years and, indeed, the new millennium. Issues that threaten the economic viability of the entire helicopter industry, and particularly our small business members, seem to loom large around every corner. Issues include access to airspace and airports, and improved landing sites; the worldwide dumping of surplus military helicopters and parts into the private sector, with little or no regard for the disruption of market forces and the likelihood of a serious and widespread diminution of aviation safety. Also, the need for a better understanding of the operational economics of providing helicopter services by everyone involved in the industry, particularly the need for realistic pricing to ensure continued viability; the critical need for a single standard of safety; the need to aggressively promote noise reduction practices and respectful flying habits through HAI's Fly Neighborly program; and the need to stay engaged in ongoing and constructive dialogue with well-meaning environmentalists and private landholders around the globe who unrealistically and unreasonably object to the presence of helicopters in their aural or visual fields.

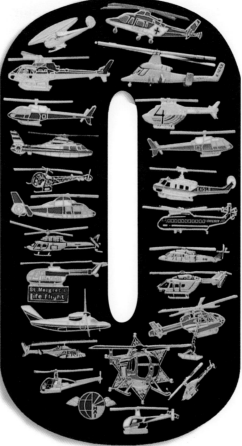

HAI Staff

Front Row (left to right): Alec G. Dickey, Vice President Marketing/Expositions; Henry J. D'Souza, Chief Financial Officer; Frank L. Jensen, Jr., President; Elizabeth W. Meade, Executive Vice President; Edward F. DiCampli, Vice President Information Systems; Glenn H. Rizner, Vice President Operations. Second Row: Stephen R. Vernem, Accounting Assistant; Marilyn F. McKinnis, Director of Communications; William B. Wanamaker, Legislative Affairs Manager; Kate A. Miller-Haselby, Director of Membership; Kristine M. Driver, Communications Assistant; Debbi L. Marquardt, Exhibits Manager; Patricia G. Willibey, Executive Assistant to the President; Michelle A. Mullins, Receptionist; Stephanie P. Minor, Executive Assistant to the Executive Vice President; Laura T. Blanchard, Assistant to the Vice President Operations. Third Row: Andrea S. Pimm, Graphic Designer; Scott W. DiBiasio, Operations Staff Assistant; William C. Sanderson, Director of Heliports and Technical Programs; Kimberly M. Newell, Advertising/Exhibits Sales Manager; David R. Barber, Information Systems Assistant; Jacquelyn L. Curry, Membership Assistant; Joseph Corrao, Director of Regulations; Jitao (Jeremy) Xu, MMIR Programmer; Brian D. Rettmann, Administration Services Assistant; Carol M. Pietro, Receptionist/Secretary.
(Not Pictured: Richard M. Wright, Jr., Director of Safety and Flight Operations; Kelly S. Stivers, Information Systems Manager)

There are clearly challenges that confront the civil helicopter industry as we head into the 21st century. We have, without question, a full plate. But with the continued support of the membership, and the dedication of HAI's headquarters staff, we're confident we'll be able to meet these challenges head-on, to the continuing benefit of HAI and the civil helicopter industry worldwide.

Clearly there was a need to work together. As envisioned by the founders, HAI has become the most visible and influential organization in the world dedicated exclusively to civil helicopters.

So as we close the book on the first 50 years, and as we look forward to helping write the many chapters to come, we salute all who have served the helicopter so well and faithfully during the past five decades: it's been a job well done. Working together, we can continue to advance civil helicopters for the benefit of all.

Having fun at HELI-EXPO.

Heli-Hound educates
children about helicopters

131

HELIFOR INDUSTRIES LIMITED

Helifor Industries, a subsidiary of International Forest Products Limited (Interfor) of Vancouver, British Columbia, began operations in 1978. Utilizing heavy-lift aircraft leased from Columbia Helicopters, Helifor's primary focus has been helicopter logging on the coastal areas of British Columbia. The 1997 fleet consisted of three Boeing 107-II Vertols and one Boeing 234 Chinook. Helifor also owns four MDHC 500 Ds used for supporting the logging operations.

Operating continuously for the past 20 years, Helifor has achieved many goals and set numerous production and flight time records, including a high time flight hour month for the Boeing 107 of 338.3 hours and a high time flight hour month for the Boeing 234 of 276.4 hours. Helifor has logged over 60,000 hours on its heavy-lift fleet, averaging over 2,300 hours per aircraft in the 10-month season of helicopter logging in British Columbia.

Other heavy-lift work has included motion picture support, forest fire suppression, ski lift and power line construction, barge salvage, and diamond mine support.

Helifor operates off remote-based, fully contained floating camps with all the modern conveniences of home. Pictured is the Chinook camp "Eclipse" logging alongside the Boeing 107 camp "Paragon." Eclipse was the first camp for Helifor and has been in operation since 1978. "Odyssey" camp operates mainly on the central and north coast of British

Columbia. Helifor's fourth operation, which began in 1997, is called "Horizon." Rounding out the Helifor team is "Calypso" camp, which is used primarily for the timber falling crews.

Safety is paramount at Helifor. Crews are highly trained professionals with many years of experience. The logging crews are the best in the business and take great pride in the tasks they perform. The aircraft maintenance engineers have a combined 290 years of experience. Helifor's 25 pilots are all airline transport pilot rated and average over 9,000 flight hours each.

Helifor's success can be attributed to many factors: the vision and support of Interfor's chairman and chief executive officer Bob Sitter, the excellent working relationship and support of Columbia Helicopters, and the dedication, commitment, and skill of Helifor's employees, many of whom have been with the company since its inception.

Helifor congratulates the Helicopter Association International on its 50th Anniversary.

Chinook camp "Eclipse" logging alongside the Boeing 107-II camp "Paragon."

HELIPRO CORPORATION

When Sandy Strukoff and Hugh Whitfield founded S&H Helipro Ltd. in July 1988, they literally spent their first years on the road. In a bread delivery van equipped as a mobile workshop, they traveled the back roads of Canada and the U.S. repairing helicopters in the field.

Encouraged by their initial success, in 1989 they bought a hangar and workshop in Langley, British Columbia, to undertake larger and more complex projects.

In 1991, Helipro Corporation International was formed in Bellingham, Washington, to provide a facility for customers. An FAA repair station, it introduced Bell Helicopter-approved repair fixtures. Sikorsky and McDonnell Douglas fixtures were later added. Early contracts included repairs to sightseeing helicopters damaged by a violent storm in Hawaii.

With its growing reputation for quality and overnight field response, Helipro grew to 45 employees.

Gradually, the company pursued more ambitious programs.

Strukoff and Whitfield had long contemplated shortening the cabin of the Sikorsky S-61N and S-61L to improve payload and performance. Following two years of development, Helipro's first S-61 Short flew on February 11, 1996. Six S-61 Shorts were modified for heli-loging use by mid-1997, with more on order for 1998.

After both the FAA and Transport Canada certified the S-61 Short, international customers encouraged development of an offshore version custom-tailored for over-water missions.

S-61

Helipro has used strategic partnerships to provide its customers with one-stop airframe, component, and engine support.

Helipro Component Services Ltd. is managed by Jim Campbell and Mike Druet, two experienced component industry specialists. It overhauls and repairs Sikorsky and Bell components.

Helipro Completions Inc. repairs and supports the full Bell product line at facilities near Houston, Texas. It is a partnership with a New Zealand company.

Helipro technicians routinely fly overseas to repair helicopters at customers' facilities. Self-sufficient, they travel with pre-packaged repair kits containing virtually every tool, part, and manual required.

Field work ranges from 9,000-hour inspections of S-61Ns in Greenland, Holland, and Malaysia, to S-76 repairs in Trinidad and Thailand, and Bell UH-1H structural repairs in Latin America.

The future of the company is overseas. A helicopter repair and modification facility will open in Europe by the year 2000 to support customers in the North Sea and Africa.

S-61 Short, on ramp.

ICARO S.A.

In 1980, ICARO began commercial aviation operations and, in 1981, was issued an operating permit for tourism flights. In 1982, ICARO began non-scheduled public air taxi and cargo transportation service between Quito and the rest of the country to provide a link to the country's major economic and social centers — there were no links via ground or air prior to this service. This activity also satisfied a great need of the oil companies for transporting their personnel to the Ecuadorian Oriente.

In 1984, ICARO proposed to the Director General of Civil Aviation that helicopters be used for specialized work flights involving the hydrocarbon and mining companies' exploration and production activities, and for other natural resources in the country's interior. The Ecuadorian government expedited the legal bureaucratic processes and invited international companies in.

Two Alouette III helicopters were leased and began operating in October 1984, supporting seismic work. In 1985 the oil and mining operations expanded, so ICARO lease/purchase optioned nine Alouette III helicopters and three larger capacity Puma SA-330J helicopters. Then a recession hit and oil activities between 1992 and 1995 resulted in little if any helicopter use.

ICARO began "related operations service" in 1995 and in January 1996 lease optioned a Bell 205 and a Bell 206 L-3. A Bell 206 L-3 has been purchased from the Bell factory and negotiations for a second Bell 206 L-3 are under way.

Cap. Esteban Saltos has been appointed helicopter operations manager, and with the assistance of the noble and determined ICARO personnel, their transparency and ethics, will to work, spirit of service, and great love of aviation, ICARO looks forward to a strong and healthy future.

Cap. Esteban Saltos, helicopter operations manager and a Bell 206 L-3

Based on the initiative and private efforts of a group of friends and inspired by their love of flying, ICARO S.A. was established as a civil pilot aviation school in Quito on September 21, 1971. Led by Captain Guido Saltos Martinez, the instructors teach at what they refer to as "the highest" school of civil aviation in the world — Quito has a 12,000-foot altitude.

The Director General of Civil Aviation issued Resolution No. 028 on January 29, 1972, authorizing ICARO to operate. On September 1, 1972, the first class of private pilots graduated and the dreams of 25 students came true. This group included such distinguished professionals as Captain Diego Quirola, Architect Camilo Villamar, Engineer Ignacio Davila Rojas, Engineer Juan Espinoza, Mr. Fausto Gortaire, and others.

During its 26 years of operation, ICARO has produced more than 2,000 pilots. Many are presently working for commercial companies such as Ecuatoriana de Aviacion, Saeta, Aeca, and Tame. Some are commanders and others are copilots, a source of satisfaction and pride for everyone at ICARO.

PROFILE

ITC-AEROSPACE, INC.

From the emerging markets of Southeast Asia and South America, to the more developed markets in Europe, Australia, and North America, ITC-Aerospace, Inc. has become one of the most responsive sources of funding for helicopters and fixed-wing aircraft.

Being Japan's largest lessor of helicopters, ITC serves the global aviation community with innovative and flexible lease, finance, and sales packages for all of the major types of aviation assets.

Founded in 1988 as a firm specializing in the sales and finance of helicopters and regional aircraft, ITC has rapidly expanded to become Japan's premier dealer in this important aviation market segment.

It is now considered by the aviation industry as one of the world's leaders in sales, finance, and leasing of helicopters and fixed-wing aircraft. With a staff of highly experienced, qualified, and multi-lingual aviation specialists at Tokyo Head Office and other offices in Singapore, the U.S., the U.K., and the Philippines, ITC has been able to achieve an average delivery rate of over 30 aircraft per year.

Helicopters and fixed-wing aircraft under lease are currently dedicated to major operators in the United States, Canada, Spain, Mexico, Brazil, Australia, New Zealand, Malaysia, India, Thailand, the Philippines, and Taiwan, as well as Japan. ITC plans to continue its fleet and market activity into the future.

KAMAN CORPORATION

In the fading light and swirling snow of January 16, 1947, Charles H. Kaman watched his first helicopter hover inches off the ground. The K-125 shook ferociously on its first brief flight. It nevertheless flew in time to satisfy the backers of the young Kaman Aircraft Corporation, and it began a half-century of helicopter evolution. Today, HAI and Kaman Aerospace share 50 years of helicopter history and a bright future.

The evolution of Kaman helicopters began in East Hartford, Connecticut, in 1943 when the 24-year-old head of the Hamilton Standard aerodynamics department watched the Sikorsky VS-300 fly. Charles Kaman was captivated by the freedom of helicopter flight but challenged by the power wasted in an anti-torque rotor and by the pilot effort needed to control the machine. He knew intermeshing rotors used by Anton Flettner in Germany were an efficient alternative to the tail rotor. He also thought small ailerons on each rotor blade — servo-flaps — could help control helicopters with less effort.

When his employers showed no interest in the aerodynamic servo-rotor, Kaman set up the Kaman Aircraft Laboratory to get the wartime permits to buy materials with which to build and test his concept after hours. A 14 foot-long hand-carved spruce plank became a helicopter rotor. The engine and chassis of a wrecked Pontiac and the rear end of an old Dodge truck became the powertrain for a mobile test stand. A bathroom scale measured lift.

Trials with servo-flaps set close to the blade were disappointing. However, moving the flaps away from the bladehub to increase their moment arms twisted the big airfoil all along its length to change pitch and lift. Working flaps on both blades in unison would provide collective pitch to climb and descend. Using them differentially produced cyclic control for roll, pitch, and yaw. Moving the flaps took far less effort than twisting the entire blade from the root.

Charlie Kaman conducted an impromptu demonstration of his invention in his mother's driveway for the engineering manager of United Aircraft. He was told bluntly the company had no need of another inventor. With meager financing from two friends, the upstart engineer left his job and incorporated Kaman Aircraft Corporation (today the Kaman Aerospace subsidiary of Kaman Corporation) on December 12, 1945. Work continued in a gymnasium at Bradley Field in Windsor Locks, Connecticut.

Kaman's first helicopter put on an effective flying display before backers on Good Friday 1947. The synchropter with intermeshing rotors and servo-flaps promised an aircraft so easy to fly that thousands would buy them. But while the single-seat K-125 proved the elements of everyman's helicopter, tighter regulations pushed the cost of certification beyond the reach of a small company. When the U.S. Navy Bureau of Aeronautics issued a small servo-flap rotor study contract in May 1947, the K-125 began a tour of U.S. military bases. The three-seat K-190 first flew in April 1948. It was certified by the Civil Aeronautics Administration (CAA) in April 1949, and was followed by the more powerful K-225 a short time later. The CAA Restricted Use license would not permit general sales of the helicopter. Kaman began leasing aircraft in 1949 to spray farms in Florida, North Carolina, New York, Connecticut, and Maine. By 1948, Kaman had 25 employees working on more powerful machines.

Also in 1949, the government of Turkey paid $27,500 to become the first customer to buy a Kaman helicopter. In 1950, the U.S. Navy bought two K-225s and the U.S. Coast Guard one. A navy K-225 later became the world's first turboshaft helicopter with a Boeing 502 engine.

In September 1950, while developing the HOK-1 observation helicopter for the Marine Corps, Kaman received a U.S. Navy contract for 29 of the K-240 or HTK-1 trainers. An HTK-1 became the world's first twin-turbine helicopter in March 1954.

Kaman moved to its current location in Bloomfield, Connecticut, in 1953, and flew the Kaman K-600 or HOK-1 that year. The H-43B Huskie won a 1956 Air Force competition for a crash rescue helicopter, and Huskies were stationed at Tactical Air Command bases to fight fires and rescue aircrews. The Lycoming XT53 turboshaft flew in an HOK in September 1956 and led to the turbine-engined H-43B ordered by the U.S. Air Force. Delivery of the last H-43A in July 1959 marked the end of the reciprocating engine at Kaman.

Kaman pilots K-190 in Washington, D.C., July 1949. Charles H. Kaman built the servo-flap rotor test rig to prove his control concept.

HH-43Bs and armored HH-43Fs performed thousands of crew rescues and medical evacuations during the long war in Southeast Asia. The H-43B set numerous altitude, rate of climb, and other records, and was the first helicopter to go through its service life without a single accident attributable to the aircraft design. Huskies also served in foreign air forces, and some found their way into commercial logging where the lifting efficiency and relative quiet of intermeshing rotors were important. Kaman uses two Huskies today to train K-MAX pilots.

A 1956 U.S. Navy requirement called for a long-range, adverse weather utility and rescue helicopter. Kaman proposed a single-rotor design to save deckspace and achieve higher speeds and in 1957 won a contract to produce the HU-2K-1 (later the UH-2) Seasprite. UH-2As and Bs flew from ships in the Gulf of Tonkin to rescue aviators downed off and in Vietnam. In 1965 a single-engine Seasprite was modified with two T-58 turboshafts and became the prototype for the HH-2C and HH-2D rescue helicopters.

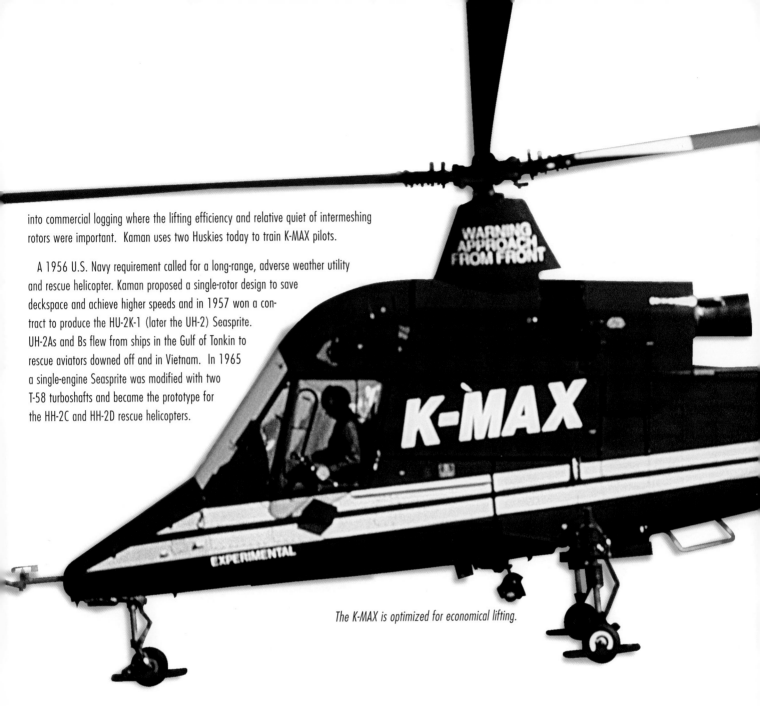

The K-MAX is optimized for economical lifting.

After the war in Southeast Asia, the navy's Light Airborne Multipurpose System (LAMPS) used the Seasprite as an extension of the ship. The LAMPS I helicopter proved a powerful asset through the Cold War and two conflicts in the Persian Gulf.

Kaman flew twin General Electric T700 turboshafts on a YSH-2G in April 1985, and the U.S. Naval Reserve received its first Super Seasprite in December 1992. Egypt, Australia, and New Zealand have ordered advanced SH-2Gs for their navies, and the powerful Super Seasprite is a contender for more international orders.

The K-1200 Multi-Mission Intermeshing Rotor Aircraft demonstrator first flew in December 1991 and gave Kaman a new commercial helicopter. It was certificated by the FAA in 1994. The single-seat, single-engined K-MAX is a cost-effective medium- to heavy-lift helicopter for logging, construction, and other external load work capable of lifting 6,000 pounds and operating at altitudes up to 15,000 feet. Like the first operators of the K-225, the first K-MAX operators leased their helicopters. By 1997, the K-MAX fleet had accumulated more than 26,000 flight hours in North and South America, Europe, Japan, and the Arabian Gulf.

Charles Kaman has received numerous awards and honors for his contributions to aviation, including the National Medal of Technology, presented to him in July 1996 by President Clinton. In August 1995, he was given the Distinguished Public Service Award by the U.S. Department of Defense, and in September of that year he was named an Honorary Fellow of the Royal Aeronautical Society. In December 1997 he was awarded the Wright Brothers Memorial Trophy. Today, with the K-MAX and the SH-2G programs, Kaman's vision continues to shape helicopter industry.

PAPILLON GRAND CANYON HELICOPTERS

Papillon Grand Canyon Helicopters' origin can be traced to 1957, when a young engineer named Elling Halvorson began a construction company specializing in remote-area, high-logistic projects. In 1961 Halvorson secured a contract to construct a relay station in the transcontinental telephone system on a mountain peak above Tahoe, California. To complete this job, Halvorson purchased the first 47G3B1 helicopter built by Bell. By 1963 he had won the contract to build a water pipeline stretching 14 miles across some of the most difficult terrain in the world — the Grand Canyon.

To construct the Grand Canyon pipeline, all equipment, materials, and workers had to be flown to remote sites. Helicopters manufactured by Bell, Hiller, and Sikorsky were used to accomplish this feat in the mile-deep gorge.

Having flown over 25,000 hours of flight time, this project remains the largest helicopter supported construction project in the United States.

Everyone who flew into the Grand Canyon during the pipeline project was overwhelmed by the breathtaking views and photo opportunities made possible only by helicopter.

By 1965 Grand Canyon Helicopters was formed to provide on-demand aerial tours; thus was born the first helicopter company devoted solely to the sightseeing industry. Over the years, various aircraft have been used including Hiller, Sikorsky, Hughes, Aerospatiale, and Bell.

Papillon expanded its operations in 1985 to the Hawaiian Islands under the name Papillon Hawaiian Helicopters, Ltd. Shortly after beginning its Hawaiian operation, Papillon became the premier helicopter company in the islands, operating a fleet of 25 Aerospatiale AS-350B and AS-350D helicopters and three Bell JetRangers. In June 1994, the Hawaiian division was sold.

In 1995 a multi-phase expansion and modernization program began, including several proprietary enhancements to the Bell LongRanger helicopter. Among the new innovations were Vista View windows, Bose sound systems, and a striking rainbow color scheme.

The modernization program continued in April 1996 with the unveiling of a state-of-the-art heliport and hangar complex. The facility includes a luxurious passenger lounge, safety briefing area, interpretive museum, photo processing lab, and gift shop. The flight line has 12 active landing pads to accommodate the fleet of 26 Bell jet-powered aircraft.

In 1992 Elling Halvorson, in his commitment to quiet aircraft technology, embarked on an ambitious project to design and manufacture a new generation of super-quiet helicopters. The result of this project, the Whisper Jet® (S55QT), is scheduled for commercial operations in the summer of 1998. The aircraft seats nine passengers and offers a smooth, quiet flight with unparalleled views of the Grand Canyon through over-sized windows and a "glass-bottom" floor window.

Today, as the next generation of Halvorsons "join Elling at the controls," the company is recognized as an innovative world leader in helicopter flightseeing. During its 33 years of operations, Papillon has safely flown millions of passengers and provided them with the "experience of a lifetime."

Brenda Halvorson, President

Elling Halvorson, Chairman

PETROLEUM HELICOPTERS, INC.

As HAI celebrates its 50th anniversary, Petroleum Helicopters, Inc. (PHI) observes its 49th year of world leadership. The two organizations have experienced all the memorable moments in helicopter history.

PHI was launched in 1949 by the late Robert L. Suggs to support oil industry seismic crews in Louisiana's coastal marshes. When the industry moved offshore, fast, safe, efficient ways to transport personnel and equipment were essential. In meeting that need, PHI quickly established itself as the world leader in commercial helicopter operations, and has maintained that position for almost half a century.

The company's technological and procedural innovations have contributed to the progress of every segment of the oil and gas industry. The commercial helicopter industry has benefited profoundly from PHI's pioneering accomplishments.

management information, and the most efficient and effective use of all company resources.

With Suggs' guidance, PHI began a program of growth through expansion, diversification, and acquisition in the domestic oil and gas, international, aeromedical, and technical services markets. A million dollar safety incentive program ensured continuance and expansion of the company's world leadership position in helicopter safety. Customer service training for all employees was instituted, and "partnering" with customers became part of the PHI Standard.

"At the heart of the strategic plan," Suggs says, "is a team of motivated and talented men and women. This is our greatest asset, and the strongest guarantee of customer satisfaction."

Robert Suggs guided PHI until his death in 1989. The years immediately following were challenging ones for PHI with the loss of its founder and long-time leader, along with an unexpected decline in the domestic petroleum industry. In a move that gave the men and women of PHI a renewed sense of continuity and confidence, Carroll W. Suggs, widow of PHI's founder, stepped in to fill the void created by her husband's death.

Bell 407

Carroll Suggs not only brought to the task pride in the company's history, but also the realization that continued industry leadership could be ensured only by responding to new challenges and seizing new opportunities.

Suggs and a strong management team established a new PHI Standard and a strategic plan based on development of a world-class, service-oriented, and customer-driven organization that would preempt all competition at identifying and responding to customer needs. With the goal of becoming "The Total Helicopter Company," PHI reorganized for greater accountability, a more systematic flow of

The plan is working. It sustained PHI's leadership position in serving the offshore oil industry and enhanced the company's ability to respond to the industry's resurgence and its changing needs. Growth in PHI aeromedical services is surpassing that of all competitors. Expansion in the international division has given PHI a strong, growing global presence. A new world market for PHI's technical services division has been established. With more than 8 million flight hours, the company's safety record remains the best in the world.

"We are The Total Helicopter Company," Suggs says, "with a new corporate vision, organizational structure, mission, goals, and approach to the challenges of today's marketplace."

In 1949, the Bell 47 was a state-of-the-art aircraft for the domestic oil and gas market.

PRATT & WHITNEY CANADA

Pratt & Whitney Canada (P&WC) congratulates the Helicopter Association International (HAI) on its 50th anniversary and its efforts on behalf of the helicopter industry.

In the late 1960s, P&WC entered the helicopter market with its first PT6T Twin-Pac® model, the PT6T-3, certified in 1970. Since then, the PT6T-6, PT6T-6B, PT6T-3B, PT6T-3BE, PT6T-3D, and PT6T-3DF models have been added to the product line, with the latest models providing improved hot/high performance through continuous product improvements. These turboshaft engines power the Model 212/412 helicopters manufactured by Bell Helicopter Textron, Agusta, and IPTN (Indonesia).

The success of Bell's 212/412 helicopters powered by the PT6T Twin-Pac gave P&WC a dominant presence in the medium helicopter market, and the extraordinary Twin-Pac service experience established the reliability and durability standards in helicopter operations.

In the early 1980s, P&WC started developing the PW200, a new generation turboshaft engine that follows the design and development principles so thoroughly proven in 30 years of PT6 turboshaft and turboprop experience. Helicopter operators had a strong hand in the PW200 design, through regular consultations where they expressed their technical preferences. Reliability, maintainability, and low ownership cost were high priorities from the beginning.

Since then, the PW200 turboshaft series has been selected by five helicopter manufacturers to power their New Generation Light Twin helicopters, thus establishing P&WC as the prime turboshaft engine supplier in this market.

Boeing selected the PW206A in 1989 for the MD900 Explorer and the PW206E in 1996 for the MD902. The PW206B was selected by Eurocopter for the EC135 in 1991. The aircraft was certified in June 1996. In 1993, Agusta chose the PW206C to power the A109 POWER, which was certified in May 1996. The PW206D was selected in 1996 by Bell Helicopter Textron for

the Model 427 and was certified in December 1997. First production engines were delivered in January 1998. The latest addition to the family is the PK206C, which was selected in 1997 by Kazan for the ANSAT.

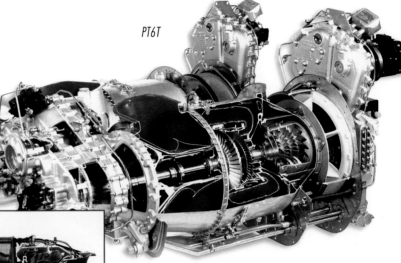

PT6T

PW206B

P&WC is now expanding its PT6 turboshaft family with the PT6B-37 engine and the PT6C-67 series. In February 1996, the PT6B-37 engine was selected by Agusta to power its single-engine A119 Koala. The PT6B-37, rated at 1,002 thermodynamic shp for take off, is a direct derivative of the PT6T-3D. The PT6C-67 series, rated from 1,200 to 2,000 shp, will offer proven PT6 reliability, low operating costs, and competitive performance in a cost-effective package tailored for helicopter operation.

In September 1996, PZL-Swidnik of Poland selected the PT6C-67B turboshaft to power its twin-engine W-3 Sokol helicopter. P&WC plans to certify the PT6C-67B in the second quarter of 1998. Bell Helicopter Textron/Boeing Co. chose the PT6C-67A to power the new Bell Boeing 609 Civil Tiltrotor. Engine certification is expected at the turn of the century.

P&WC, with its PT6 turboshaft and PW200 series engines, has become the main engine supplier in the commercial light twin and medium twin helicopters.

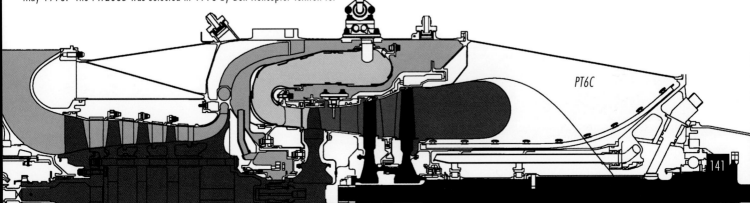

PT6C

SIKORSKY AIRCRAFT CORPORATION

Sikorsky Aircraft Corporation Today

Sikorsky S-92 Helibus™

Sikorsky Aircraft Corporation, a subsidiary of United Technologies Corporation, is the world leader in the design and manufacture of advanced helicopters for commercial, industrial, and military uses.

Sikorsky helicopters occupy a dominant international position in the intermediate to heavy range of 9,900 pounds (4,500 kg.) to 70,400 pounds (32,000 kg.) gross weight. They are used by all five branches of the United States armed forces, military services, and commercial operators in more than 40 nations.

Based in Stratford, Connecticut, Sikorsky has outlying manufacturing facilities in other Connecticut locations, as well as Florida and Alabama. The total area of buildings owned or leased by Sikorsky comprises more than 3.5 million square feet. Revenues in 1996 were $1.6 billion.

The Sikorsky and Boeing Helicopters team is developing the U.S. Army's new armed reconnaissance helicopter, the RAH-66 Comanche, which conducted its first flight in January 1996.

An international team led by Sikorsky is developing the S-92 HELIBUS, which is aimed at the medium-lift commercial and government markets. The team members are: Jingdezhen Helicopter Group/CATIC of the People's Republic of China, Mitsubishi Heavy Industries (MHI) of Japan, Aerospace Industrial Development Corporation (AIDC) in Taiwan, Embraer of Brazil, and Gamesa of Spain.

S-76C+ Corporate Version

Core programs are based on the H-60 aircraft, the U.S. Army BLACK HAWK and the SEAHAWK series for the U.S. Navy. H-60 derivative aircraft are being fielded for a multiplicity of missions with other branches of the U.S. military. Sikorsky's CH-53E and MH-53E heavy-lift aircraft are used by the U.S. Navy and Marine Corps to transport personnel and equipment, and for anti-mine warfare missions.

The U.S. Federal Aviation Administration certified the commercial S-76C+, the helicopter's latest variant, in the summer of 1996. S-76 variants can be found around the world serving executive transport, offshore oil, and government search-and-rescue missions.

RAH-66 Comanche

STANDARD AERO

As the Helicopter Association International (HAI) is proud to celebrate its 50th anniversary, Standard Aero begins its seventh decade of operations. The HAI's evolution to become the largest helicopter association in the world is paralleled by Standard Aero's growth from a small aero parts machine shop to one of the largest independent gas turbine engine overhaul companies in the world.

Standard Aero entered the helicopter industry in 1963, when the company began to overhaul the General Electric T-58 engine for the CH-124 Sikorsky Sea King helicopter. In addition to this program, the organization added Lycoming T-53 and T-55 engine repair and overhaul capabilities to provide support to the Canadian Armed Forces rotor-wing programs.

Standard Aero's greatest success in the helicopter market began 30 years ago, with the addition of the Allison 250/T-63 engine program. The program was initially developed to support the Canadian Armed Forces fleet of Allison T-63 engines. Since then, Standard Aero has grown into one of the largest Allison 250 Authorized Maintenance Centers in the world with facilities in Canada, Mexico, Singapore, Australia, the Philippines, and the United States.

The company's philosophies have evolved as the growth and expansion has occurred. The organization is no longer dependent on government programs but instead a healthy mix of commercial and military business. The assembly lines of the early days have been abolished, making way for a more efficient cellular design. The employees own the maintenance processes and take pride in the product and the organization.

In an attempt to provide operators with increased value for their maintenance dollar, Standard Aero focused on doing more than just fixing engines. With quality, reliability, and costs being of utmost importance to operators, the organization developed a number of tools to aid helicopter operators with their maintenance efforts and management of their direct engine operating costs. The development of the custom build standard and engine monitoring devices, CrossCheck and the Engine Doctor, have proven invaluable to operators in allowing them to make real-time maintenance decisions.

The commitment to innovation also opened the door for Standard Aero to be a part of rotor-wing history. In 1994, Standard Aero provided Ron Bower with a custom build engine for his initial around-the-world, record-breaking journey.

In celebration of HAI's grand success, Standard Aero is proud to be a continued supporter of the organization and its members. The civil helicopter industry can be confident that they are represented by a world-class association. The employees of Standard Aero wish the Helicopter Association International the best of luck during this year of celebration and we look forward to celebrating the next 50 years supporting HAI and its members.

Allison 250 turboshaft engine overhaul (1970).

TURBOMECA ENGINE CORPORATION

Powering on.

Turbomeca is no stranger to the helicopter industry. Since its start in 1938, the name Turbomeca has been synonymous with small and medium gas-powered turbine helicopter engines. In fact, they were one of the first to witness the emergence of the modern helicopter industry.

The beginning of the modern helicopter movement can be traced back to April 18, 1951, with the first flight of the Ariel III. It was the world's first helicopter to be powered by a gas turbine engine — the Arrius II. Another historic company achievement occurred in 1952 when Turbomeca introduced the Artouste turboshaft engine. The Artouste not only powered the Sikorsky S-52-5, it also powered the world-renowned Aerospatiale Alouette II and III helicopters. The Artouste family of turboshaft engines played a major role in earning Turbomeca its reputation for sturdy, highly reliable engines.

The sixties marked another significant breakthrough for the helicopter industry and Turbomeca — the development of the Astazou II and the Turmo IV. The high-performance Astazou II was installed on the Alouette II starting in 1961. More than 1,300 of these engines were manufactured over a period of 18 years. And in 1965, the Turmo IV turboshaft for the SA330 Puma helicopter was developed. A total of 2,800 Turmo engines were built and enabled Turbomeca to establish a foothold on the highly competitive medium helicopter market.

Turbomeca continued to make significant industry strides in the seventies with the introduction of Arriel and Makila turboshaft engines designed for light, medium, and heavy helicopters. As the universally- acclaimed leader in its power class, the Arriel was the original powerplant chosen for the Aerospatiale Ecureuil and Dauphin, the Agusta A109K2, and the Sikorsky S-76A. It was also selected to re-engine the Astar (the U.S. version of the Ecureuil) and the Sikorsky S-76A+.

The Makila, the Turmo's successor, also helped solidify the company's reputation for designing

reliable and high-performance engines. Known for its simplicity and ruggedness of design, combined with excellent performance and low direct operating costs, the Makila became the engine of choice for Aerospatiale's Super Puma helicopters.

Aerospatiale Djinn with Turbomeca engine.

During the eighties, Turbomeca began a long-standing Rolls-Royce partnership with the creation of the RTM 322 and MTR 390 for heavy-duty 7- to 15-ton helicopters. These two engines further confirmed Turbomeca's technological lead and established a strong presence in the helicopter defense marketplace. Also during this time period, Turbomeca expanded its product line by producing the Arrius. The Arrius was the first engine in its class to provide twin-engine helicopter pilots true one engine inoperative (OEI) power when they needed it. Plus, it was engineered to reduce operating costs and enhance flight safety, without sacrificing helicopter operators' strict demands. In all, the Arrius serves as another example of how Turbomeca was able, with its technological expertise, to produce high performance from a simple, rugged design.

Today, Turbomeca is the power of choice for the Eurocopter EC120, EC135, AS350, AS355, BK117 C1, AS365, AS332; Agusta A109K2 and A109 Power; Boeing - MD901; and the Sikorsky S-76. And as Turbomeca powers forward, it is striving to be a leader in the research and development of helicopter turbine engines. Not only today, but well into the future.

Aerospatiale Ariel helicopter with Turbomeca Arrius II engine.

P R O F I L E

VICKERS INCORPORATED

The Technical Development Company (Tedeco) was founded in 1952 by Dietrich W. Botstiber, who was chief mechanical engineer at Piasecki Helicopters. In the early years of rotary flight, failure detection was a simple threaded magnetic plug in the lube system sump, which was inspected during oil change. Tedeco's first product was a self-closing valve into which the mag plug was inserted, allowing frequent inspections without oil loss. This simple, inexpensive device was an instant success in the industry.

Armed with the expertise gained from the development and in-service application of the self-closing mag plug, Tedeco went on to produce a broad range of fluid system products such as fillers, breathers, level indicators, gauges, sight glasses, level switches, and optical level sensors.

As the helicopter industry progressed, the basic magnetic plug evolved into the chip detector, a passive electrical device that provided a "Chip" indication in the cockpit. Although a significant improvement, it had an inherent shortcoming in that it could not distinguish insignificant wear particles from potentially failure-related debris. This necessitated many unscheduled landings to physically check the collected material.

In 1977, Tedeco introduced the Zapper® Electric Chip Detector, whose principal feature was its ability to clear normal, noncritical wear debris accumulations from the detector while continuing to indicate failure-related particles. This is still the most widely used failure detection device for helicopters.

In an effort parallel to the Zapper®, Tedeco also developed two distinct Quantitative Debris Monitors (QDM®), which collect and electronically indicate ferromagnetic debris.

In QDM systems, ferromagnetic debris generates a voltage pulse proportional to particle mass as individual chips are captured by a magnetic sensor. These low-level signals are then amplified and processed as required for interface with aircraft monitoring systems.

The IQ™ system differs from QDM in that the electronics assembly continually monitors changes in the inductance of the sensor's magnetic circuit caused by the accumulation of ferrous debris and provides an analog output. This difference in operating principle allows IQ systems to track and trend debris accumulation over time.

In 1985, Tedeco was purchased by Aeroquip Corporation and in 1990 was transferred to a sister company, Vickers Incorporated. The operation became known as Systems Monitoring Division. In 1997, the Tedeco name resurfaced because of its recognition in the industry.

Product improvement efforts in the 1990s have produced the Smart Zapper™, a microprocessor-based unit that verifies the integrity of the entire system while allowing greater flexibility in selecting an energy pulse profile for each detector.

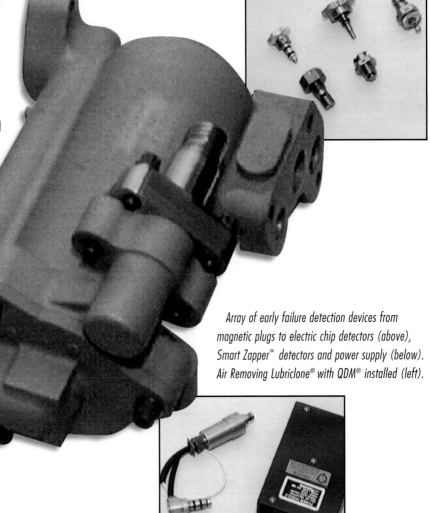

Array of early failure detection devices from magnetic plugs to electric chip detectors (above), Smart Zapper™ detectors and power supply (below). Air Removing Lubriclone® with QDM® installed (left).

145

N4499N

PAN AM

Westland 30

6

Westland Helicopters Ltd., 30 Series 100-60

THE SEVENTIES

*"I'm president of nothing
without people."*

Andre Lachapelle, Trans-Quebec Helicopters, 1979

> *A banking industry attitude of "show me, don't tell me" dogged the commercial operators when it came to financing new aircraft.*

Twenty years after it became familiar as the flying ambulance of the Korean War, the helicopter was firmly established worldwide as a major factor of the 1970s in rescues and commercial operations, after military service in Southeast Asia and places that did not appear on most maps.

By 1970, a safety-minded Helicopter Association of America (HAA) was providing helicopter operators management courses each mid-year and had made the Safety Committee a standing body of the association with instructions to prepare the first safety manual.

It would take a while for these industry initiatives at self-improvement to be visible at the working level. Human nature being what it is, a banking industry attitude of "show me, don't tell me" dogged the commercial operators when it came to financing new aircraft. Their concerns included image and safety.

HAA management and safety courses, the hiring of two safety specialists, and various other steps were intended to address precisely the issues of perceived safety and operating effectiveness.

On April 13, 1970, the crew of Apollo 13, four-fifths of the way to the moon, told Mission Control: "We've got a problem here." Apollo 13 landed safely four days later.

Bell 430

On June 11, 1970, the U.S. presence in Libya ended as the last units left Wheelus Air Base.

On June 22, 1970, President Nixon signed a law lowering the voting age to 18.

The industry moves toward self-improvement were not enough to convince federal agencies that the private sector could handle the many necessary tasks, including the highly visible challenge of providing emergency medical services.

In August 1970, the U.S. government launched a multi-department helicopter program called Military Assistance to Safety and Traffic. Known as MAST, it included the Departments of Defense; Transportation; and Health, Education, and Welfare, which encouraged military units to provide emergency helicopters to local communities. The idea was that military units of all kinds had resources that were often standing idle. If these could be made available to the civilian public, it would save lives.

The program began in five western states, using helicopters and medical personnel from active and reserve military units. Not only would local communities have the benefit of rapid evacuation, but they would be treated by trained medical specialists. MAST got off to a good start, but set a very bad precedent in terms of government encroachment into the private sector.

As 1970 moved along, an increasing number of commercial operators took the option of requesting a safety survey, which the insurance industry preferred calling an "evaluation." The survey covered operations, training, maintenance, facilities, and safety, as well as the management and organization of the operation. Management was then briefed on the findings and told what had to be fixed.

Application of the standards set up by HAA were a condition of continuing membership in the industry association, which had lingering difficulties getting operators to respond to requests for operating and safety data.

In October, the association took its new HAA Management Guide and Operations Manual to London, seeking Lloyd's approval.

That same month saw the election of Alan Bristow, head of England's Bristow Helicopters, as the first HAA director from outside the western hemisphere. Within months, at the January 1971 annual meeting, Bristow was named chairman of the newly established International Committee.

The executive director's position was filled in April 1971 by HAA past president Bob Richardson, who worked with HAA President Glenn McPherson of Okanagan Helicopters in managing a smooth transition for an ever-growing helicopter association. By May 1971, the helicopter association had hired Ed Hutcheson to run its safety operations.

On November 9, 1970, Charles de Gaulle died.

On December 2, 1970, the Environmental Protection Agency (EPA) began operating.

On April 1, 1971, the Occupational Safety & Health Act (OSHA) became effective.

Did You Know?

Horatio Alger has many nationalities, speaks many languages, and sometimes flies a helicopter.

In the Canadian province of Quebec, a young man named Andre Lachapelle had worked hard in the construction business and saved his money until he owned a small share in a cement company. In 1970 he encountered a man who owned both a commercial license and a single Bell 47 helicopter that the "commercial operator" flew almost as a hobby. Lachapelle bought both the commercial license and the helicopter by selling his share of the cement plant.

Within nine years he went from near-zero financially to the presidency of Trans-Quebec, a commercial helicopter operation valued in 1980 at $10 million. Through careful bidding, acquisitions, spinoffs, and other shrewd business practices, he steadily increased the value of his company, which had 180 employees as the decade closed.

Lachapelle never forgot what it was that made the company succeed.

"I'm president of nothing without people."

Issues of the day ranged from the dramatic to the mundane, from the estimated 70 percent of helicopter accidents that were caused by pilot error, to slow-paying federal agencies causing financial grief to their commercial helicopter contractors.

It was generally assumed at the time that the ongoing war in Southeast Asia was generating a great many experienced helicopter pilots who could easily make the transition into commercial operations. However, there are significant differences in military and civil operations and their piloting skills.

Accidents attributed to pilots were addressed bluntly by HAA President-elect J. Arlo Livingston, who noted on the front page of the association's newsletter that "as a small operator working in the bush country, I would like to make a few observations which have been arrived at by some costly experiences. There are quite a number of helicopter pilots available in the U.S. with military background. Some of these are excellent material but do require considerable training to engage in a commercial operation successfully. In our operation, we have found that it takes at least one year before the pilot, with approximately 1,500 helicopter hours, is capable of doing all the various jobs in which we are engaged, and this with considerable briefing and supervision. I am sure that the same problem exists in agricultural work, offshore drilling, construction and the many other facets of helicopter operations. Therefore, the only conclusion we have made is that the pilot has to be briefed and have training on each kind of work to be done."

Jim Ricklefs, Hal Conners, Pete Brown, all HAI past presidents

On the critical issue of safety, collective industry attention to the problem resulted in a significant improvement for HAA members from 1969 to 1970: an improvement of 27.4 to 22.3 accidents per 100,000 flight hours. For helicopter operators generally, the rate was 35.08 in 1969 and an estimated 28 accidents per 100,000 flight hours in 1970.

Wire strikes were (and remain) a chronic hazard to helicopter operations, and in the summer of 1971 alone nine people were killed in 10 wire strike accidents in the U.S. All 10 aircraft were either destroyed or substantially damaged in the mishaps, which often occur where pilots are unfamiliar with takeoff or landing locations.

That same summer, helicopters reduced accidents in ground transportation in their own way. A pair of helicopters was leased for a year by the New York Metropolitan Transportation Authority and used to patrol long stretches of track for the Long Island Railroad (LIRR) and Penn Central Lines. Normally-dry statistics often tell a dramatic story, as they do here.

June is traditionally a bad month for railroad vandalism because of vacationing students who get into mischief. In the first three months of helicopter patrols, airborne railroad police reported almost 4,000 incidents. In May 1971, there were 43 injuries to passengers and crew from vandalism, down from 94 the previous May. In June 1971, personal injuries dropped 73 percent on the Penn Central, and 81.5 percent on the LIRR, compared with June 1970. In that same three-month period of April-May-June, broken train windows declined from 6,382 to 2,690 over 1970. The use of helicopters for security patrols obviously paid off.

Helicopters were quietly working their way into many other economic roles during the first few decades of their commercial history, and in most cases were not only environmentally friendly but actually reversed environmentally damaging practices involving other modes of transportation.

Significant reductions in vandalism and injuries to railroad passengers and crew members were welcomed results when helicopters began patrolling railroads in 1971.

For The Record

1970 - Apollo 13 lands safely in Pacific after near-catastrophic journey to moon •

U.S. Forest Service calculations of the period indicate that the cost of logging 1,000 board feet of lumber via helicopter was about $60. To do the same job in the traditional way cost $7 to $12. However, when the cost of environmental damage caused by logging roads, central loading sites, and other indirect logging operations were included, the cost became almost equal . . . and esthetic considerations clearly gave the nod to selective helicopter logging.

It was Erickson Lumber Co., parent of the helicopter firm that removed and replaced the Freedom Statue on the Capitol dome in Washington, D.C., that first used heavy-lift helicopters for logging, at the urging of Columbia Construction Helicopters. Erickson subsequently bought its own helicopters and diversified into other heavy-lift work. Columbia and Carson Helicopters then joined in the logging business along with Erickson, with great environmental benefits following in their wake.

On April 19, 1971, the Messerschmitt-Bölkow-Blohm BO-105 was certificated by the Federal Aviation Administration (FAA) and MBB's U.S. distributor, Boeing Vertol, announced plans to demonstrate the twin-turbine helicopter to U.S. operators beginning in June. Two BO-105s in West Germany were even then patrolling the Autobahn system and making medevac flights.

Aerospatiale's SA-330 Puma, a transport-class helicopter sold in the U.S. by Vought Helicopter Corp. of Dallas, Texas, was certificated by the FAA in September 1971. The 17-passenger twin-turbine aircraft was leased by PHI from Vought in April 1972 for an evaluation of its offshore performance. The Puma was in heavy use by French, British, and other military establishments. Aerospatiale hoped to crack the commercial market as an offshore utility machine.

The January 1972 HAA annual meeting saw the election of Arlo Livingston of Livingston Helicopters as president for a two-year term. Industry icon Joe Mashman of Bell Helicopters was named to the Board as a special advisor, and Don Atwood of Allison became an ex officio director, the first from an engine manufacturer. Before the end of the year, Mashman was also named chairman of a new HAA instrument flight rules (IFR) committee.

The association also recognized law enforcement members with establishment of the Hughes Law Enforcement Award, which was presented for the first time at the following annual meeting.

February 1972 was the best year Bell Helicopter ever had, with the Texas firm selling 105 commercial helicopters valued at $23 million. The significance of Bell's single-company record was that the combined sales of Beech, Cessna, and Piper general aviation airplanes for the month were only $22 million.

On May 2, 1972, J. Edgar Hoover died.

On May 15, 1972, Democratic presidential candidate George C. Wallace was shot while at a Laurel, Maryland, shopping center and left paralyzed.

On June 17, 1972, the downfall of President Richard M. Nixon began when five burglars were caught at Democratic National Headquarters in Washington's Watergate complex.

On August 12, 1972, the last American combat ground troops left Vietnam.

Rescues were big news in 1972, as they are in virtually every year, but some have higher media profiles than others.

*"Flight For Life" Alouettes
Denver, Colorado, 1979*

While the drama of rescues and emergencies caught headlines, there continued the unheralded daily rounds of scheduled helicopter passenger airlines. Civil Aeronautics Board data for May 1972 indicated that the three scheduled helicopter airlines then operating had overall traffic increases of 14.5 percent over May 1971. Chicago Helicopter Airlines had a 42.9 percent increase in revenue passenger miles, while New York Airways (NYA) traffic increased 10.8 percent and San Francisco Helicopter Airways (SFO) levels jumped by 19.2 percent. NYA alone carried nearly 32,000 revenue passengers during the month.

Undramatic but life-sustaining are daily ministrations of the aviation mechanics who keep flying machines flying. In a sign that helicopters were increasingly considered part of the mainstream aviation world after a quarter century, the FAA annual award for aviation mechanic named Era's David Botens the 1972 regional winner. He was a rarity in the helicopter world at the time.

For The Record

HUMANITARIAN HELICOPTERS

On February 24, 1972, helicopters made at least 150 landings on the roof of the burning 29-story Andraus office skyscraper in Sao Paulo, Brazil, to rescue trapped people. Eleven helicopters — owned by Pirelli S/A and six other civil operators, along with four government helicopters — rescued more than 450 people. Despite landings every 90 seconds on the single heliport in darkness and smoke, there were no helicopter mishaps. The helicopter rescues involved nearly a quarter of all the people in the building because flames had cut them off from escape routes. Five panicked people jumped to their deaths from the upper floors during the first 30 minutes of the fire.

The disaster-turned-miracle was due to the presence of a helipad on the roof of the burning building, and to the courage of more than a dozen pilots who flew into the thick smoke, fire-induced turbulence, and tangle of wires on the rooftop. The Pirelli corporate heliport was nearby and became a command center for the four-and-a-half-hour operation. Political leaders elsewhere in the world saw the lesson, but many still did not pass laws requiring rooftop helipads on tall buildings.

In 1973 another high-rise fire occurred in Sao Paulo but there was no rooftop landing area — 200 people perished.

Eventually, U.S. cities like Los Angeles and Chicago passed laws requiring all buildings over 75 feet tall to have rooftop clear areas for helicopter operations.

The smoke had hardly cleared from the Andraus building in Brazil when helicopters once again showed that — above all and anywhere in the world — helicopters save lives.

In the Swiss Alps, a cable car encountered severe turbulence and began swinging violently enough to entangle the cables. The entire system abruptly stopped. It was 8:10 p.m. on March 11 and still a bitter winter. The cable car stranded 800 feet above Mt. Schilthorn trapped its 70 passengers until daylight, when a rescue would be attempted.

Two helicopters from Air Zermatt lowered mechanics to the roof of the stranded cable car, but the mechanics found that the car could not be freed in a short time. It was then decided to evacuate the passengers by helicopter. Air Zermatt helicopters, aided by helicopters from Swiss Air-Rescue, made 40 flights in the high mountain air, carrying two people per flight. Passengers were placed in a harness at the doorway to the cable car, then winched up into the hovering helicopter and flown to an assembly point. By noon all the passengers were evacuated.

In May, half a world away, a mountain climber was injured at the 17,300-foot level of Mt. McKinley in Alaska. With rescue resources limited, a call went out to Anchorage Helicopters and the commercial operator responded with an Alouette III flown by Gene Lloyd, rescuing the injured man. A month later, the same Alouette III flew search missions for three missing climbers on Mt. McKinley at an altitude of 20,500 feet.

Mass-casualty rescues draw media attention in direct proportion to the proximity of the dramatic event to centers of media concentration such as New York, London, Paris, Los Angeles, Tokyo, Moscow, or Washington, D.C.

In June, Tropical Storm Agnes roared up the east coast of the United States, disrupting transportation and communications. Dozens of helicopters flocked to areas of crisis, and one commercial operator alone, Ronson Helicopters Inc., had seven helicopters in emergency service throughout the stormy period.

Police Bell 412 performing water rescue

RotoWay Exec 162 Fs
in flight

HELICOPTER VERSATILITY

"Versatile" should probably be listed in the thesaurus as a synonym for "helicopter."

• SFO Helicopter Airlines flew a Sikorsky S-61N slowly along the vineyards of the San Joaquin Valley at 100-ft. altitude in order to keep air moving and prevent a killing frost.

• Decair Helicopters moved a rare grand piano to a sixth-floor apartment in Connecticut because the building's elevator was too small and the stairway too narrow. A Bell 206 sling-loaded the 1,200-pound piano to the roof, then it was muscled down one flight of stairs to the top-floor apartment.

• An entire prefabricated bank building was airlifted by a Sikorsky SkyCrane to a site in Woodbridge, New Jersey. The building was shaped like a flying saucer, 26 feet wide, 12 feet high, and weighing 13,500 pounds. The temporary bank was being used while a permanent bank was under construction and was completely outfitted with carpeting, teller windows, cabinets, seats, and telephones. Power and phone connections were waiting, and 30 minutes after the bank was delivered, it opened for business. When the permanent building was ready, the "saucer bank" was moved again by SkyCrane to Toms River, New Jersey, 60 miles away, for similar duties.

• The most extensive short-term application of timber fertilizer ever completed was done by Evergreen Helicopters. Four Bell 205s broadcast 20 million pounds of granular fertilizer on 60,000 acres of trees in Oregon and Washington for the Weyerhaeuser Company.

• Over the jungles of Ecuador, a 2,500-foot cable had to be moved 28 miles to a drilling site across an area known as "The Garden" with no roads or rivers. There was almost no way to do it because the specially built, inch-and-a-quarter-diameter cable could not be cut or divided. Heli-Ecuador was called. It was eventually decided to have each end of the wire spooled onto a drum and slung beneath two helicopters, with a 200-foot length of wire linking the two spools. The commercial operator brought in a Sikorsky S-58T and a Bell 205A, arranged the spool weights according to the lift capacity of the helicopters, and delivered the cable without incident.

• Over the waters of the Chesapeake Bay, the second span of a pair of bridges at Annapolis, Maryland, had been completed and now came time for dismantling construction equipment atop the 374-foot-tall suspension towers. A Sikorsky SkyCrane — which had also poured much of the 45,000 cubic yards of concrete for the bridge footings — lifted the derricks from the towers. The job took 20 minutes.

• On and over the North Sea in the summer of 1973, KLM Noordzee Helikopters placed its one-thousandth harbor pilot aboard a vessel inbound to Rotterdam since the service began in 1968. The service saved ships and harbor pilots a long, arduous boat trip and transfer over often dangerous seas.

Harbor pilots also began arriving and departing oceangoing vessels at ports in Germany as Helikopter Service A/S of Norway contracted with the German government to replace pilot boats. Other ports using commercial helicopters to deliver and pick up harbor pilots included Hong Kong and Melbourne, Australia.

• On and over the South Atlantic, Court Line Helicopters rendezvoused near the Cape of Good Hope with vessels 12 miles offshore to provide them with cargo, mail, and personnel transfer. The commercial helicopter saved oceangoing vessels a very expensive port call to pick up vital items.

• In Nigeria, Volkswagen chartered a Bell 214 from Rotorflug to move parts from ships in the clogged Lagos harbor to the firm's new automobile manufacturing plant.

• In Jedda, Saudi Arabia, Carson Helicopters offloaded 600,000 tons of cement in a year from ships in the congested harbor. The job involved eight twin-turbine S-58T helicopters.

Typical of the kinds of uses found for government helicopters that resulted in clearly unfair competition with commercial helicopter operators were these:

The State of Colorado bought two surplus H-13 helicopters from the U.S. Army and planned to reassemble their parts into one helicopter to be used by the State Department of Fish and Game for surveillance and personnel transportation. The safety of such a machine made completely of cannibalized parts was so obviously questionable that it is surprising it got past the initial idea stage. Commercial operators had been providing such helicopter services under contract to federal and state agencies for years.

Kansas Air National Guard used a CH-54 and its crew to lift an air conditioning unit to the roof of a state office building after the state had sought and received a bid from a commercial operator for the job.

The U.S. Army provided a UH-1 Huey helicopter and crew for standby medical service at a commercially sponsored World Ski Cup competition on Crystal Mountain, Washington. This was done despite a long-standing Defense Department policy of not competing with private-sector enterprises.

Around the world again in the Japan of mid-1972, there were 459 general aviation aircraft, of which 295 (more than three-fifths) were helicopters. Japanese whirly birds had begun to branch out into aerial surveying and photography, but still did mostly agricultural work in the densely populated country.

Agriculture had been the first love of the commercial helicopter operator since the 1940s, and now it seemed to be at a turning point, at the initiative of the very federal government that had so strongly encouraged its early use.

As Don Larson, chair of HAA's agricultural committee warned, "Ag committee action has been almost entirely DEFENSIVE, hard work. Weekly review and briefing on federal and state legislation seems to come in bales now instead of letters. All ag operators should take the time to familiarize themselves with regulations, not only in their own state, but particularly the federal. The Occupational Safety and Health Act became effective in April 1971. Remember the name OSHA, as it is called, and also the Federal Environmental Protection Act of 1971 (EPA). These are really tough and could put us all out of business."

The federal government in 1972 presented yet another threat to the civil helicopter community. This was the planned expansion of the MAST program using military resources to assist civilian communities in emergencies.

Bell 412 operated by Inova Medical Aircraft

In an ironic sense, the controversy swirling around MAST was a mirror-image of the posse comitatus controversy in law enforcement. The U.S. Constitution prohibits the use of military resources for civil law enforcement, yet here were military resources being used for civil emergency relief when no disaster situation had been declared by the federal government. The constitutional analogy was thin, but it was there.

The commercial helicopter industry finally went on record opposing the MAST program and urging its termination. It was a delicate, multi-faceted problem, as the industry's association noted: "Through February 1972, the pilot program proved to have pluses and minuses."

HAA acknowledged that MAST in 19 months had carried 1,125 patients in 891 missions, but noted that most were transports of medical patients, not traffic accident victims as the program had initially envisioned. It was also pointed out that a helicopter was not always available when a local community needed one, so faith in the system was never solidified; and when a military helicopter was available at the required time, the local community's own emergency medical system had to be highly developed in order to take advantage of that benefit.

What triggered the commercial helicopter industry's public opposition was the announced plan to expand MAST to 20 more states beyond the original five in the pilot program. Despite arguable results of the initial period — mostly a matter of interpretation — some federal officials liked those results. Commercial operators very bluntly did not like the results even before they learned that a bill had been introduced in the Congress to expand MAST into an almost unlimited and permanent national program. It would have threatened bankruptcy for many commercial operators who had invested in equipment for emergency medical services, and would have pulled the rug from under hospitals that had done essentially the same thing.

"While it is awkward to complain about a program that saves lives," said the industry association, "the Helicopter Association of America is opposed to the reliance by communities on MAST. As long as MAST is available, local governments avoid developing their own civilian helicopter emergency transportation programs. [MAST] really isn't 'free' to the public; MAST encourages military units to expand their operations beyond what is needed for training purposes; [and] military helicopters are bigger and more expensive to operate than necessary to do the civilian medical job. So the tax-paying public ends up paying more than it would for purely civil emergency programs. And, sooner or later, the military units either will be moved, put on full military assignment, or cut back severely. Then the local community will find itself without MAST and no civil programs to fill the hole in its emergency services."

Eventually, federal efforts to provide military resources for local community operations faded away, but that was not necessarily true at other levels of government.

The State of California, through Governor Edmund G. Brown Jr., proposed using the state's National Guard helicopters to provide "free" medical transportation as a public service. The reaction was similar to that which greeted the federal MAST program, and eventually that idea also faded away.

What did not immediately fade away was the fuel crisis of 1972 and its lasting impact on the world. Along with the fuel crisis, the industry got a shock when the federal government launched an Aviation Cost Allocation study, intended to make users pay for those parts of the national aviation system that they used.

The U.S. government wanted to tax aviation fuel across the board and apply portions of the received monies to pay for air traffic control, airports, radar coverage, and other parts of the national aviation system.

The industry responded in detail, noting that commercial helicopter operators make little use of the airways system. A survey of 87 operators showed that 24.4 percent of more than 700 commercial helicopters were based outside the airways from 50 to 100 percent of the time, and more than 55 percent were based outside controlled airways 100 percent of the time. Helicopters often do not require air traffic control, airports, control towers, radar tracking, or other airplane necessities. Helicopters, the industry added, use proportionally far more fuel than airplanes, meaning the burden would be unfairly carried by helicopter operators.

The federal government also expanded its policy of making surplus military helicopters available to government agencies at the state and local levels. Commercial operators opposed the practice on the grounds that military aircraft had undergone service far more arduous than most civil helicopters and their actual safety was in question by the time they got to local governments. Among the pitfalls were missing records on maintenance, repairs, over-stress conditions, and other safety problems. Liability alone was a major hazard for local governments, many of which were completely unaware of what they were getting in the way of liability and cost.

Then there was FLIR. The U.S. Forest Service (USFS) proposed using military CH-47C Chinook helicopters to conduct tests of electronic guidance systems and fire-retardant spreading tests. USFS said commercial

operators had no helicopters capable of using the forward-looking infra-red (FLIR) equipment. Operators countered that the Bell 205, among others, could do the job, and if the 205 was not satisfactory, then commercial operators should be allowed to use Chinooks under bailment from the military.

Fairchild-Hiller now had delivered 200 of its five-place FH-1100 utility helicopters, a design originally created for the army's light observation helicopter (LOH) program. Most FH-1100 customers were commercial operators, corporations, law enforcement, and construction firms around the world.

Notwithstanding the fact that the Helicopter Association of America had had several presidents from outside the U.S. and now had members from 21 countries, an October 1972 motion to change the name of the organization died with no action taken. KLM's Dr. Menno Kamminga was named an ex officio member to emphasize "the importance of having international representation on the Board."

In November, Petroleum Helicopters Inc. (PHI) placed an order for 30 Bell JetRanger II models and three Bell 205A helicopters for more than $5 million to serve the growing demand for offshore support. The expanding need for offshore support included waters of Southeast Asia, where Cordon International also expanded operations off Indonesia, Thailand, and Borneo. PHI's was the biggest single order in commercial helicopter history.

By the end of 1972, in spite of many challenges, HAA had grown to 200 regular members, 73 associate, and 50 sustaining, for a total of 323 members from 21 countries.

The joke of 1972 following the OSHA, EPA, MAST, FLIR, surplus military helicopters, fuel shortages, Aviation Cost Allocation, and other government-inspired crises was a simple statement: "I am from the government and I am here to help you."

The joke could have been carried over, as 1973 began with another government-inspired crisis. Bell Helicopter Textron refused to accept IFR certification from the Federal Aviation Administration for its Bell 212 until "FAA makes a more realistic interpretation of existing requirements."

Speaking at the 1973 and 25th anniversary meeting of HAA in Las Vegas, Nevada, the FAA's flight standards director told operators there would be no changes for the foreseeable future in the agency's requirements for IFR flight . . . requirements that were designed for airplanes. Commercial operators sought a limited-class helicopter IFR model certification that FAA was not willing to adopt. The HAA Board asked IFR Committee Chairman Joe Mashman to have his committee find a way through or around the impasse and spearhead the effort to gain some FAA changes.

Hughes-500

As HAA noted after years of exasperation, "The Federal Aviation Administration claims to understand the difficulties encountered by the commercial operator in this challenging [offshore support] area of operation. The agency has implemented some restrictions that make this claim difficult to substantiate."

The first commercial operator to actually fly work missions on IFR instrumentation was Norway's Helikopter Service A/S, which provided offshore support in the North Sea. As far back as 1968, Norway's Directorate of Civil Aviation had approved this operating mode, so it was clear that IFR missions were feasible in daily operations.

Renewed interest in international activities had come to the surface in 1972 with the formation of HAA's International Committee, chaired by KLM's Dr. Menno Kamminga. The following year — its Silver Anniversary — HAA launched a drive to acquire more international members, of which it already had 29 regular and associate members.

For The Record

1973 - Supermarket bar codes introduced • Secretariat wins the Triple Crown •

"Civil aviation is international by its nature," wrote Kamminga, pointing out that helicopter development was driven by inventors from a great many countries. He said a more international membership and a name change would gain recognition by the International Civil Aviation Organization, a body of the United Nations, and greater worldwide stature. He urged a name change for HAA into something "more truly reflecting its international character."

In 1973 a new-old helicopter went into resumed production. Heli-Parts Inc. set up a subsidiary in Porterville, California, called Hiller Aviation, to produce the piston-engined UH-12. Heli-Parts bought all rights, tooling, spares, type certificates, and other data from Fairchild Industries, which had bought Hiller Aircraft. There were about 2,000 original UH-12 models in service when Heli-Parts decided to resume production.

On August 14, 1973, the U.S. bombing of Cambodia came to a halt, ending 12 years of American combat in Indochina.

On August 29, 1973, an earthquake hit areas southwest of Mexico City, killing 500 people and injuring 1,000 others. Helicopters played a major role in rescues.

With the proliferation of new helicopter models, modifications, supplemental equipment, and improved versions, the lack of standardization in cockpit layouts, control locations, and instrument displays became an increasingly critical safety issue. The problem was evident not only among aircraft of different manufacturers but also in variations among models produced by any one manufacturer.

"In calendar year 1972," wrote HAA's safety consultant, "the pilot was listed as a cause or factor in approximately 67 percent of U.S. helicopter accidents. While this is basically a true statement, due to the fact that the actions of the pilot caused the accident, a more thorough and detailed investigation of some accidents would reveal that the decision or action of the pilot was generated by erroneous stimuli or non-standardized cockpit displays, controls, or switches."

An illustration of a helicopter cyclic stick showing eight switches for such functions as hoist, Inter Communications System (ICS), trim, landing light, emergency floats, and other operations was provided. The electric cargo release, he noted, is located in five different positions in five different helicopter models. With that as a jumping-off point, helicopter operators launched a campaign to get manufacturers to standardize cockpit displays and controls.

Helicopter models certificated for IFR flight in mid-1973 were the following:

- Aerospatiale Puma 330 certificated by FAA (USA) and SGAC (France), and already in IFR service.
- Bell 212 certificated by FAA, CAA (UK), DCA (Norway), and MOT (Canada), and already in IFR service.
- MBB 105D certificated by CAA and LBA (Germany), with FAA pending. Deliveries under way.
- Sikorsky S-58T certificated by FAA and CAA, with deliveries under way.
- Sikorsky S-61 certificated by FAA, CAA, DCA, and MOT, and already in IFR service.

Hand-in-hand with the need to standardize helicopter cockpit layouts and instruments was the need to have those instruments help the machine reach its greatest potential. Thus, Joe Mashman's IFR committee crystallized the need into six focal points:

1. Establish a means of certifying helicopters for various levels of traffic density as relating to crew requirements and installed equipment;

2. Relax present aircraft IFR stability requirements when the type of operation ensures equivalent safety;

3. Encourage rotorcraft manufacturers to provide IFR capability in the design concept of new aircraft models;

4. Provide the FAA air traffic control system and helicopter operators with a guide for routes and procedures that will enable helicopters to operate under IFR conditions, within our present air traffic control system, with minimum impact on fixed-wing traffic;

5. Establish a realistic criteria for determining helicopter ability to fly in icing conditions; and

6. Encourage the acceptance of our FAA's helicopter certification standards by other nations of the free world.

Reflecting the mood of operators after the hard-line FAA position delineated at the January meeting in Las Vegas, this was a clear plan of action for the development of helicopter operations through the end of the century and beyond.

The saga of scheduled helicopter airlines in America during the 1970s is one of marginal-at-best economics, frustrating political climates, and a safety record dictated by Murphy's Law.

In late 1973, pioneer scheduled helicopter airline Los Angeles Airways (LAA), which had ceased providing scheduled service for Los Angeles International Airport (LAX) in December 1970, went into bankruptcy and sold its assets to Carson Helicopters. In October 1973 LAA's operating certificate was revoked, leaving Los Angeles with no mass transit worth the name, and no helicopter shuttle service, but an abundance of freeways.

In mid-1975, a new and unrelated commuter company, Los Angeles Helicopter Airlines, began operating an hourly service to and from LAX under authority of the state Public Utilities Commission.

One thing LAA left behind was a $41 million breach-of-contract lawsuit against Hughes Tool Company, which LAA said had reneged on an agreement to buy the airline.

The demise of LAA left the only scheduled helicopter airlines certificated by the Civil Aeronautics Board (CAB) operating in New York, Chicago, and San Francisco, and SFO would not be operating for very much longer.

In August 1976, SFO's mechanics went on strike. To the surprise of the mechanics, however, the company's board of directors decided that the company's operating economics had never been very good in the first place. The shareholders voted to liquidate the carrier's assets and go out of business. In June 1977, SFO sold its three Sikorsky S-61s to British Airways Helicopters and had the CAB approve its application to suspend service. Presumably, the mechanics scattered and found jobs elsewhere, but the Bay Area joined southern California in losing scheduled helicopter service.

In mid-1977, Pacific Seaboard Airlines applied to CAB for an exemption to operate 14-passenger helicopters over the routes previously served by LAA and SFO Helicopter Airways, but permission to do so was denied.

On March 5, 1976, the British pound fell below the equivalent of $2 for the first time.

On April 5, 1976, Howard Hughes died.

In May 1976, Bell Helicopter marked its 25th anniversary.

On May 24, 1976, Britain and France began transatlantic Concorde service.

On July 4, 1976, Israeli commandos raided Entebbe airport in Uganda, rescuing almost all the passengers and crew of a hijacked Air France jetliner.

Then it happened again. It seemed like a sports event's instant replay of the February 1972 Andraus building fire in Sao Paulo, Brazil. On July 23, 1973, fire broke out on the 14th floor of the 36-floor Avianca building in

Standardized cockpit displays, controls, and switch locations and functions enhanced flight safety.

Columbia Helicopters Boeing 234

Bogota, Colombia. It was spotted by a commercial traffic helicopter from HELICOL on routine patrol. The blaze spread through Bogota's tallest building, trapping all those on the 15th through 36th floors. Helicopter rescues from the roof were coordinated by HELICOL. The saving of 400 lives was made more notable by the fact that Bogota is at 8,600-foot altitude and the fire made the altitude, turbulence, and visibility more difficult hazards. Included in the rescue were not only commercial and military helicopters, but also Colombia's Presidential Bell 212.

At the beginning of 1974, Billy Rowe of Campbell Air Service was elected president of the 421-member HAA, and Bill Baxter of Alan T. Archer was seated as the first ex officio Board member to represent the insurance industry.

The new HAA officers and directors were just in time to hear the Nixon Administration announce it would shelve the Aviation Cost Allocation study begun in 1972 that had thrown general aviation into turmoil. The administration had wanted user fees from various sectors of aviation to fully pay for the cost of maintaining the system, and the allocation study had shown that although airlines were close to paying for their share of the national aviation system, general aviation was well short of what the administration wanted.

Because helicopters seldom use most of the airways and airports system, the helicopter operating industry had reacted sharply and uniformly, and the message was delivered by HAA Executive Director Bob Richardson. The Nixon Administration's decision to forget the idea was welcome news to those already flirting with financial red ink.

Heliports may have been a major official concern of commercial operators since they banded together in 1948, but in the everyday working environment, few of them really needed heliports. Human nature prompts people to take action only when their interests are directly involved. An estimated 17 percent of all commercial operators were near major metropolitan areas, but HAA Heliport Committee Chairman Art Schneider of Island Helicopter Corporation warned the remaining 83 percent that time would bring the day when "the problems of heliport establishment, legally, would assume major importance."

In September 1974, the HAA Heliport Research and Development Council was founded in St. Louis, Missouri. A major stimulus for forming the group was a pending bill in Los Angeles to set regulations that would severely restrict helicopter operations. A new surge of organizational energy went into heliports.

Organizational energy was seen in other quarters as Brazilian commercial helicopter operators formed their own association — Associacao Brasileira de Helicopteros — and modeled it after the U.S. group. Not surprisingly, the Brazilian group said it was motivated by lack of government recognition of the economic and social contributions of the commercial operators.

1975 - Home computers, light beer, and disposable razors introduced •

By 1975, with PHI's Frank Lee having been elected HAA president, it was estimated that more than a million lives had been saved by helicopters in rescues and emergency medical service flights. It was also in 1975 that the number of registered civilian helicopters in the U.S. exceeded 5,000 for the first time, and the number of commercial operators grew 23.1 percent over the prior year. Hospital heliports were up to 564, for a 15.8 percent gain over 1974.

Throughout the mid-decade year, consolidation of the operating industry and evolution of the manufacturing sector continued as smaller commercial operators were bought by larger competitors and various manufacturers licensed builders in other nations to produce specific models. Agusta, Dornier, Fuji, Helibras, Hindustan Aeronautics, Kawasaki, Nurtanio, and Westland were among licensing companies working with primary manufacturers to build helicopters worldwide.

Civil helicopters increased again in number by 8.4 percent during 1975 over 1974 in the U.S., Canada, and Puerto Rico. Manufacturers said 5,222 helicopters were in use by 1,891 operators, compared with the 1974 level of 4,819 helicopters in use by 1,536 operators.

It was on October 17, 1975, that Petroleum Helicopters, Inc., logged its two millionth flight hour. The milestone was relatively easy for PHI because of its sheer size, but the record was still a symbol of the industry's advances.

Export of U.S.-made helicopters also rose in 1975, this time to new records, as the five major manufacturers (Bell, Boeing-Vertol, Enstrom, Hiller, and Sikorsky) shipped 437 aircraft valued at $220 million. The helicopters went to 37 nations, including Canada (64 helicopters), Italy (50), Israel (45), Mexico (30), and Singapore (25). The comparable value for 1974 exports was about $124 million.

Within the domestic helicopter industry were extremely perceptive and creative minds in the spirit of pioneers like Igor Sikorsky, Arthur Young, Frank Piasecki, Stanley Hiller, and others.

In 1975 Frank Robinson was dubbed an "overnight success". . . in the same sense that a show business star is an overnight success after working hard for 20 years. "The industry has bypassed the light helicopter," he told the "New York Times." "There are a tremendous number of people who would like to learn to fly them, but nothing is available." Robinson had benefitted from 19 years' engineering experience with big helicopter manufacturers.

Frank Robinson and a few engineer friends sat around his living room and designed a piston-powered helicopter weighing 720 pounds, or about the weight of a large motorcycle. Robinson had found businessman C.K. LeFiell to finance the project. They envisioned the final product costing about $20,000. It was to be an ideal helicopter for personal use, pipeline patrol, training, forestry, law enforcement, executive transport, air taxi, and photography.

Robinson told the newspaper he was confident his helicopter would find a profitable market.

Three years' worth of production — 261 helicopters — was sold out before the first Robinson R-22 was delivered. To the surprise of very few, however, the price was up to $34,000 by mid-1978, and by the end of the year, HAA's Bob Richardson was citing a price tag of $40,000 for the Robinson helicopter.

R22

Dr. Menno S. Kamminga, KLM, became the first European to chair HAA in April of 1976. HAA achieved a milestone in April of that year when the American National Standards Institute (ANSI) printed "External Load Operating Standards for Rotorcraft." The helicopter industry thus became the first group to take a safety operating standard through the ANSI machinery since the passing of the Occupational Safety and Health Act of 1970. HAA received recognition from the U.S. Department of Labor for taking the initiative in the matter. The achievement was significant in that it avoided many potential confrontations between helicopter operators and organized labor, particularly in the construction industry.

The January 1977 meeting saw the election of Richard Wien, Era Helicopters, as HAA president, and within months the Board met outside the western hemisphere for the first time when it convened in Amsterdam that May.

On February 1, 1977, New York Airways (NYA) began rooftop service from the heliport on Manhattan's Pan Am Building. Three flights hourly were scheduled to JFK Airport and one hourly flight each to Newark and LaGuardia, all using Sikorsky S-61 helicopters.

The service proved very popular, and NYA had a 33 percent increase in traffic the month it inaugurated the Pan Am rooftop service, compared with February 1976.

The world-famous service came to an abrupt end 105 days later on the afternoon of May 16, 1977. Five people were killed when a NYA Sikorsky S-61L, idling atop the Pan Am Building in midtown Manhattan, toppled over due to a collapsed landing gear. Four people died on the heliport and part of a main-rotor blade flew into the street below, killing a woman. Use of the heliport was immediately halted, even though use of an airport would not have been stopped under the same circumstances.

The National Transportation Safety Board absolved the commercial operator, New York Airways.

NYA flew 3.804 million revenue passenger miles (RPMs) in the first nine months of 1978. The previous year's figure had been 3.618 million RPMs. NYA's load factors, down in 1977, were back up from 39.1 percent to more than 50 percent in the first three-quarters of 1978. For all of 1978, NYA flew 4.973 million RPMs, which was a 7.5 percent increase over the 1977 level. Passenger load factor for the 1978 year was 45.4 percent.

Nevertheless, the Pan Am rooftop heliport was not used for regular passenger services again.

Far from Manhattan, British helicopter traffic, in support of North Sea offshore operations, jumped from 500 movements a day in 1976 to 1,500 in 1978.

Don Sides of Madison Aviation was elected HAA president in 1978, heading an association that had grown to 589 members. Under his administration, HAA issued a position paper in June, spelling out HAA's stance on surplus and public aircraft and on replacement parts.

On May 12, 1978, the U.S. Commerce Department said hurricanes would no longer be named exclusively after women.

On May 17, 1978, women were included in the White House honor guard.

On May 26, 1978, the first casino in the eastern U.S. opened in Atlantic City, New Jersey.

On July 13, 1978, Lee Iacocca was fired as president of Ford Motor Co.

On July 25, 1978, the world's first test-tube baby, Louise Brown, was born.

While helicopters are vital to the missions they perform, the aviation maintenance teams are the life-sustaining support that keep flying machines flying.

Westland 30

Although the bogus helicopter parts problem had been around for years and would remain a presence for many more, it became a higher-profile issue in the mid-1970s. The definition of bogus, depending on the term's source, meant anything from deliberately counterfeited parts to military surplus parts not certified for civil use. It covered parts salvaged from crashed aircraft and parts improperly marked or tested. HAA formed a committee, chaired by Vin Colicci, to keep track of the problem that threatened to injure or kill operators and pilots.

The appeal of bogus parts, of course, was their lower initial cost over genuine parts, but the difference in cost could mean life or death. Bell embarked on a campaign to remove bogus Bell 47 parts from the marketplace. In April, Bell filed a $35 million lawsuit against 11 firms that had knowingly manufactured and sold helicopter parts under Bell's name, trademark, and other forms of identification. Bell referred to the defendants as a "conspiracy" and said they had also shipped bogus parts to other countries. Some of the bogus parts were flight-safety critical, including tail rotor drive shafts and transmission parts.

There was an "Oops!" in the manufacturing sector of the industry near the end of 1978. In an effort to give its S-76 a name in addition to a number, Sikorsky called it the "Spirit," only to discover the name was offensive to some religious groups in other countries. The name was quietly dropped in favor of the model number. (A similar episode occurred when General Motors marketed its Chevrolet Nova model in Latin America and found that "Nova" translates as "doesn't go" in Spanish.)

On August 19, 1978, a theater fire set by Islamic extremists in Abadan, Iran, killed more than 400 people.

On December 8, 1978, former Israeli prime minister Golda Meir died.

On February 11, 1979, Ayatollah Ruhollah Khomeini took power in Iran.

On March 19, 1979, the U.S. House of Representatives began TV broadcasts of its day-to-day business.

On March 26, 1979, the Camp David peace accord was signed by Israeli Prime Minister Menachem Begin and Egyptian President Anwar Sadat.

Vin Colicci of Helicopter Services took over the HAA presidency in January 1979, and before he left office, HAA had a pilot loss-of-license insurance program in place and ready for launch.

A major FAA attitude change seemed to occur in 1979, as the Rotorcraft Regulatory Review was launched by the agency. The director of flight standards took a completely different tack from that of his predecessor and told the HAA convention in January that his agency was moving to have its helicopter IFR stance better reflect the operating capabilities of helicopters. At the same time and at the same convention, FAA's director of safety regulations acknowledged that the agency's rules still frequently missed the point concerning helicopters.

A thorough review of Federal Aviation Regulations (FARs) was accomplished as part of the Rotorcraft Regulatory Review by HAA's Regulations Committee, chaired by Sikorsky's Ted Dumont. The association submitted 200 recommendations, which was 38 percent of all those received.

Within months, it became necessary for commercial operators to petition the FAA for relief from six provisions of a new Part 135 section of the FARs. The six (along with a dozen others not so onerous) were written with air taxi and commuter airplane safety in mind. Helicopters mostly perform special tasks under visual flight rule (VFR) conditions. HAA asked FAA, on behalf of the operators, for relief from requirements that the helicopter have a second pilot, gyro instruments for night VFR operations, thunderstorm detection equipment, one-engine-inoperative (OEI) performance, 45-minute fuel reserves, and certain maintenance inspections.

FAA quickly recognized the problem and granted the industry request.

No sooner had that battle been won than HAA was among the first to petition FAA for needed changes in Part 91 rules.

In March 1979, FAA certificated the Robinson R-22, which now had a price tag almost double its original target figure, due in part to the fact that half of its six-year development period had to be devoted to testing and analysis for certification.

Enstrom 480

The burden of federal regulations was not limited to new designs. FAA reported that 354 air taxi operators had gone out of business rather than comply with the new Part 135 regulations. The number represented nearly 10 percent of all air taxi operators in the U.S., and these were the same rules from which HAA had sought relief for helicopter operators.

In another of its joint initiatives with other industry groups, HAA worked with the National Agricultural Aviation Association (NAAA) toward the end of the decade to achieve national standardization of agricultural chemical containers. In the past, each helicopter and airplane pilot had to consult secondary references to decipher labels on pesticide and herbicide containers.

A jolt for U.S. manufacturers came in May 1979 when the U.S. Coast Guard awarded a $215 million contract to France's Aerospatiale for 90 HH-65A Dauphin 2 (Model AS-366G) short-range recovery helicopters. Bell Helicopter immediately protested the Coast Guard award and filed a lawsuit.

Iran and the Ayatollah's revolution were not only among the top headlines of 1979 for the world at large, they had a specific financial impact on the helicopter manufacturing industry. Agusta, Bell, and others had many millions in contracts with the Shah's government. When the new hard-line government took power, Bell evacuated all its personnel from the country.

Two of the more competitive personalities in the commercial helicopter operating business collided head-to-head at the end of the 1970s. Alan Bristow decided to enter the Gulf of Mexico offshore support market, long the domain of PHI's Bob Suggs and, to a lesser extent, Air Logistics and Era. After a period of intense competition running into the 1980s, Bristow quietly backed away.

During the latter half of the 1970s, bogus parts became an increasingly high-profile issue and it became necessary for someone to carry the fight to the source of the problem.

Bell Helicopter Textron reached an out-of-court settlement with some of the defendants in its bogus parts lawsuit, filed early in 1977. It was late September 1979 when the Fort Worth, Texas, company announced that a permanent injunction had been issued against four California companies. All stencils, dies,

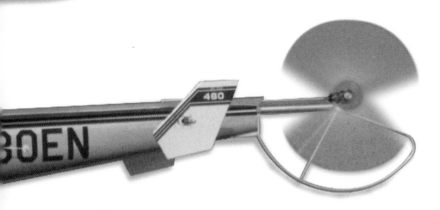

stamps, and other items that duplicated or closely resembled any used by Bell for its spare parts were ordered to be surrendered.

A British court had previously found in favor of Westland Helicopters in a legal action against some of the same defendants, who allegedly sold and/or misrepresented falsely labeled parts intended for use in helicopters of the British military. The bogus parts problem was more than an academic exercise in labeling. It was estimated in 1979 that 15 percent of all new helicopter costs were attributable to the need for the manufacturer's product liability insurance.

Thus, against the backdrop of a crusade to safeguard the integrity of classic helicopter technology, the 1970s came to a close with the introduction of new technology. It was epitomized by Paramount Helicopters' use for the first time of fiberglass main rotor blades on a Bell 214B in Oregon logging operations.

Sikorsky president Gerald Tobias put a framework around post-Vietnam helicopters that would enter commercial service en masse in the 1980s. Tobias told an HAA audience in Tucson, Arizona, in 1975 that compared with helicopters of the 1955-65 era, the technology introduced with the S-76 gave operators twice the range, half the fuel consumption, 25 percent higher cruise speed, half the maintenance hours, less horsepower per unit of payload, half the seat-mile cost, overall payload improvement of 23 percent, half the labor cost due to automation, 35 percent fewer parts per pound of weight, 65 percent reduction in rotor head vibration, and a 300 percent increase in test-flight hours monthly because of improved instrumentation.

In keeping with that spirit, Sikorsky said it forecast a 600 percent increase in its production rate by the end of the 1980s, including 1,250 commercial S-76 models. The firm decided near the end of 1979 to shut down its production lines for the S-61 and S-64 models, selling the S-64 rights to Erickson Air-Crane Co. in 1992.

Did You Know?

Federal Aviation Administration tabulation of 6,454 helicopters operating in the U.S. as of December 31, 1978, shows the following distribution by manufacturer. Note that the FAA list had major flaws that eventually became almost traditional. Inconsistency in the FAA registration numbers has always confused the task of statisticians, upon whose work many critical decisions are based.

Agusta (including Agusta-Bell)	17
Air & Space	22
Bell (1,554 piston, 1,609 turbine)	3,163
Boeing-Vertol	6
Brantly (137 Model B-2, 16 Model 305)	153
Continental Copters (Tomcat)	35
Delackner (DH-5)	1
Enstrom	369
Fairchild-Hiller (FH-1100)	85
Hiller-Frye (UH-12, etc.)	702
Hughes (Models 300, 500, etc.)	1,043
Kaman (H-43 etc.)	19
Kawasaki (KV-107-II)	4
Kellett (G1-B)	2
Lawyer (Scorpion, Bensen, Etc.)	15
Lockheed (L-286)	2
McCulloch (J-2)	38
MBB (BO-105)	61
Piasecki (HUP-3, etc.)	8
Pitcairn (PA-39, PCA-2)	2
Sikorsky (328 piston, 91 turbine)	419
Sud Aviation (Alouette, etc.)	239
Texas Helicopter Corp.	19
Topping (Helicom, Scorpion)	9
Vertol (H-21, etc.)	20
WSK-Swidnik (Mi-2)	1
TOTAL	**6,454**

Elsewhere in the agency's own figures is a total for U.S. helicopters of 7,688, of which 5,029 were piston and 2,659 were turboshaft. The difference in the two "official" totals was a substantial 1,234 helicopters.

Bell began deliveries of twin-turbine helicopters, the Model 222 (and increased its 222 production commitment), while flight tests continued on the four-blade Model 412 and the heavier Model 214ST.

Corporate decisions to increase production might have been spurred by a forecast of DMS, a market research firm, that predicted in 1979 that "the commercial helicopter market will continue to represent one of the few aerospace market segments where non-American manufacturers are competitive in the U.S." In fact, NASA testimony delivered to the Congress at about the same time predicted that nearly 40 percent of all light helicopters operating in the U.S. might soon be non-American made.

Another market research firm, Forecast Associates, foresaw a 15,000-helicopter world market, with twin-turbine helicopters being favored, by 1985.

Clearly, those kinds of numbers would not develop with only a single market, such as offshore support. Commercial operators sought other markets for their services, and it was surprising how many of these developed.

From the very outset, helicopters had been used for aerial photography. Now the needs of television news organizations, as well as Hollywood movie producers, put increased pressure on the industry to develop sophisticated platforms for doing film and videotape production. Not long after, live TV from helicopters would become almost commonplace and would be so unobtrusive that viewers would hardly realize the technique had been developed, and few would wonder where the camera was located!

Consolidation of the industry throughout North America and the rest of the world continued. In Canada, Okanagan bought Bow Helicopters, as well as the helicopters of New York Airways and Boise Cascade Corp., making Okanagan the most dominant commercial operator in Canada. The operator's activities were centered throughout the 1970s on mining activity in the West, as well as the James Bay hydroelectric project. Offshore oil/gas support slowed during the middle of the decade, but later resurged. Legal issues delayed some work off the east coast of Newfoundland, but those had been resolved by the end of the decade.

Helicopter commercial operations is one industrial activity that can be significantly affected by events elsewhere, including the weather. A mild winter in 1976-77 brought with it a low snow pack, which in turn told operators such as Okanagan that they would probably have substantial fire fighting work in the coming season. Like most large commercial operators (the firm had 500 employees in 1977), Okanagan had ongoing flight work in many places besides its home country of Canada, including New Zealand, the Red Sea area, and India.

Corporate operators often put their helicopters through daily grinds that would surprise many who are not familiar with the aircraft and its capabilities. An example is Colonial Sand & Stone Inc., a construction materials corporation in the New York City area operating a Bell 206 JetRanger. In addition to making customer sales and service calls at construction sites, Colonial used its helicopter to link its outlying quarries and other locations.

Timex Corporation in Connecticut, 65 ground miles from the nearest airline terminal, found that it could move key executives (as well as critical spare parts) around much more efficiently with its single helicopter than it could with a fleet of cars and trucks. The company calculated that its 5,000 helicopter flight hours saved an estimated 20,000 hours of personal transportation time by its executives, simultaneously avoiding production shutdowns.

Despite the glowing descriptions of post-Vietnam helicopter technology coming to the commercial arena from manufacturers, commercial and corporate operators saw things differently from those who built and sold the machines.

"Manufacturers with vision," are what the helicopter industry needs, Mobil Oil's Dave O'Keefe said, referring to 1975-era technology. The operator attitude regarding glowing recitations of the blessings of technology resembled the old saying about one man's meat being another man's poison. Bob Suggs of PHI said "the manufacturers are way, way behind where they should be."

Vin Colicci, of Copters Unlimited and Helicopter Services, said maintainability was an issue between operators and manufacturers. He said the manufacturers are "standing still and in some cases going backward in maintainability." Colicci described a helicopter airspeed indicator that required the removal of 18 screws to replace its light bulb, at a labor cost of $51.

From Norway, Morten Hancke of Helikopter Service A/S, cited a pivot stud that increased in price by 728 percent in less than two years.

The manufacturers were put on notice that regardless of press releases on the benefits of technology, their customers were dissatisfied. Commercial operators wanted to share the prosperity of the manufacturers.

The industry rule of thumb was that any piece of equipment that could not be flown at least 500 hours a year was a bad investment.

On November 4, 1979, Iranian militants stormed the American Embassy in Tehran and took 66 hostages.

On November 21, 1979, Islamic mob attacked the U.S. Embassy in Islamabad, Pakistan, setting the building afire and killing two Americans.

On November 28, 1979, Air New Zealand DC10 airliner on a sightseeing flight over the South Pole crashed into a mountain in Antarctica, killing all 257 aboard.

On December 27, 1979, Soviet forces seized control of Afghanistan.

By the final year of the decade, the number of commercial operators in the nation had climbed to 1,126. During the 1970s, the number of commercial operators in the U.S. had doubled, with the greatest single-year increase being a 450-operator jump in 1978.

The industry was preparing at this point for the great Northeast Corridor project. The plan was to set up discrete, low-altitude navigation aids and procedures to allow helicopters to operate like airliners between Washington, D.C., and Boston.

Throughout the late 1960s and the early 1970s, Americans saw more helicopters than ever before in history. That did not mean they really understood this very capable machine, because they had seen it used only in certain ways.

But the machine was becoming increasingly visible. In 1977, the manufacturers produced 940 helicopters valued at $454 million.

As the 1970s wound down and the Vietnam War became a receding memory, there were still misconceptions about helicopters. The most prevalent of these were handily dismissed by aviation writer Dan Manningham, who listed five of the most common:

"1) Helicopters are slow. If you think helicopters aren't fast you are probably using an inappropriate speed comparison. Helicopters are really designed to compete against surface transportation. Think of them as a 100-knot station wagon operating free from all the constraints of surface routing and congestion.

"2) Helicopters are expensive. Compared with what? Nothing is expensive if it saves, or makes, money.

By the end of 1978, employment in the helicopter manufacturing industry reached 26,600 people and it was expected that the figure would rise by 8.6 percent in 1979. By the end of the 1970s, helicopter manufacturing employment reached 28,900 workers.

The number of helicopter pilots in the U.S., said FAA, was 33,764 at the end of 1978. Pilots who were helicopter-only qualified numbered just 4,874, while the others held various additional ratings.

On June 4, 1979, PHI logged three million flight hours by its 305 helicopters. The milestone was equivalent to 543 round trips to the moon, or 12,300 trips around the earth at the equator.

Three million hours is also equivalent to 342 years.

"3) <u>Helicopters are uncomfortable.</u> That's another one of those comparative things. Is it more comfortable to sit or ride in a Continental or even a Rolls for two hours than it would be to ride in a helicopter for 10 to 30 minutes? If you haven't had a ride in the latest helicopter models, you're in for a treat.

"4) <u>Helicopters are noisy.</u> That statement should read: 'Older helicopter designs were often noisy.'

"5) <u>Helicopters are bad neighbors.</u> The truth is that helicopters are good Samaritans and better friends when introduced with the proper community relations attitude."

As the 1970s closed, the decade ahead seemed to clearly promise prosperity and growth. Energy companies were reaching farther from shore for oil/gas to supply growing economies throughout the industrialized world.

As HAA saw things developing, "The size of the commercial [helicopter operator] industry will treble or quadruple over the next decade, and a major factor influencing this growth is the introduction of third-generation turbine-powered helicopters."

There was every reason to think so, as all indicators pointed upward.

If there was any slackness to helicopter sales in the mid- to late-1970s, it was attributed to anticipation of newer models coming along soon, such as the Bell 222, Agusta 109, Sikorsky S-76, Aerospatiale A-Star, and the MBB BO-105. Still more designs were expected to emerge from helicopter manufacturers in a steady stream, like the Dauphin 365, BK-117, and an anticipated S-75 civil version of the Sikorsky UH-60 Black Hawk military transport helicopter.

Commercial operators in remote-area and offshore support eagerly awaited these as the hoped-for answer to technology that couldn't quite do the job at the desired cost. Everything from the S-75 to the Bell 214 Big Lifter were lined up with the Chinook, ready to tackle the jobs of the 1980s.

Bristow Helicopters ordered five long-range, 44-passenger Boeing Vertol models for offshore support, at a total price tag exceeding $55 million. The British operator also changed the name of its recently acquired U.S. operation, Offshore Helicopters, to Bristow Offshore Helicopters and moved its offices in anticipation of new business.

The Norwegians were talking of following suit with an order for three Chinooks for their own offshore support requirements, and several U.S. operators leased the long-legged Chinook for Arctic exploration.

Columbia Helicopters awaited the civil Chinook and its 14-ton external lift capacity, anticipating that the $7.5 million price tag per aircraft would be recouped by handling jobs that previously had to be passed up.

The same upbeat attitude also prevailed in the public sector, where police departments, environmental agencies, and forestry services all needed the new capabilities of the post-Vietnam War helicopters.

Commercial helicopter operators in logging, construction, offshore support, emergency medical services, and corporate flight departments were looking to buy new equipment, and the equipment was certainly there, with new black boxes, sleek aerodynamic styling, and electronics to dazzle the marketplace. Order books were full; backlogged orders were the topic of trade press articles; and speculators began dealing in delivery positions, hoping to buy low and sell high to make a profit.

In hindsight, it was all quite remarkable.

With such a resounding end to the 1970s, it was no wonder that the memories of early decade oil embargoes, shortages, and taxes were dim indeed.

As the 1970s closed, the decade ahead seemed to clearly promise prosperity and growth.

Hughes 300C

EQUITABLE

N1113U

300C

175

Hughes 500 filling Bambi Bucke

THE EIGHTIES

*"Just say the report of my death
has been grossly exaggerated."*

Mark Twain, 1897

The FAA unveiled the National Airspace System (NAS) in January 1982.

The roller-coaster 1980s opened on an economic high, but the decade brought considerable turmoil for the commercial helicopter operating industry particularly in the early years, when double-digit inflation and a new political administration in Washington both made their marks in the history books.

It was as though helicopter buyers went out to lunch on July 4, 1981, and did not return for several years.

Not until nearly the end of the decade could operators or even manufacturers relax, though the latter had military work as a financial cushion. One of the axioms of operators is that economic security is always relative, and one can be in severe financial difficulty before a rotor blade makes a complete revolution.

On March 27, 1980, a North Sea floating oil field platform, the Alexander I. Keilland, capsized in a storm, killing 137 workers.

On April 15, 1980, French philosopher and author Jean-Paul Sartre died.

On April 20, 1980, Cubans arriving in the Mariel boatlift reached Florida.

On April 24, 1980, the U.S. tried to free American hostages in Iran, resulting in the deaths of eight U.S. servicemen.

On May 5, 1980, a siege at the Iranian embassy in London ended as British commandos and police stormed the building.

Boeing 234

The new decade was not starting out well.

To make certain the association was not caught unprepared by any future developments, the Helicopter Association of America (HAA) — under the presidency of Delford Smith of Evergreen Helicopters — set up a Long Range Planning Committee in 1980 headed by Joe Mashman. It was the same year that the association first held its industry exposition in a convention center rather than a hotel ballroom because of the size of the exhibit hall needed.

For The Record   1980 - Mount St. Helens erupts • 3-bedroom home costs $64,600 • John Lennon dies •

In 1980, U.S. commercial helicopter operators fell into one of several categories, which — though simplified here to make the point — were fairly accurate in describing the industry: near the Gulf of Mexico the operators provided offshore oil/gas support; across the Rocky Mountains they worked in the over-thrust belt; Midwest operators sprayed crops; Northwest operators harvested timber; East Coast operators did a lot of executive/charter work.

Civil aircraft sales in 1980 would outpace military aircraft sales for the first time since the 1930s. Large transport helicopters were seen as an especially bright spot in the market picture. Dramatic changes were foreseen in the number of imported helicopters, which rose from only 42 in 1976 to about 215 imports in 1979.

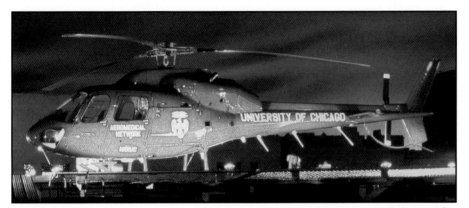

Eurocopter A-Star

Imported helicopters received a big boost in the U.S. market when the General Accounting Office backed up the Coast Guard in its selection of France's Aerospatiale AS-366G for its short-range recovery mission.

Bell was busy with other projects, and the industry soon heard reports of a twin-engine Bell 206L model on the drawing boards, as well as a four-blade Bell 214 and other new products.

Air Logistics, which had received the first production Sikorsky S-76 of 12 on order, calculated that it could carry 12 people on a 150-mile offshore mission a half hour faster than earlier-technology helicopters of the same capacity, while burning half the fuel.

Salary for a Sikorsky S-76 pilot as the 1980s opened was about $36,000 annually, according to a Midwest corporate operator. Both Sikorsky and its training contractor, American Airlines, had trouble keeping instructor pilots because they were hired away by S-76 customers who wanted their experience. Sikorsky, meanwhile, claimed five world records for the S-76, including point-to-point travel from New York to Boston and to Washington. Lack of public heliports in Washington and Boston forced the helicopter to use National and Logan Airports, said Sikorsky pointedly, estimating that 8,000 civil helicopters would enter service in the decade.

Norway reversed its decision of only a few weeks earlier that it would buy the Boeing Vertol Chinook for offshore support in the North Sea, but that was not enough to dampen the overall market. One of every 10 U.S. helicopters was at the time working in the Gulf of Mexico, and the number was increasing dramatically.

Indeed, corporate helicopter ownership increased significantly by 1979, with twin-engine types favored as they became more available.

The Helicopter Association of America urged the Congress to increase funding for the Federal Aviation Administration's (FAA's) research and development programs by $125 million over the next five years, putting the association in the position of recommending more money for the agency than FAA itself had sought.

Any notion at the outset of the 1980s that the helicopter business was the same seat-of-the-pants venture it was in the late 1940s was dispelled.

In 1980, Sikorsky President Gerald Tobias told an audience in Washington, D.C., that helicopters had rescued one million people worldwide since WWII.

Tobias said it was well documented that 673,000 people were rescued by helicopters in Southeast Asia during the war there; an estimated 10,000 medevacs were flown in the Korean War; there were 12,000 other U.S. military rescues between 1964 and 1975; about 26,000 U.S. military rescues were made during disaster relief operations and about 19,000 in domestic U.S. Military Assistance to Safety and Traffic flights; an estimated 20,000 offshore rescues were made by commercial helicopter operators; a well-documented 40,000 offshore rescues were made by the U.S. Coast Guard; another 118,000 were non-U.S. military rescues, 15,000 non-U.S. civil rescues, about 64,000 East Europe and China rescues, and an unknown number in the Soviet Union and other non-reporting countries.

Alan Bristow said at the time that his customers demand the capacity of the Boeing Chinook, and that was why he ordered it. He added that the military flying experience is almost useless to a commercial operator. The military flies in a year what commercial operators fly in one or two months, he said.

Bristow was only a minority shareholder in Bristow Offshore Helicopters, but just the addition of his name to the company gave competitors something to think about. While this was going on, one of his S-76s set the London-Paris speed record in both directions.

As the decade opened, the U.S. Forest Service put down $10 million in a contract with Frank Piasecki to prove the concept of his Heli-Stat, a marriage of four H-34 helicopters and a navy surplus blimp envelope. The idea was to minimize environmental damage by having the Heli-Stat lift loads that no helicopter could handle. On an early flight, the Heli-Stat suffered a mechanical malfunction that resulted in a crash, ending the project.

The HAA meeting of that January broke all prior attendance records and was proclaimed a commercial success, mirroring the industry it served. If the manufacturers' public projections and estimates are valid, sales at the three-day event totaled $400 million.

In the economic euphoria of the new decade, Sikorsky announced a replacement model for the S-61, Hughes announced a new 14 to 24-passenger Model 2000, Bell and Sikorsky each announced sales exceeding $100 million while Messerschmitt-Bölkow-Blohm (MBB) said sales exceeded $60 million, and Robinson sales were pegged at $1.5 million. The Robinson amount, however, paid for 31 helicopters.

Talk of economic hard times was dismissed.

Bell Helicopter had, in fact, accumulated the largest commercial backlog in its history, with annual dollar sales in the hundreds of millions. In 1965, Bell sales totaled $10 million, in 1970 sales reached $28 million, and the predicted level for 1984 only in markets outside the U.S. was about $300 million.

Carl Dougherty of Petroleum Helicopters Inc. (PHI) was elected HAA president in 1981, and soon after the association began publishing its "RotorGram" newsletter, while the monthly "ROTORnews," begun in 1966, was now changed to a bimonthly frequency. In May the association had its first European Helicopter Operators Management Course, held in Switzerland.

Things were not economically bright everywhere. New York Airways (NYA) had stopped all scheduled passenger flight operations, sold off its S-61 helicopters, and was down to two full-time employees. A group of investors was talking with NYA's creditors, but things looked gloomy. Columbia Helicopters was a one-time suitor, but walked away from the situation after an evaluation. Various efforts to start regular, profitable passenger helicopter services in the New York City area reappeared often in succeeding years at the instigation of determined entrepreneurs, but determination was not enough to make it work. New York was the Big Apple in many ways, and one of those ways was to show how things could be done. Absent a successful experience in high-profile NYC, it was not so easy to make the idea work elsewhere.

British Airways Helicopters considered a London-Paris-Brussels-Amsterdam route using stretched Chinooks carrying 70 passengers between city centers.

Commercial operator optimism in other sectors was generally high at the beginning of the decade, as reflected in a survey by the Allison division of General Motors. The biggest problem seen by 68 percent of operators was their operating cost, of which 22 percent cited the cost of parts, about 21 percent the cost of fuel, and 22 percent insurance costs. Another 19 percent identified government restrictions as their biggest problem. Despite their recitation of problems, about 61 percent of those responding to Allison's survey said they had a positive outlook toward the future, and only 9 percent had a negative viewpoint. At least 46 percent said they planned to buy a new helicopter in the near term.

Golf great Arnold Palmer tees off after purchasing a new
Model 500E executive helicopter.

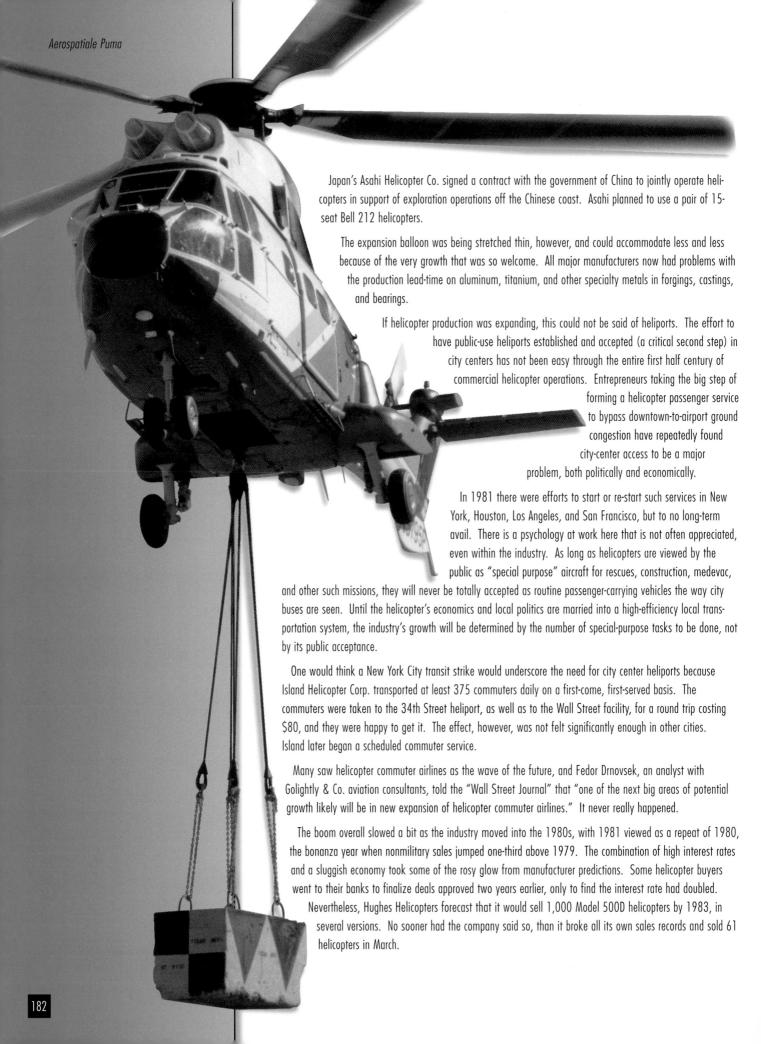

Japan's Asahi Helicopter Co. signed a contract with the government of China to jointly operate helicopters in support of exploration operations off the Chinese coast. Asahi planned to use a pair of 15-seat Bell 212 helicopters.

The expansion balloon was being stretched thin, however, and could accommodate less and less because of the very growth that was so welcome. All major manufacturers now had problems with the production lead-time on aluminum, titanium, and other specialty metals in forgings, castings, and bearings.

If helicopter production was expanding, this could not be said of heliports. The effort to have public-use heliports established and accepted (a critical second step) in city centers has not been easy through the entire first half century of commercial helicopter operations. Entrepreneurs taking the big step of forming a helicopter passenger service to bypass downtown-to-airport ground congestion have repeatedly found city-center access to be a major problem, both politically and economically.

In 1981 there were efforts to start or re-start such services in New York, Houston, Los Angeles, and San Francisco, but to no long-term avail. There is a psychology at work here that is not often appreciated, even within the industry. As long as helicopters are viewed by the public as "special purpose" aircraft for rescues, construction, medevac, and other such missions, they will never be totally accepted as routine passenger-carrying vehicles the way city buses are seen. Until the helicopter's economics and local politics are married into a high-efficiency local transportation system, the industry's growth will be determined by the number of special-purpose tasks to be done, not by its public acceptance.

One would think a New York City transit strike would underscore the need for city center heliports because Island Helicopter Corp. transported at least 375 commuters daily on a first-come, first-served basis. The commuters were taken to the 34th Street heliport, as well as to the Wall Street facility, for a round trip costing $80, and they were happy to get it. The effect, however, was not felt significantly enough in other cities. Island later began a scheduled commuter service.

Many saw helicopter commuter airlines as the wave of the future, and Fedor Drnovsek, an analyst with Golightly & Co. aviation consultants, told the "Wall Street Journal" that "one of the next big areas of potential growth likely will be in new expansion of helicopter commuter airlines." It never really happened.

The boom overall slowed a bit as the industry moved into the 1980s, with 1981 viewed as a repeat of 1980, the bonanza year when nonmilitary sales jumped one-third above 1979. The combination of high interest rates and a sluggish economy took some of the rosy glow from manufacturer predictions. Some helicopter buyers went to their banks to finalize deals approved two years earlier, only to find the interest rate had doubled.

Nevertheless, Hughes Helicopters forecast that it would sell 1,000 Model 500D helicopters by 1983, in several versions. No sooner had the company said so, than it broke all its own sales records and sold 61 helicopters in March.

The rest of the industry agreed with the Hughes perspective and churned progressively along. Hiller Aviation Inc. bought the rights to the five-place FH-1100 from Fairchild Industries and moved production to Porterville, California. The former army competitor had found a welcome in corporate markets.

The boom for some aircraft began to unravel, it seemed, in mid-1980. Bristow and Norway's Helikopter Service A/S both canceled orders for a total of eight Boeing Vertol Chinooks worth $143 million. The helicopters were to have been jointly operated.

It wasn't long before Bristow ordered 35 Aerospatiale AS-332L Super Tiger (originally Super Puma) models.

The Chinook tremor was easy to dismiss as an isolated phenomenon in a busy marketplace, until Bell halved the order for Avco-Lycoming engines to power its Model 222. The cut was attributed to technical problems, and PHI had indeed limited the helicopter to 90 knots airspeed.

After delivering 136 of these aircraft in 19 years, Sikorsky shut down S-61L/N production in June 1980. The last of the original breed went to Siller Brothers, a commercial logging operator in California.

Operator demand for the S-61 was not satisfied by a long-term program to create a replacement, so the manufacturer looked at mating the Black Hawk dynamic system with the S-61 airframe to give operators the internal volume and nacelles (sponsons) they liked so much, along with the newer technology of the dynamic system. The idea did not come to fruition.

Bell, meanwhile, delivered its 25,000th helicopter, a Model 222, to Omniflight, and at the same time delivered the first Model 412.

Double-digit interest rates, a slow economy, and humiliation of the previous administration at the hands of the new rulers of Iran gave the White House to Ronald Reagan in November 1980.

Moving in to fill the gap left by the Sikorsky S-61 were several new-technology designs, including the joint ventures of MBB and Kawasaki to produce the BK-117 and that of Westland and Agusta to build the EH-101 large transport helicopter. Robinson R-22 orders now exceeded 850, and one-third of those were for export.

The industry's collective voice, the Helicopter Association of America, was now the Helicopter Association International (HAI) and it had new strength and influence . . . though not enough to easily surmount all obstacles. The stubborn resistance to city-center heliports was deep and diverse, not amenable to a solitary stroke of effective lobbying or persuasion. HAI was now holding annual meetings that drew thousands of registrants and hundreds of exhibitors.

Almost every FAA decision-maker who mattered was now appearing on HAI panels at the annual meeting, or at least was circulating among the operator-attendees. Operators were able to directly address, question, or criticize FAA officials in post-panel Q&A sessions.

On August 3, 1981, U.S. air traffic controllers went on strike despite warnings from President Ronald Reagan that they would be fired. Two days later, firings began.

On August 30, 1981, Iran's president and prime minister were killed by a bomb.

On October 6, 1981, Egyptian President Anwar Sadat was assassinated.

On November 11, 1981, stuntman Dan Goodwin scaled the outside of the 100-story John Hancock Center in Chicago in nearly six hours.

A European Helicopter Association had been formed, but some operators on the continent wanted to stay with the U.S.-based HAI.

"We will abandon all ideas of a European Helicopter Association," said KLM's managing director, "if the HAI can adequately meet our requirements." H.S. Jonker pointed out the intricacies of some international problems that had few, if any, counterparts in the U.S. "We have an almost invisible political structure with different

The XV-15 Tiltrotor hovering over the Capitol grounds.

parliaments and governmental infrastructure in each nation," he noted on behalf of the 21 percent of association members who operated outside the U.S., "and we don't want to go back to the concept that each count has his own castle." At the time of the changeover, there were more than a thousand members of HAI.

Hughes Helicopters tripled its independent research and development (IR&D) funding in one year, including research on composite main rotor hubs. Bell put $73 million of its own money into IR&D funding in 1981 alone, the highest figure in the firm's history.

The Reagan Administration's Commerce Secretary Malcolm Baldridge said while it might be true that foreign firms were taking a bigger share of the helicopter market, they were also bringing capital into the country. "While we're all pulling for Bell Helicopter Textron," he told a news conference, it must be remembered that "Aerospatiale gave jobs to American workers."

As if concern about French helicopters was not enough, the General Accounting Office (GAO) forecast that Japan was a far more likely player of substantial impact on worldwide civil aircraft markets. The only question, said GAO, was how big Japan's share would be.

The fact that the export flow went both ways was demonstrated when Helikopter Service A/S of Norway once again placed an order for Boeing Civil Chinooks, worth an estimated $40 million.

Gian F. Blower, senior director of Italy's Elitos Helicopters, was elected HAI's twenty-eighth president at the 1982 annual meeting.

On April 2, 1982, Argentina seized the Falkland Islands in the south Atlantic.

On May 21, 1982, British troops attacked the Falklands.

On September 30, 1982, H. Ross Perot, Jr., and Jay Coburn finished the first round-the-world helicopter flight in Fort Worth, Texas, in a Bell 206L.

"Logging represented a great amount of our business — about 80 percent — until September '81," said Columbia Helicopters. "Suddenly, business went to near zero."

Hughes had good results with its anti-torque, no-tail-rotor design using blown air, which made it all the way to production models. There were other examples that ultimately benefitted commercial operators, the military, and other users as well.

The granddaddy of all successful vertical lift concepts of the 1980s, however, was Bell's tiltrotor. This idea, conceptualized by England's Sir George Cayley in the early 19th century, promised to eventually help the downtown heliport serve destinations much further than the nearby airport. The tiltrotor conceivably could take people from a city center directly to their ultimate destination in another city center several hundred miles away — from Washington to Boston, San Diego to San Francisco, or Portland to Seattle for example — without an airport intervening. To be sure, British Airways wanted a stretched Chinook, but Boeing simply could not see a market for the idea, and Sikorsky was not rushing into production with civil versions of the Black Hawk.

Bell first flew the XV-15 tiltrotor research aircraft in May 1977, then showed its capabilities at the 1981 Paris Air Show. By the end of the century the concept had advanced to the point where military tiltrotor transports were flying and committed to production by a Bell-Boeing team. The tiltrotor promises to benefit commercial operators in many ways, such as long-haul offshore and remote-area support, but conventional-style helicopters will always be required.

Much of the technology used by commercial helicopter operators was originally developed with military funding, and so it was with the tiltrotor concept. That did not mean, however, that money would be pouring into every technology development program in sight.

The specter of government competition did not go away with President Reagan's promise to "get government off the backs of the people." Commercial operators in California — where Reagan had once been governor — learned that the U.S. Air Force was giving the state 12 surplus UH-1F helicopters for fire fighting, vegetation management, and other tasks in direct competition with the commercial operators who once provided those services. The issue was controversial, complex, and costly, depending on who did the explaining and the bookkeeping.

It wasn't long before HAI succeeded in getting legislative language introduced before the Congress as part of the Defense Appropriations Bill to stop most instances of Pentagon competition with the private sector. That did

Numerous industry groups began during the first half century of commercial helicopter operations. These included the European Helicopter Association, Helicopter Airline Association, Helicopter Operators of Texas, Helicopter Safety Advisory Conference, Appalachian Helicopter Pilots Association, National EMS Pilots Association, and Mid-Atlantic Helicopter Association. Each had carved out a narrow niche, but in many cases the niche was too narrow and the organization faded away. HAI's position was to encourage and support these special-purpose organizations and welcome them as affiliates of HAI.

not stop the army from going forward with plans to provide massive helicopter support to the Olympic Games in Los Angeles, despite an HAI protest. The unfavorable consequences to the private sector affected both economics and public relations — the army pilots were not trained to fly neighborly.

To the astonishment of those who had expected otherwise from the new administration, things appeared to be eminently worse for helicopter manufacturers as the Pentagon considered what to do with as many as 8,000 surplus military helicopters. A Federal Trade Commission (FTC) academic contractor's report, prepared by a Dartmouth College economics professor, said private-sector helicopter producers "must not be allowed to use their position to control the growth of a second-hand market if the economic benefits are to be realized."

While it is debatable if such an apparent windfall would have been to the long-term benefit of commercial helicopter operators — and it did not appear that the Dartmouth professor had spoken with a single operator — the fact was that the conclusion sounded as though it had been written in the Kremlin, despite its many factual errors.

As is the case with many such ivory-tower ruminations, the report was not heard of again outside the halls of the FTC. However, the matter of thousands of surplus military helicopters, primarily from the U.S. Army but including the former Soviet machines as well, is a stark reality.

To many commercial operators, the Dartmouth study was strictly an academic exercise, because there was less business for which to compete. Bristow Offshore Helicopters was one operator that drastically cut back its Gulf of Mexico operations, selling off 17 Aerospatiale AS-350 models. Others among the Gulf's 35 commercial operators, initially certain that Bristow's experience was unique to that company, gradually did their own pruning of operations in the Gulf. Considering the proportion of U.S. domestic commercial operations represented by Gulf offshore support, it was a major step.

The folklore at the time claimed that if an offshore rig wanted ice cream, they'd order it flown out by helicopter. That was no longer the case, as oil companies began sharpening their pencils to justify the costs of helicopter operations. The Baltimore Canyon offshore exploration off the east coast of the U.S. had not produced anything of commercial interest, and the Alaska pipeline was now finished. Some promising markets had slowly faded away.

Loran E. (Pat) Patterson of Continental Helicopters was elected HAI president in 1983 and told his fellow operators that "the helicopter industry has been beset by external economic forces that have placed limitations upon all of us."

The fallout of those "external economic forces" was fewer purchases of new commercial helicopters, of course, and steps to maximize utilization of existing fleets. Manufacturers began trimming production rates and schedules, intensifying their marketing, and introducing new products in response to the sagging economy. Hughes reduced its production rate on the Model 500D and laid off 650 commercial employees.

Some of these measures helped, some did not.

An official of Agusta Aviation Corp. said the economic situation was like trying to thread a needle in an earthquake.

There was some good economic news in that Agusta made a deal with Sikorsky to produce the S-61 model under license. This gave Agusta more work and revenue, removed pressure from Sikorsky to produce a replacement for the now-terminated S-61 production line, and gave operators an option for acquiring a new S-61. At nearly the same time, Sikorsky sold most rights to the S-58/S-58T product line to California-based Helicopter Parts, Inc., for about $5 million.

The soft market had cost Sikorsky in other ways, however, as orders for the S-76 fell from a high of 444 to about 375 as the company eliminated "marginal speculators."

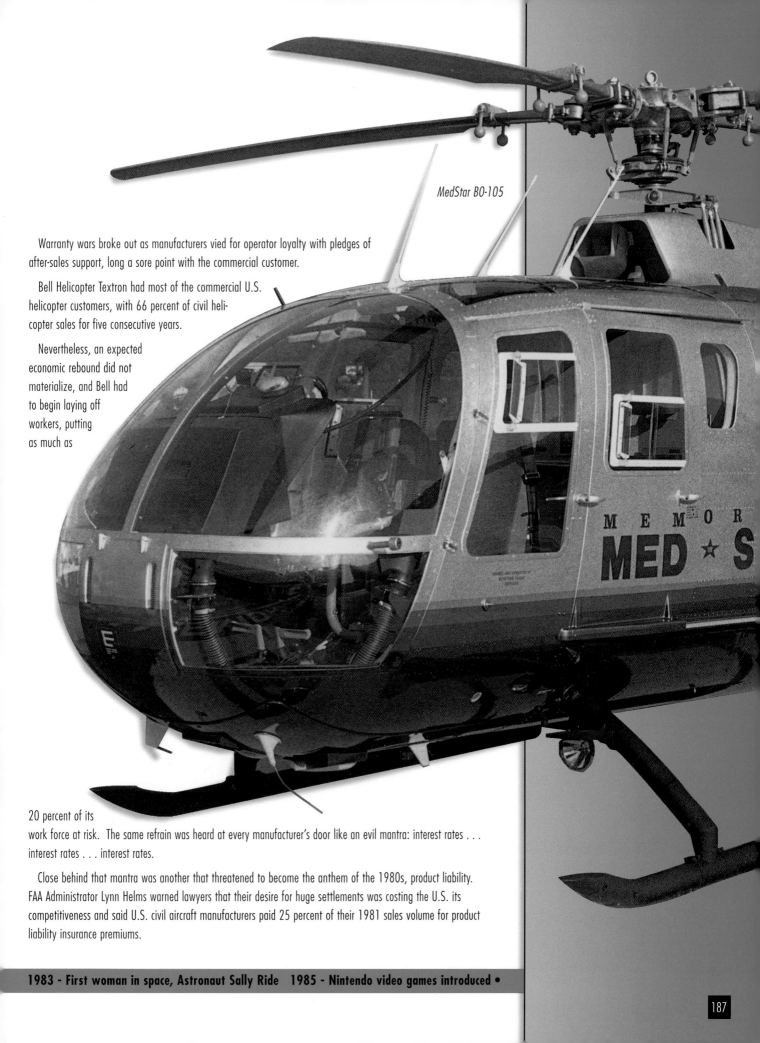

MedStar BO-105

Warranty wars broke out as manufacturers vied for operator loyalty with pledges of after-sales support, long a sore point with the commercial customer.

Bell Helicopter Textron had most of the commercial U.S. helicopter customers, with 66 percent of civil helicopter sales for five consecutive years.

Nevertheless, an expected economic rebound did not materialize, and Bell had to begin laying off workers, putting as much as

20 percent of its work force at risk. The same refrain was heard at every manufacturer's door like an evil mantra: interest rates . . . interest rates . . . interest rates.

Close behind that mantra was another that threatened to become the anthem of the 1980s, product liability. FAA Administrator Lynn Helms warned lawyers that their desire for huge settlements was costing the U.S. its competitiveness and said U.S. civil aircraft manufacturers paid 25 percent of their 1981 sales volume for product liability insurance premiums.

1983 - First woman in space, Astronaut Sally Ride   1985 - Nintendo video games introduced •

187

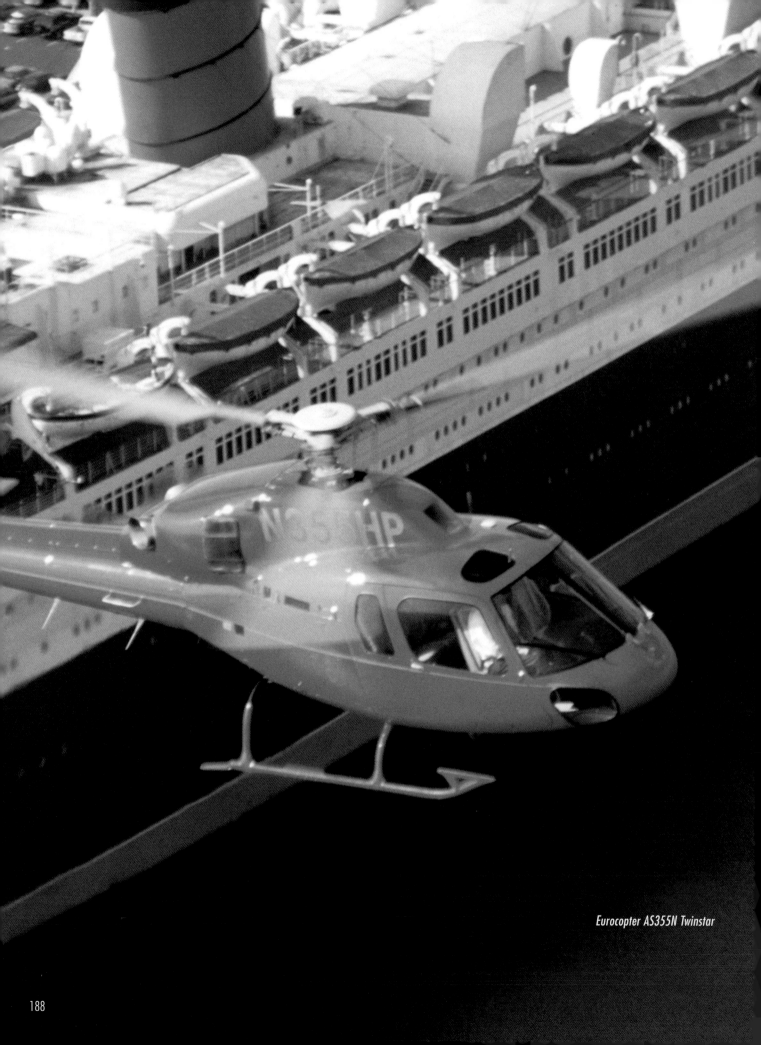

Eurocopter AS355N Twinstar

The following numbers for commercial helicopters will give an indication of how the 1980s plummeted:

In 1982, Sikorsky delivered only 29 Model S-76s (ten in December alone), compared with 42 of the same model in 1981 and 85 in 1980.

Bell delivered 195 Model 206 helicopters in 1982, compared with 476 delivered in 1981 and 550 throughout 1980. The company delivered 80 units of all other models in 1982, compared with 297 in 1981 and 164 in 1980.

Hughes delivered 122 Model 500 helicopters in 1982 (including a controversial sale of 30 helicopters to Iraq), compared with 134 throughout 1981 and 229 in 1980. The Model 300 series delivered 54 in 1982 (including 30 to Iraq), compared with 50 in 1981 and 136 in 1980.

Aerospatiale reported 111 deliveries of all models for its French and U.S. facilities for the first five months of 1982, compared with 298 for all of 1981 and 242 for 1980. Numbers for all of 1982 were not available, but the trend was nevertheless clear.

The story was the same for every manufacturer, no exceptions, with some variation by model and time period. The trend was steeply downward.

Operators responded to the plunge by buttoning up and hanging on.

On May 9, 1983, Philippe Jeantot of France arrived in Newport, Rhode Island, after sailing alone around the world in 159 days in a 56-foot cutter. He repeated in 1987.

On May 31, 1983, American heavy-weight boxing champion Jack Dempsey died.

On July 22, 1983, Dick Smith ended a solo flight around the world in a Bell 206, landing in Fort Worth after logging 35,258 miles and 320 hours flight time. Smith was the first person to circumnavigate the world, solo, by helicopter. He timed his epoch flight so that he would be at specific locations on the anniversary of historic aviation events.

As if interest rates and a recession were not enough, the manufacturing industry took another body blow when the New York State Supreme Court found that a helicopter manufacturer may be liable for proven business losses of an owner/operator in case of a product defect. The court drew a distinction between cases where a defective part is merely ineffective, and cases where it causes an accident.

Manufacturers across the land made note of this finding.

Headlines proclaimed that 30,000 businesses in the U.S. went under in June 1982. Helicopter operators, averaging three dollars of debt for every dollar of equity, were extremely vulnerable to joining those failed businesses, and many did. Even those with long-ago debt at lower interest rates were now forced to pay much higher rates when re-financing.

Along with the straight bankruptcies, there were mergers and acquisitions among the operators. Fugazy bought Decair, KLM bought a minority interest in Schreiner Airways, and Bristow affiliate United Helicopters bought 49 percent of Okanagan. But the mergers and acquisitions mania hit the big time with United Technologies, Martin Marietta, Allied Signal, and Bendix Corp. When the fog cleared enough for commercial helicopter operators to look around, many could not tell where they should go for service.

To paraphrase "Business Week," waiting for the helicopter buyer to show up was like "waiting for Godot." Sikorsky had delivered only eight S-76s in the first half of 1982. This made it all the more remarkable that the firm had its first year of sales exceeding $1 billion. That was due, of course, to military work on the UH-60 Black Hawk and other programs, but still it helped salve the trauma of the recession.

Bell 412 on patrol

A Helicopter Airline Association was formed to wield some collective clout, both politically and economically, but the qualifying members were really too few to have the desired impact on the situation. The association's goals included primarily operating issues such as noise ordinances and heliport availability. For any organization to succeed, a minimum critical mass is required, and 35 helicopter passenger services were close to that minimum.

NYA's successor, New York Helicopter Corp. (NYHC), a subsidiary of Island Helicopters, had far better luck flying a mixed fleet of Dauphin 2s and S-58T helicopters around New York and its airports. The company was expanding despite the recession elsewhere in the industry. NYHC carried 800 passengers the day after the blizzard of 1983 shut down East Coast airports, including JFK and Newark.

Blizzards of a different sort were seen for the first time along the coast of the Gulf of Mexico as union organizers papered local areas with pamphlets urging Air Logistics pilots to join the Oil, Chemical, and Atomic Workers (OGAW) union. The election was held in February 1984 and was supervised by the federal government. In the end there was no union set up at Air Logistics or any other Gulf operator. Most likely, a gloomy national economic picture influenced many of the pilots in this most personal of economic decisions.

On August 18, 1983, Hurricane Alicia slammed into the Texas coast, leaving 22 dead and more than $1 billion worth of damage in its wake. Helicopters rescued scores of people.

On August 21, 1983, Philippine leader Benigno Aquino was assassinated.

For The Record

1985 - Wreck of the Titanic discovered • Rock & Roll Hall of Fame opens in Cleveland •

Other significant economic decisions of the 1980s included that of the Howard Hughes estate to sell off Hughes Helicopters. Hughes had previously made arrangements to hand its Model 300 product line over to Schweizer Aircraft, and was instead concentrating on the Model 500 series and the AH-64 Apache attack helicopter. The sale was made more palatable by the fact that Hughes expected to turn a profit in 1983 for the first time in its history. The buyer was at first rumored to be Raytheon Corp., then Kaman Corp., but the eventually successful suitor was McDonnell Douglas.

While industry figures were in a selling mood prompted by a poor economy, Alan Bristow sold a part of his holding in Bristow Helicopters to British & Commonwealth Shipping (B&CS), which already owned two-thirds of the helicopter operator's stock. Bristow's sale of shares brought the B&CS overall ownership of the company to 75 percent and reduced Alan Bristow's personal share to about 13 percent.

Bristow's timing preceded by several months the helicopter operator's laying off pilots for the first time in its history. British Airways Helicopters (BAH) had earlier followed that route in response to slack demand. Worldwide, Bristow cut 70 pilots of its 500 total, and 50 of the layoffs were in the U.K.

On the North Sea, nevertheless, BAH and Helicopter Service A/S were busily flying 219,400 passengers on civil Chinooks in offshore oil/gas support during their first two years of operation. The big birds had a monthly average of 139 flight hours and a dispatch reliability of 93 percent.

British Caledonian, for its part, responded to the slump by selling off about two-thirds of its fleet.

Slowly the economy turned, ever so slowly.

Sikorsky announced the sale of 15 corporate S-76s. Bell said deliveries of its Model 222 were at 11 aircraft for the second half of 1983, compared with only three aircraft in the first half. Additionally, Bell was chosen by the Canadian government to establish a helicopter manufacturing industry that would bring "immense economic and technological value" to the country.

Did You Know?

Despite economic bad news of the early 1980s, it was obvious that helicopters were the wave of the future for rapid medical missions. By 1982, more than 900 hospitals had heliports on the premises, compared with only 34 in 1965.

Sikorsky S-76

Overcapacity on the North Sea slowly was taken up by demand, so slowly that not all the operators caught it. New tax incentives helped, as they usually do, and so did the glamour-less old workhorse, the S-61, which "just refuses to go away." The old-technology helicopter kept new-technology machines like the Bell 214ST and Aerospatiale Super Puma from easily getting into the market because they couldn't touch its economics. The Bell 214ST, however, was considered second only to the Boeing Chinook in desirability for long offshore missions.

Enstrom 480

The S-61 was like the DC-3: it was obsolete, but the aircraft hadn't noticed.

On March 11, 1985, Soviet leader Konstantin U. Chernenko died. Politburo member Mikhail S. Gorbachev was chosen to succeed him.

On March 20, 1985, Libby Riddles became the first woman to win the Iditarod Trail Dog Sled Race, going from Anchorage to Nome, Alaska, in under 18 days.

On April 12, 1985, Senator Jake Garn of Utah became the first senator to fly in space as the shuttle Discovery lifted off from Cape Canaveral, Florida.

It appeared the North Sea offshore support sector of the British helicopter industry may have kept its dark glasses on for too long. The number of idle rigs off the British coast dropped from 44 in 1985 to only 17 within two years, catching the helicopter operators off guard in their 1987 capacity calculations. The offshore explorers were not only resuming prior activity levels at production platforms, they were

expanding into new areas with exploratory drilling rigs. The independent exploratory rigs each needed their own dedicated helicopter.

Helicopter operators, however, had limited their capacity and personnel in 1985 to meet the reduced demand and forgot to check in with the oil industry often enough. The long lead times required for buying new helicopters, hiring and training pilots, and gearing up for more activity put the British operators in the position of possibly losing business to foreign helicopter operators simply because they couldn't handle it.

Economic recovery usually gives signs of its arrival, and in the aviation community one of those signs is attendance at major industry events. HAI's January

1984 meeting drew 9,532 registrants, a small but reassuring gain over the 1983 figure of 9,227.

Consensus was that a gradual but definite turnaround in sales for the helicopter industry came in June 1983, although the traditional offshore sector was not leading the way. That distinction was held by the emergency medical services and corporate sectors.

Medevac statisticians announced that 95,000 patients were flown a total of eight million miles by helicopter in the first 10 years of hospital-based aeromedical transport service.

One outcome of the recession was that pricing of helicopters became much more creative and difficult to define in a few words. The quoted price of the newly introduced S-70C, for example, was "based on the operator requirement for various financing options." (The first S-70C was ordered by Erickson Air-Crane Co. for utility work.) The monthly payment was now more important to operators than the total price, while leasing and lease-backs began to assume a larger role than ever. It became extremely difficult to determine when a helicopter was "sold" or even "delivered" because of the creative transactions.

Allison's Fritz Harvey differed with some of his colleagues in the business when he said the slump had been a severe depression, not a recession. But airframe manufacturers stuck to the sales projections and slowly things did improve.

Boeing Vertol showed faith in its Chinook by flying about a dozen reporters and VIPs to the HAI show in Las Vegas in a Chinook. The high-profile flight was virtually unprecedented in scope and was a huge success, both for the company and for the industry as a whole.

General Motors was so confident that helicopter and airplane re-engining programs of Soloy Conversions would be a money-maker that the company — parent of Allison — bought 15 percent of Soloy. Dozens of Hiller and Bell conversions using the Allison turbine engine were already flying.

Because the operating costs of turbine engines were low and the capacity of helicopters powered by those engines was greater than was previously possible, many believed that viable commuter and air taxi operations were now possible. Now, they seemed to think, if only we could do something about the lack of public heliports in cities where the customers are.

Confidence was surging throughout the industry. Keystone Helicopters, betting that a recovery couldn't possibly be too far off, tripled the size of its base in West Chester, Pennsylvania, and began marketing an enclosed test cell for turbine engines.

Shortly thereafter, the parent company of Island Helicopters, New York Helicopter, and several other firms declared Chapter 11 status.

Before long, Air Logistics unit of Offshore Logistics put its Conroe, Texas, maintenance base up for sale. Offshore Logistics lost $18.8 million in just the first quarter of 1984. In addition to 50 layoffs in its maintenance staff, Air Logistics lost a major contract, again showing the volatile and fickle nature of the business. Despite the bad news, Air Logistics bought 10 Sikorsky S-76 models for offshore support.

Manufacturers believed the worst was over, but that did not help commercial operators, who continued throughout the 1980s to be uncertain about the stability of their economic health.

Economic benefits may not have been contagious and the dark days may not have been completely gone, but HAI did its best to pass along good news by having a half-price membership sale for new members with five or fewer aircraft and public service operators with fewer than 14 aircraft.

The association was honored by FAA with its Silver Award for Distinguished Service for its organizing and spon-soring of its "Fly Neighborly Program," an innovative noise reduction program. HAI was the first association ever to receive the FAA award.

Without accurate industry data it was difficult to tell what was happening, and the customary repository for such data in a regulated industry was the federal government . . . specifically FAA. Largely in response to urging by HAI, the agency held a conference and announced a new approach to industry statistics, which FAA admitted had been way off base in the past and bore little resemblance to private-sector data measuring the same thing. FAA's new approach was to use multi-source private-sector data, modified to fit FAA needs.

The new method showed that FAA projections for the number of helicopters expected to be registered in 1995 was 17,164.

About six months later, FAA released its annual aviation forecast, which showed that the number now expected to be registered in 1995 was only 10,500 helicopters. No one knows what changed in a few months.

(What was the actual 1995 number of civil helicopter registrations? It was 10,605, remarkably close to the FAA's second projection a decade earlier!)

The problem, of course, was to decide which of FAA's projections one should have believed in the mid-1980s.

HAI by this time had worked with other organizations and successfully improved the safety record of emergency medical services (EMS) helicopters to the point that there were entire years in which no EMS accidents occurred. Such a record cannot be sustained indefinitely, of course, but it does show what can be accomplished.

The Transportation Research Board (TRB) studied helicopter relationships to the national transportation picture and concluded that the federal government holds the key to helicopter development because it has the option of nurturing the industry in the same way it has nurtured the fixed-wing industry for so many years. Such a policy, said TRB's report, would be of great benefit to the general public. However, "disunity in the government" and a lack of consensus in the helicopter operating community were seen as detriments to the development of discrete helicopter airways as part of an integrated, optimized national airways system.

Just as bogus parts had always been a problem with the aircraft industry, there eventually came to light a bogus-helicopter problem. Bell Helicopter reported to FAA that some identification plates from wrecked Model 47 helicopters had been illegally removed and attached to other Bell 47s so often that 43 of that model were reported completely destroyed at least twice. The motive, to no one's surprise, was money via insurance.

The Robinson R22 saw sales soar as the decade progressed, with new buyers climbing by 50 percent. That aircraft — simple, straightforward, and using familiar technology — must have looked good to some commercial operators whose helicopters were grounded due to problems with new high-technology turbine engines.

And so it always goes in a high-technology field where every effort is made to squeeze the last percentage point of performance from systems that are mated with other systems. The problem is that a commercial helicopter operator must try making a living and meeting a payroll with revenues from those often-over-extended technologies. Over-extended in both technology and sales promises, the operator might add.

"To those manufacturers who have taken positive action to help reduce operating costs, I offer sincere appreciation. Together, we may yet save this important industry," wrote HAI Chairman Chuck Johnson of Era Helicopters. "To those relatively few manufacturers who do not seem to understand the need for simplicity, reliability, and maintainability, I extend an urgent request that you climb down from your ivory tower and examine the situation within your marketplace."

The turbine engine problem was eventually brought under control by manufacturers and it slowly evaporated.

On April 15, 1989, students in Beijing launched pro-democracy protests upon the death of former Communist Party leader Hu Yaobang, who had been forced from power for refusing to crack down on student unrest.

On April 19, 1989, a gun turret explosion killed 47 sailors on the USS Iowa.

On May 19, 1989, the Dow Jones Industrial Average passed the 2,500 mark.

On May 31, 1989, House Speaker Jim Wright announced he would resign.

On June 3, 1989, Iran's Ayatollah Ruhollah Khomeini died.

July 1, 1985: the HAI highest elected position transitioned from "president" to "chairman of the board." Thus, Chuck Johnson was HAI president in 1984 and became HAI chairman when re-elected into office in 1985. In May 1985, the HAI chief staff executive transitioned from "executive director" to "president," and that title was bestowed upon Frank Jensen.

In a survey of commercial operators, engine reliability was the most important worry for 83 percent of the respondents.

The U.S. Supreme Court did not rush to the aid of commercial operators when it unanimously reversed several lower court opinions and found that FAA could not be sued for aircraft product defects that caused accidents. This was true even though FAA had certificated the product in question, the court said, and FAA is the federal agency that policed air safety. The court said only the aircraft owner can ensure safety, and therefore it is the aircraft owner who is responsible for any failures. Left untouched by the finding was the possibility of direct neglect by the federal government, such as a failure by an air traffic controller. That left little with which a commercial operator could be cheered.

Avco settled a lawsuit against a commercial maintenance center that was selling piston engine parts as Avco originals when they weren't.

It was just after he retired following 40 years at Bell that Joe Mashman let loose a blast at the manufacturers and the federal government for "backsliding" in the development of civil vertical lift aircraft. Mashman was one of the earliest of Bell's test and demonstration pilots and his perspective could hardly be dismissed.

Mashman said NASA was ignoring most of the needs of commercial operators. As he told the HAI Board after a meeting with NASA to review the agency's research, "None, and I emphasize none, of their goals and the means of achieving them held any promise of significantly affecting civilian helicopters in the area of economics and usefulness." Mashman's credentials prevented his being disregarded. Nor did his employer of 40 years and others in the manufacturing sector escape.

Most of the manufacturers, he said, had gone over to a military focus. "The military doesn't give a damn about noise," he said, singling out the issue that caused much of the community problem for urban-area operations. Ironically, Mashman's industry was heavily dominated by offshore and utility operators, who have little more concern for noise than the military. The noise concerns voiced by Mashman were largely those of corporate and urban-area operators, but the economic and performance points applied to all commercial operators and were well stated.

"I'm surprised it's news," commented manufacturer Frank Robinson on Mashman's report. "It's been that way for years." Other manufacturers passed up the opportunity to reply.

Robinson had his own criticism, however, and it was that common target he called "runaway litigation" that was "the biggest impediment" to improved helicopter designs. His own company, he said, was "scared to death to make any changes. We actually have to prove that a design change will not make it safer." Robinson was referring to the legal ploy of claiming that a product improvement implies a faulty design in the first place. Someone, he said, "would have to be crazy" to develop a new civil helicopter.

With that observation ringing across the engineering department, one hardly knew what to make of Robinson Helicopter Co.'s disclosure that it was developing a four-place, piston engine helicopter to be called the R44 and would be ready for certification within about three years of launch. The company's willingness to go ahead with the project was probably influenced by the fact that Robinson helicopters had an excellent safety record, which was made possible by a factory-supervised flight instructor training program and a Robinson-backed insurance plan. Further, Robinson helicopters — which had become the lead

Enstrom traffic helicopter
rescues injured swimmer

199

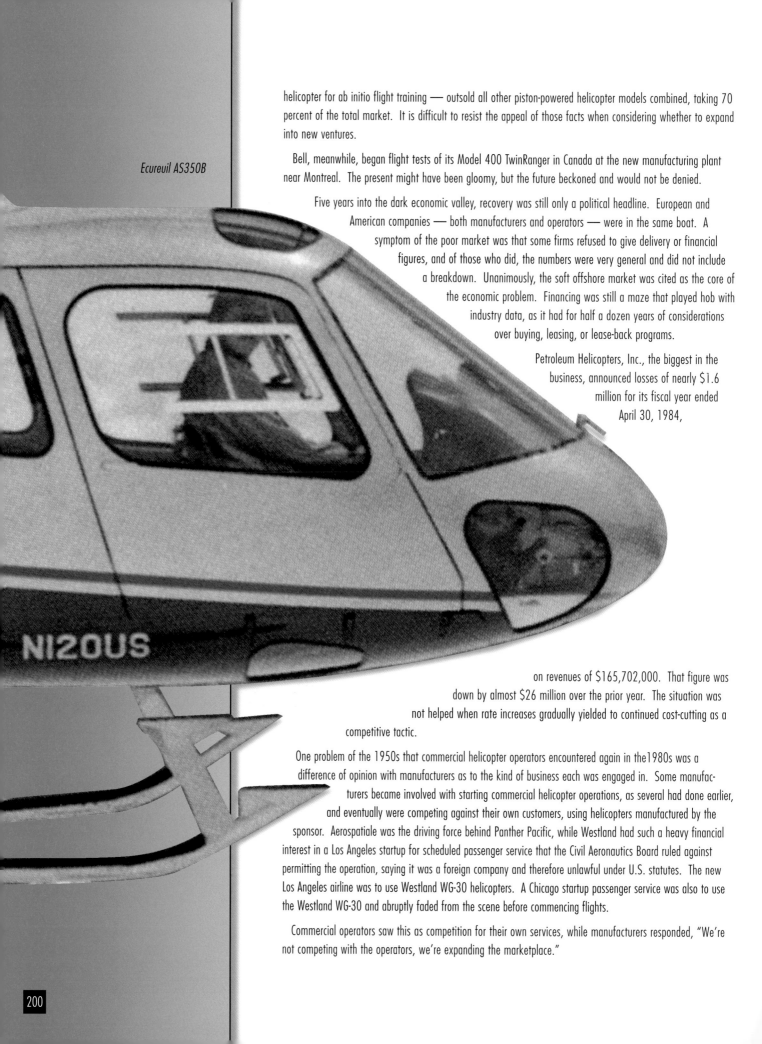

helicopter for ab initio flight training — outsold all other piston-powered helicopter models combined, taking 70 percent of the total market. It is difficult to resist the appeal of those facts when considering whether to expand into new ventures.

Bell, meanwhile, began flight tests of its Model 400 TwinRanger in Canada at the new manufacturing plant near Montreal. The present might have been gloomy, but the future beckoned and would not be denied.

Ecureuil AS350B

Five years into the dark economic valley, recovery was still only a political headline. European and American companies — both manufacturers and operators — were in the same boat. A symptom of the poor market was that some firms refused to give delivery or financial figures, and of those who did, the numbers were very general and did not include a breakdown. Unanimously, the soft offshore market was cited as the core of the economic problem. Financing was still a maze that played hob with industry data, as it had for half a dozen years of considerations over buying, leasing, or lease-back programs.

Petroleum Helicopters, Inc., the biggest in the business, announced losses of nearly $1.6 million for its fiscal year ended April 30, 1984,

on revenues of $165,702,000. That figure was down by almost $26 million over the prior year. The situation was not helped when rate increases gradually yielded to continued cost-cutting as a competitive tactic.

One problem of the 1950s that commercial helicopter operators encountered again in the1980s was a difference of opinion with manufacturers as to the kind of business each was engaged in. Some manufacturers became involved with starting commercial helicopter operations, as several had done earlier, and eventually were competing against their own customers, using helicopters manufactured by the sponsor. Aerospatiale was the driving force behind Panther Pacific, while Westland had such a heavy financial interest in a Los Angeles startup for scheduled passenger service that the Civil Aeronautics Board ruled against permitting the operation, saying it was a foreign company and therefore unlawful under U.S. statutes. The new Los Angeles airline was to use Westland WG-30 helicopters. A Chicago startup passenger service was also to use the Westland WG-30 and abruptly faded from the scene before commencing flights.

Commercial operators saw this as competition for their own services, while manufacturers responded, "We're not competing with the operators, we're expanding the marketplace."

Prosperity is where one finds it, and one type of helicopter operator doing rather well in those bleak economic days were the casinos, one of which started a regular shuttle service between Manhattan and Atlantic City using three Sikorsky S-61s. Another casino, the Golden Nugget, had a lavishly outfitted Aerospatiale Super Puma and a Sikorsky S-76 for what they termed "premium players." The entire fleet of the two biggest casinos in New Jersey flew "a significant number of hours" and a number of other casinos were looking around for helicopters to add to their premium services.

To understand the casino interest in providing the very best for its players, consider the casinos' collective winnings at the time. For the month of July 1984, 10 casinos in Atlantic City, New Jersey, had a gross win of $200.04 million. That was not the total cash flow, that was the win (gross income) of those 10 casinos in one city in a single month. The "drop," or the total money bet, was $620,055,600 for the month. Resorts International won $26.2 million for the month, and the Golden Nugget won $25.5 million. That kind of money could buy any helicopter on the market. Not all casinos elected to buy their own helicopters, however. The Atlantic City Hilton, The Sands, and Harrah's all contracted with commercial operator Damin Aviation to provide on-call service for premium players.

Lingering problems with the introduction of a variety of new helicopters and their systems prompted Air Logistics general manager David O. Smith to propose a new type of warranty for the industry. He said the introductory period is worst on the operator who buys a new aircraft and risks the chance that "teething problems" could cost him far more than any savings offered by new technology. Smith suggested a three-phase warranty where the new machine would not only be fully covered by the manufacturer for such problems, but that lost revenue would also be replaced.

In the second, or "product improvement," phase, helicopter designs are usually past their teething problems and the manufacturer is on his best behavior. This is when operators buy the aircraft far more readily, forgetting all about the teething problems that caused so much aggravation. In the final phase, Smith said, a helicopter is so thoroughly debugged that operators with a problem cannot even get the manufacturer's attention.

Smith, who had been Sikorsky's commercial sales director, proposed the three-phase warranty as a form of "variable annuity" in which the operator could decide where the best coverage should be.

Economic pressure forced PHI and Air Logistics, the two biggest Gulf market operators, to raise their rates for the first time since 1980, and while Air Logistics mailed its new rate sheet to all clients, PHI retained the long-standing secrecy on its two-tiered rate structure. The new rates for both firms were accompanied by raises for pilots.

Economic moments-of-truth come in many forms, and one of the most notable occurred when Aris Helicopters president Steve Sullivan put up $7,000 of his own funds to match an FAA grant to the city of San Jose and the County of Santa Clara for a heliport system study. Neither of the two local governments was able to generate the $7,000 to match FAA's $70,000, so Sullivan donated it.

Wanda L. Rogers became chair of HAI, the second woman ever to hold that position. Under her 1986 stewardship the association launched its safety hotline, providing instantaneous access to flight safety information. She was succeeded in the top leadership spot by Steve Sullivan of Aris Helicopters in 1987.

Regardless of competition between government agencies, manufacturing corporations, and commercial operators within their own bailiwicks, there was always one kind of competition that commercial operators should not have had to worry about — the competition between commercial operators and their own government at several levels. Federal agencies have chronically assumed that helicopter assets (or any other kind) controlled by an agency is that agency's to use as it wishes, even when the task at hand has nothing to do with the agency's mission. The issue arose several times throughout the 1980s, always with a new rationale for its initiation, and once again in connection with helicopters to be used in fire fighting by California state foresters. The message often sent by government executives to complaining operators was this: it might be better to forgo economics and base a strong case on the ideology of free enterprise.

An eye-catching episode in the U.K. had Alan Bristow trying to buy manufacturer Westland, which was financially struggling after the long years of a very soft world market. The offer was not accepted, and indeed Westland considered it a hostile takeover attempt. The investment group headed by Alan Bristow withdrew the offer after a closer look at Westland's finances, unsold inventory, and order book.

British & Commonwealth Shipping, which had bought Alan Bristow's commercial helicopter operation, became uneasy about the confusion of names now that Mr. Bristow was engaged in financial ventures that may or may not reflect adversely upon B&CS. A name change was considered, but then deferred.

Despite Bristow's highly visible financial activities, which gave the industry a patina of large cash flow, commercial operators continued to have a fearsome mortality rate. A survey indicated that about 10 percent of all commercial operators were out of business before 1986.

As part of that ongoing scene, Air Logistics announced it was closing down its California operations due to declining business. Within days, Air Logistics announced a major restructuring of its debt and instituted a cost-cutting program (management salary cut of 25 percent, employee pay cut of 10 percent, and a cut in fleet size from 200 aircraft to 128). More startling was PHI's rate increase of 14 to 16 percent in the Gulf of Mexico market, prompted by a loss of more than $8 million for the year. This was on top of the increase announced in May, totaling a 25 percent jump in just a few months.

In short, it was survival.

"Business has grown," said Tim Voss, president of AgRotors, "but it hasn't necessarily become more profitable."

New markets were actively pursued by those trying to diversify and find new uses for the helicopter. One of the most promising — which had been started in the 1970s and was now greatly improved from a technical standpoint — was that of electronic news gathering (ENG), benefitting from development of stabilized camera mounts and better electronic transmission systems. ENG was such a lucrative market for commercial operators, and an indispensable marketing tool for news networks, that it became almost a sub-industry itself. In many cases, the helicopter is given a high-profile name and the pilot becomes a local celebrity.

Bell 412

As with other areas of the economy, however, even ENG was a turbulent market for some operators, and it was totally beyond their control. The fact that a new market could be developed did not mean it was the salvation of an operator, and just as much hard work was required with ENG as with any other market.

"We were once very active in the television market," explained an executive with Omniflight, which had acquired Chesapeake & Potomac Airways as part of the 1980s consolidation, "but it dried up. We had a dozen JetRangers on stand-alone contracts in 1981, but have less than half that now." More stable was the New York Omniflight shuttle using a trio of Westland 30 helicopters.

Market diversification can be to a helicopter operator what a backup system is to his aircraft.

"We saw what happened to operators who are after a single market and we intentionally started diversification," said a Crescent Airways Inc. manager. The Florida operator spread out from its basic charter business and engaged in tuna spotting for fishing fleets, washing electric-tower insulators, U.S. Forest Service contract work, and doing Environmental Protection Agency collection of acid rain samples.

Environmental friendliness became an increasingly stringent consideration as the 1980s progressed through annual April 22 celebrations of Earth Day, and reports of global warming, El Nino, and major storms filled headlines. No sight is more welcome to a storm-damaged area than the fleet of rescue helicopters that magically appears immediately afterward.

As a major boon to operator members in 1987, HAI launched its Maintenance Malfunction Information Reporting (MMIR) system for reporting service difficulties, and soon had the entire system automated. The next year, Vernon E. Albert of PHI became HAI's chairman.

On November 21, 1989, the proceedings of Britain's House of Commons were televised live for the first time.

On December 13, 1989, South African President F.W. de Klerk met for the first time with imprisoned African National Congress leader Nelson Mandela.

On December 20, 1989, the United States launched Operation Just Cause, sending troops into Panama to topple the government of General Manuel Noriega.

No sight is more welcome to a storm-damaged area than the fleet of rescue helicopters that magically appears immediately afterward.

For The Record

1989 - Lucille Ball dies • San Francisco struck by earthquake measuring 7.1 on Richter scale •

Few realize the essential contribution helicopters make to the environment, largely because that contribution is often made out of sight of television cameras.

Helicopters can become so familiar while doing these jobs that after a short curiosity period, they are taken for granted, being so far removed from population centers that the public never has a chance to see and be impressed by helicopters at work. Some routine but vital environmental jobs done by helicopters include:

• Forest work with helicopters can provide new growth or harvest mature growth with no impact whatever on surrounding areas, thus reducing or eliminating the need for roads through the forest. A helicopter can hover above trees, collect cones, then re-seed using only cones from large, healthy trees and without causing damage to the trees or the surrounding areas.

• Forest fire fighting is one of the best-known examples of helicopters in an environmentally-friendly role, if only because the fire itself is news and attracts television cameras. Fire fighting requires helicopters fitted with special tanks and snorkels, or "Bambi Buckets" that allow them to refill from local lakes without having to land. The helicopter can also move firefighters around from one hotspot to another more efficiently and faster than ground vehicles can.

• Animal herding and relocation is a routine task of helicopters in New Zealand, Scandinavia, North America, and other places. Wildlife management involves sheep, reindeer, moose, bears, and other animals. In Indonesia, orangutans are relocated from urban areas to remote forests. Some flights are to count, herd, tag, or round up animals, while other flights physically pick up animals and put them somewhere else.

• Acid rain is a phenomenon known to most people, but few realize that to combat the problem, helicopters efficiently spread tons of lime on forests to save them from destruction. This antidote for acid rain introduces no roads or pollution to the forest areas.

• Helicopters engaged in "flight-seeing" allow people to see remote beauty — such as that in the western United States — without requiring them to use destructive ground vehicles or be among the hardy few who can trek into these areas. This has been a boon to the elderly, the very young, and those with mobility impairments.

HAI members continued to demonstrate that machines may be great tools, but it is the human element that makes or breaks an industry. Thirteen regular members of HAI, each a single-helicopter operator, decided to forgo a dues-reduction benefit and contribute the amount to the Helicopter Foundation International as a way of helping preserve helicopter history.

Management changes occurred in some companies. Carl Brady stepped down as head of Era Helicopters but remained active in its parent, the Rowan Companies. Peter Wright, Sr., stepped down as president of Keystone Helicopters and became chairman; Peter Wright, Jr., assumed the presidency.

Meanwhile, the 500th Robinson R22 was quietly delivered. The first R22 had been delivered less than six years earlier.

Not only was Robinson relentlessly producing a quality, new-design small helicopter, but at the other end of the size spectrum, NASA, FAA, the Defense Department, and the Commerce Department signed a Memorandum of Understanding to develop a 40,000-pound gross weight civil airline version of the tiltrotor V-22 Osprey transport. Following the most clearly defined apparent path to the future, the West German government and industry proposed a comprehensive plan for research into new vertical lift technology, focused on the tiltrotor and X-wing concepts, in order to reduce the gap between U.S. and European research for commercial exploitation.

Clearly, things were spotty throughout every sector of the industry. Some manufacturers were doing well in ways that did not bring in significant immediate revenue, such as contracts for future work. Manufacturers with high-profile military programs and public relations departments often had to explain poor civil sales, while some manufacturers like Robinson merely delivered products.

Did You Know?

Bleak though they may be, economic hard times can bring out the essential humor in people.

In 1983, when things were at their darkest for the commercial helicopter operating industry, the wisecrack most often heard at the HAI annual meeting and exposition was "Stay Alive Til '85."

In 1985 that unofficial slogan changed to "Avoid Chapter 11 Til '87."

In a way, the 1980s were a tempering furnace that put a hard edge on those helicopter operators sharp enough to survive.

In 1989, Fred Moore of Canadian Helicopters became HAI's chairman.

It would be a mistake, however, to think that small and inconspicuous was safe. Brantly-Hynes, Enstrom, Hiller, and Schweizer certainly had problems throughout the decade, with occasional management upheavals that were alternately the cause or the effect of the market climate and the resulting balance sheet.

The economic ravaging of the commercial helicopter industry in the 1980s caused the FAA to back away from its commitment to have 25 city-center instrument flight rule heliports in service by 1995. Instead, the agency anticipated about 15 heliports by 1995, all visual flight rule (VFR) only. Other backsliding was evident, and the overall message was that the federal commitment was softer than the government had insisted.

What had been a bustling free-for-all industry at the start of the decade became a smaller, wiser collection of survivors near the end. After a ferocious intervening storm, the commercial turbulence gradually calmed, and the climate became one of mergers, acquisitions, joint ventures and other mutually beneficial moves.

The commercial helicopter operators had indeed defied predictions that they would disappear as an industry. Left to face the remainder of its first half-century was a group of hardened, more businesslike enterprises whose managers kept their accounting systems on computer disks instead of in the 1940s style, where the stereotype accounting system was often a rolled-up yellow pad sticking out of the owner-pilot's back pocket.

Not only did the operators of the 1980s have to contend with greater competition and a volatile market that sometimes didn't exist at all, but there were also far more government regulations, greater customer expectations, higher helicopter operating costs, and less flexibility allowed in getting the job done.

But the job always got done.

Industry executives who had not honed their management skills in HAI operator courses were just as disadvantaged as pilots who had not taken recurrent flight training courses. The association offered more and more "survival tools" than ever, and the prevailing operators needed HAI increasingly as the world became tougher.

In a way, the 1980s were a tempering furnace that put a hard edge on those sharp enough to survive.

McDonnell Douglas 520-N

THE NINETIES

*"My definition of an educated man
is the fellow who knows
the right thing to do at the
time it has to be done.
You can be sincere and still be stupid."*

Charles F. Kettering, American inventor

Emotionally charged words reverberated all through the 1980s and carried their unnerving message into the 1990s. Words like shakeout, Chapter 11, merger, acquisition, downsize, consolidation, and other such terms that had not been heard with great frequency — if at all — in the commercial helicopter industry.

Other terms reflected a deep-seated energy and vitality in the industry despite economic concerns, such as teaming, joint venture, cooperative programs, and other mutually beneficial endeavors.

Knowing the right thing to do at the right time became a more critical survival skill than ever. Sometimes nothing helped, but the industry as a whole was resilient and had been populated from the outset by people who did not break or discourage easily. The trouble was that, as complicated as the world may have seemed in earlier years, it became borderline incomprehensible by the end of the century.

Westland Lynx,
world's fastest production helicopter

The economics, politics, and technology of the mid-century when the commercial helicopter industry was born, landed eventually in a jumble on every operator's desk with each daily dose of news. Each of those three words now had to be preceded — for the sake of accuracy — by the word "global," so that they became global economics, global politics, and global technology. Helicopter operators who did not deal with each of them in its totality did not survive. Sometimes their fate was essentially out of the operator's control.

For The Record

1990 - Iraq invades Kuwait; U.S. responds by sending several hundred thousand troops •

An example on the bizarre side was the chaos following the November 1991 mystery death of British financier Robert Maxwell, whose holdings included British International Helicopters (BIH). By the time the situation settled down in 1992, BIH had become part of Canadian Helicopter Corp., but in the meantime there were some unpredictable twists and turns. Among the suitors for BIH were Bristow, Bond, Heli-Union, and perhaps others. The state of the estate was so confusing (legally and financially) that it was 1994, well after Maxwell's death on a yacht near the Canary Islands, before it was settled.

While it was not difficult to explain the 1940s, '50s, and '60s in a relatively linear way, that was no longer possible with the transformations of the world. Describing events became a multi-level challenge involving several countries, several manufacturers, and several dozen suppliers in a multitude of countries. It became more necessary than ever to use a specific example in order to demonstrate a generality that applied to the entire industry. Multinational corporations engaged in teaming efforts with diverse government entities or market sectors in mind to produce variants of a basic airframe, engine, avionics suite, mission package, or service. Fred Moore of Canadian Helicopters was chairman of the Helicopter Association International (HAI) as the decade ended, and the way he saw things, "the right thing to do" was clear, despite the complexities: "It's true that 1989 ended on a considerably less buoyant note than the earlier years of the decade, but much better off than during the mid-1980s, when the helicopter industry was experiencing the worst period of its 40-odd year history. . . . In looking forward into the 1990s, the greatest challenge facing the civil helicopter industry, manufacturers, and operators alike, is the necessity to open new markets."

New markets couldn't have come soon enough for the beleaguered industry, which HAI summed up in a single sentence: "In particular, 1992 was a very bad year; 1993 is expected to be somewhat better, but still not back up to the 1991 level."

One measure of how the operators were doing was how the manufacturers were doing. If operators are making no money, they are not buying new helicopters, despite all the hard work they may apply to the task.

Sometimes the hard-working operators couldn't win for losing. Rocky Mountain Helicopters subsidiary, RMH Aerologging, broke all its own records in June 1991 for hours flown and revenues produced, and the company still lost money for the quarter. An RMH Aerologging Bell 214 flew 300 hours that month and lifted more than 45.8 million pounds of Alaskan timber to earn more than a million dollars for that one helicopter. The combined effects of weather, a recession economy, and politics, however, put the RMH unit in the red for the quarter. The politics came in the form of spotted owl regulations and additional environmental restrictions.

The helicopter market had "bottomed out" in 1988, the economists insisted, and a renewal of orders began as the decades changed. Throughout the latter half of the 1980s, the Transportation Research Board (TRB) had annually revised downward its estimate of worldwide civil helicopter delivery forecast. Starting with a 1985 forecast of 9,463 helicopter deliveries, the TRB downsized its estimates year by year and reached its 1990 forecast with a projection of 5,280 deliveries. There was no change at all seen in medium and heavy categories for the entire decade of the 1990s.

> "In looking forward into the 1990s, the greatest challenge facing the civil helicopter industry, manufacturers, and operators alike, is the necessity to open new markets."
>
> Fred Moore of
> Canadian Helicopters
> Chairman of HAI

The K-MAX "aerial truck" lifts a 660-gallon Bambi bucket forest fire fighting system

For longer than anyone expected, aviation trade magazines reported with certainty that the future did not look good and that the industry's resilience would be challenged. "Manufacturers have embarked on a major revamp of their product lines at a time when sales are flat and look set to continue so until sustained recovery takes place." As if anyone questioned the nature of the problem even at mid-decade, "Flight International" magazine declared: "The major issue facing the civil helicopter industry continues to be recession."

Within the ranks of long-established operators, many changes occurred during these uncertain years, reflecting an energetic market and the need to see emerging opportunities.

The Rowan Companies, parent of Era Aviation and Era Helicopters, bought a 49 percent share in KLM Helikopters BV, which, for more than 40 years, had been a wholly owned subsidiary of KLM Airlines. The reason for its sell-off, KLM explained, was that labor union influence in the Netherlands was so strong that it was difficult to make any profit. That prompted further reports that KLM would sell its remaining 51 percent ownership.

Sure enough, Schreiner Airways arranged to buy not only the 51 percent of what had become KLM-Era Helicopters, but also bought the minority share held by Era to acquire the entire operation.

Senior managers at Bristow Helicopters, formed in 1953 and having gone through a succession of owners, bought control of that operator from its parent, the Gamlestaden financial group. Gamlestaden in turn had bought Bristow from Bricom in 1990.

The 1990s was also the decade when labor unions finally got to represent some U.S. helicopter pilots after many years of trying to gain such standing. Offshore Logistics pilots voted to join a union, while Petroleum Helicopters Inc. (PHI) pilots voted the other way.

On November 26, 1991, the U.S. flag came down at Clark Air Base in the Philippines as the United States abandoned one of its oldest and largest overseas installations.

On December 4, 1991, Pan American World Airways ceased operations.

On December 18, 1991, General Motors Corporation announced it would close 21 North American plants in the next four years and cut tens of thousands of jobs in a sweeping restructuring of the world's largest company.

On December 21, 1991, eleven of 12 former Soviet republics proclaimed the birth of the Commonwealth of Independent States and the death of the Soviet Union.

The infrastructure of the industry, however, had changed little in at least 20 years when one compares its evolution to the technological evolution of the helicopter itself. While riverfront heliports are generally considered the safest and most neighborly, Britain's Environment Secretary rejected plans for a London City Heliport, dealing a serious blow to the British industry, corporate operators, and any thought of scheduled services. The Secretary cited "noise and visual impact" as reasons for denying the go-ahead for a site near a railway bridge.

New York, the world's busiest corporate helicopter hub (1995 had 140,500 helicopter takeoffs and landings), went through several phases of helicopter infrastructure development, especially after mid-decade restrictions based on noise levels. Legal action flew in several directions, with the upshot being that the East 34th Street heliport could yield to a Pier 76 facility on Manhattan's midtown west side. That plan had hit a spaghetti-tangle of legal and political considerations by 1998, with 1997 being a municipal election year and several anti-helicopter activist groups irrationally pressuring the city to shut down all helicopter operations.

For The Record

1990 - Cold War ends • Gene therapy debuts • First McDonald's opens in Moscow •

Hughes-500

The New York situation essentially had an impact on corporate and flightseeing operators, but in the broader category of scheduled helicopter passenger services, the question of infrastructure was also seen as a chronic obstacle to industry progress. This, noted HAI, is largely a matter of perspective. One prevailing viewpoint was:

"Another long-standing issue still facing the industry is the lack of an adequate infrastructure enabling helicopters to become an integral part of the public transportation system," noted "Flight International."

HAI President Frank Jensen challenged such a pessimistic view of passenger services, however, pointing out that almost all offshore support helicopter flights operate on schedules, and the combined activities of operators such as PHI, Air Logistics, Canadian Helicopter Corp., Bristow, Era, Helicol, Helikopter Service A/S, and others in the North Sea, Asia, the Arctic, and scattered oilfield regions have carried millions of passengers safely and efficiently for nearly half a century. The obvious difference was that their points of scheduled arrival and departure did not have familiar city or airport names.

This sustained, undramatic record typically draws no media attention, while a single accident occupies the evening television news and political leaders see and hear the negative portrayals uttered by TV anchors.

Since the 1960s, British International Airways and its corporate predecessors have served the Scilly Isles and Penzance with scheduled services that have proven to be extremely safe and economically viable. Helikopter Service A/S provides scheduled passenger services between Sweden and Denmark. Greenland Air has for more than three decades flown passengers around that northern land with dispatch and safety. Helijet began passenger services in Canada and had recently extended that service to the U.S.

So, while the prevailing industry challenge in the 1980s was economics — and to some extent the infrastructure — those were joined in the 1990s by global politics. Not necessarily by domestic politics any more than usual, but by the fallout of worldwide political change.

The change seemed in those Cold War days, one might say at first glance, a Christmas gift for the world. Only later was it realized that the Christmas events of 1991 had two sides.

On December 25, 1991, Soviet President Mikhail S. Gorbachev announced his resignation. The hammer-and-sickle flag over the Kremlin came down, and Russia's blue, white, and red flag was raised in its place.

Historic perspective is often acquired by recalling once-unshakeable benchmarks and comparing them with present-day reality. Among those long-standing truisms nearly forgotten with the passage of time was the fact that in 1991 it was still called the Soviet Union. Before half of the following decade had passed, there would be commercial exchanges, manufacturing licensing agreements, wide open markets, and good fellowship all around for no-longer-communist Russia and the Commonwealth of Independent States (CIS).

What the helicopter community outside Russia and the CIS realized rather quickly was that the former Soviet states knew something — knew a lot — about helicopters. One could only wryly smile now, looking back at HAI Chairman Fred Moore's exhortation at the

Bell 412

beginning
of the decade that
the industry should
develop new markets.
Little could anyone have
guessed that Russia and 12 new republics would be happy to
take that advice! The distant fallout from changes in the global
scene would come back to haunt the commercial helicopter industry in
many countries.

Russia and its political predecessor, the Soviet Union, had run
Mi-17 helicopter passenger services almost as if they were city
bus lines, going from helistop to helistop in some regions and
picking up or discharging passengers who seemed to think nothing of it. This was in
addition to Russia's continuing widespread use of helicopters in agricultural, logging, and remote-area
support applications for just as long as the Western nations had been using them.

Russia's helicopter industry, in fact, responded better than other Russian industries to the collapse of the
Soviet Union simply because it had a more marketable product. The huge Mi-26 was clearly a very robust
machine and with proper marketing could put an entirely new face on global competition for heavy lift capacity.
Five of these aircraft were, in fact, bought by Skytech in Belgium and offered for jobs in fire fighting and other
heavy lift anywhere in the world.

Western ideas and styling were introduced into some Russian helicopter models, while other designs were
started from scratch to capitalize on newly opened Western markets. The coaxial-rotor Kamov Ka-32 was one
such example, others included Kamov's single-turbine Ka-115, a light-twin Kamov Ka-226, the Kazan light-twin
ANSAT, and still others expected to appear as Russia's industry reshaped itself. Kamov also set up the Russian
Helicopter Company to handle sales and marketing of its aircraft.

Mil-Brooke Helicopters, a Miami-based firm, became a support organization for Mil Helicopters, including the
establishment of a support and overhaul center for Mil aircraft in North Africa, where an estimated 400 Mi-2,
Mi-6, Mi-8, Mi-14, Mi-17, Mi-24, and Mi-35 types were operating, along with those in the Middle East. The
problem encountered by Mil-Brooke was one familiar to operators everywhere: no spares availability and poor
factory response to parts orders and communications.

Pratt & Whitney of Canada formed a Russian company called Pratt & Whitney-Rus to replace a joint venture it
had had with the Russian engine manufacturer Klimov. One of its first programs was to develop and certificate
the Pk206 engine intended to power Kamov's single-engine helicopter, the Ka-115. Other Kamov designs used
U.S.-designed engines, some of which were built in Russia. The Russian industry was slowly pulling itself out of
the political and economic turmoil of the early 1990s.

Therein lay the political-economic rub, as Western operators and governments said to themselves. The Soviet
Union was gone and in its place was a powerhouse of manufacturing, if only it could reorganize and focus itself
quickly enough.

Did You Know?

FAA in the 1990s
 In February 1991, the FAA
replaced the NAS plan with the
more comprehensive Capital
Investment Plan (CIP). The
deployment of new Terminal
Doppler Weather Radar systems
were implemented; Global
Positioning System satellite
technology was started.

1991 - Operation Desert Storm launched against Iraq by the United Nations •

More immediately relevant to commercial operators, however, was the size of the existing Russian fleet and the leverage that Russia could bring to bear in disposing of its surplus helicopters to small and developing countries.

Demonstrated safety was another matter.

Significantly absent was any certification of assurance of airworthiness of these aircraft. Russia had not negotiated bilateral airworthiness agreements with other large nations. Such agreements are the cornerstone of international commerce and trade in aviation.

Another unshakeable historic benchmark was the Bell 47 helicopter, first certificated in March 1946. More than 45 years later, at the Paris Air Show in June 1991, it was still necessary for the Federal Aviation Administration (FAA) to warn aviation interests around the world to beware of bogus spare parts for this workhorse, especially rotor blades. Taking for granted the aircraft's longevity and its ability to do the job was one thing, but it was clear that eternal vigilance could well be the price of staying alive.

Why the continuing problem with bogus spare parts for this old workhorse? Because there was a demand for them.

There was a more justifiable demand for the genuine article.

More than half a century after the Bell 47 was certificated, HAC Inc. of Pasco, Washington, introduced its new high-technology HAC-47-3 tail-rotor blade for the Model 47. It was an advanced composite blade of graphite and kevlar, using a new NASA airfoil with a swept tip. It also boasted a 4,000-hour life compared to the original item's 2,400 hours.

Thinking about the industry that had begun as modestly as the Bell 47 and was now developing civil tiltrotors — while still designing new blades for that very first machine — one could only shake one's head and marvel.

In the United States, government policy shifted once again as a consequence of that Christmas Day change in the Cold War in 1991, when the Soviet Union ceased to exist. The U.S. government continued competing with its own private industry despite periodic signs that the private sector had caused the practice to stop. Even as the century was on the verge of transition, the federal Military Assistance to Safety and Traffic (MAST) was still flying missions in competition with the industry after more than 25 years. The notion that something is "free" dies hard.

HAI had tried to tell the federal government that if it would only let private industry do the job, the MAST units could return to their proper military duties. By the late 1990s, MAST units had gradually declined in number from 29 to 14, which is what HAI had argued would happen because the military approach could not supplant the commercial services in all their complex facets.

The irony was that this recurring malevolence of government competing with private industry took place repeatedly in a nation that billed itself as the beacon of free enterprise. Not only did the federal government practice the destructive policy, but many states also decided that services provided by government helicopters are "free."

The massive 1980s-1990s changeover of military helicopter fleets from older technology aircraft such as the UH-1 to the newer UH-60 family — as well as the general reduction in numbers of military aircraft — made

Bilateral airworthiness agreements . . . are the cornerstone of international commerce and trade in aviation.

1992 - Largest shopping mall in U.S. opens in Minnesota • First interactive movies introduced •

McDonnell Douglas MD Explorer

New, license-built, and resurrected helicopter models continued to appear through the 1990s, notwithstanding the problem of military surplus helicopters around the world, and Russia did not represent the only new influence in the marketplace. Manufacturers continued to start up or expand their activities beyond the licensing of manufacturing rights to existing helicopters. Agusta expected to certificate its light-turbine A-119 Koala design in late 1997, and Westland resumed work on its WG-30, which many observers thought had been discontinued in the 1980s. The civil EH-101 was flying well into the decade, having been brought to market by the Agusta/Westland partnership. Mitsubishi added its own new product, the MH2000 twin-turbine, medium-lift helicopter, to its manufacture of U.S. helicopters. The aircraft uses a pair of Japanese MG5-100 turboshaft engines. Bell Helicopter joined forces with Korea's Samsung to build the Model 427, and signed an agreement with Norway's Helikopter Service A/S to develop an offshore-support version of the Model 609 tiltrotor.

Some manufacturers began to design and produce indigenous aircraft, including IPTN (formerly Nurtanio) in Indonesia, Helibras in Brazil, and Hindustan Aeronautics in India. Their governments' encouragement was based largely on the desire to foster indigenous industries and raise the skill levels of workers throughout their society.

The phenomenon of introducing new aircraft in the midst of economic uncertainty could also be seen within the United States, where Kaman took its proven intermeshing rotor system and applied it to the single-seat K-MAX for utility lift missions. Helipro Corp. brought out the S-61 Short, a modified Sikorsky model intended specifically for offshore support and heavy lift work. Schweizer Aircraft introduced its Model 330SP with a three-abreast seating configuration and a single turbine engine to try capturing the appealing light turbine market.

It was with some sense of irony that the industry that had been taken aback in the 1980s over the U.S. Coast Guard choice of a French helicopter using American engines now heard virtually the reverse. Sikorsky announced in 1997 it was halting production of its Pratt & Whitney-powered S-76B and offering the market only its S-76C+ . . . which is powered by a French Turbomeca engine. Not only did the Sikorsky production line switch to the French engines, but Keystone Helicopters was chosen by several operators to convert their S-76 models to that same French engine.

Diversification in order to acquire technology or expertise not already in hand is a classic business strategy, so just as General Motors had bought a share of Soloy Conversions in earlier years, Toyota Motor Corp. now acquired a 76 percent stake in Japan's largest commercial operator, Aero Asahi Corp. The surveying technology of Asahi, which had about 88 helicopters and 12 airplanes in its fleet at the time of the sale, was reportedly of interest to Toyota, and the automobile maker wanted to expand its aircraft business in any case.

Other makers of hardware also bought operating companies to hedge their economic bets, as did Air Methods when it acquired Mercy Air Services and entered the air medical field. Joint ventures and diversification became the order of the day as large corporations — many of which had once been three or four smaller corporations — tried to share pieces of a smaller, more complex technology pie.

Kaman K-MAX under construction

thousands of helicopters "available" for disposition. If the Soviet Union had gone, with it went the threat that required such a large U.S. military helicopter fleet. As if that were not enough, Russia saw a huge world market for the innumerable helicopters still in its own military inventory, with the result that multitudes of Mi-8s, Mi-17s, and other transport helicopters appeared in service around the world.

No one would have rejected the Christmas gift of 1991, but still. . . . The massive problems facing the helicopter industry in the 1990s, therefore, included the huge glut of surplus military helicopters on both sides of what was once called the Iron Curtain. The threat to established manufacturers was obviously the threat of lost sales due to the surplus aircraft. The threat to commercial operators was the not-so-obvious threat of very dubious safety standards. There was not only commercial business involved when foreign interests used surplus aircraft (whether or not the users were qualified) but also the question of whether the helicopters were assuredly safe. The two superpowers distributed excess and surplus military helicopters to other nations and to local jurisdictions within their own countries . . . extremely "penny-wise and pound foolish."

Aircraft of any kind used by a government entity within the United States are called "public aircraft." Since the passage of the National Aviation Act of 1926, public aircraft are exempt from laws concerning maintenance, airworthiness, safety standards, and other requirements, including the qualifications of the pilot. Surplus military aircraft that are turned over to a local government fall into this category.

As the 1990s progressed, an estimated 6,000 airplanes and helicopters had become designated "public aircraft" in the U.S., either commercially bought or military surplus models. Most are helicopters used by federal, state, or local law enforcement, medical, agriculture/forestry agencies, or other civil government operations. All are exempt from compliance with Federal Aviation Regulations regarding airworthiness and certification, and in most instances the pilots of these aircraft are not required to hold an FAA-issued pilot's license. This may have been workable in 1926 when the entire "public aircraft" fleet numbered a few biplanes, but 1996 was a different world!

To be sure, common sense dictates that many government agencies ensure that their aircraft are safe and safely flown, but as the wag once noted, common sense is not very common.

An example of a local government attitude when confronted with an obvious violation of "common sense" safety standards was the case of California's forest service and its aircraft fleet in the late 1980s and early 1990s.

Government documents obtained by the Associated Press (AP) under federal and state public records acts in 1993 revealed that FAA had restricted an aerial tanker used by the California Division of Forestry (CDF) to test flights over unpopulated areas of Arizona in 1988 and 1989.

It was officially designated an experimental aircraft by FAA. "We like to keep experimental aircraft in areas where they pose the least possible danger to people on the ground," said an FAA spokesman in explaining the rationale for the restrictions placed on CDF's operation. AP found, however, that CDF awarded contracts for the aircraft to be flown as a fire fighting aerial tanker during both of those years within California. FAA subsequently launched an investigation of the violations.

When CDF officials were questioned about their acknowledged violation of FAA safety restrictions on the tanker, a CDF official said the department had declared the plane exempt from FAA restrictions in both years because federal assessment of the tanker was slow and it was needed for fire fighting in California. CDF said under federal law and court precedent the state can exempt its aircraft from FAA rules. "We put that plane to good use saving lives and property in California. We wouldn't have flown it if we had any concerns about its safety," the state agency said.

Such a statement by a private-sector aircraft operator in the same circumstances would result in charges of criminal negligence, yet such off-the-wall government operations are rather common. The double standard is not hard to discover as FAA continues to heavily penalize commercial operators for much less egregious violations. The agency fined one operator $10,000 for failing to notice smoke coming from the engine of an MD-500 when a subsequent flight required an emergency landing. Another operator was fined $15,000 when its mechanics removed and cleaned the wrong magnetic plug after a warning light illuminated and a subsequent flight required an emergency landing. In neither case were there any injuries.

The "common-sense" standard is definitely not standard among operators of "public aircraft" but woe to the private-sector operator who trips over a regulation.

It was quickly realized at HAI and other responsible aviation organizations that the problem of "public aircraft" was neither small nor theoretical. The dumping of many thousands of helicopters from both superpowers into the world market would unavoidably create havoc, not only with private-sector balance sheets, but with international standards of safety that all aviation groups had struggled so hard to develop and maintain.

China became an unwilling case in point for the relationship between substantial increases in aircraft and the vital topic of safety.

China's air passenger traffic grew by 33 percent in 1992 and the Xinhua news agency said the country's total number of passenger aircraft reached 340 in 1993, up 27 percent over 1992. The rapid increase in civil aviation led to increased risks as over-burdened airports and air traffic controllers struggled to handle the boom.

A high-priority program was designed to triple China's airport capacity to handle an estimated 180 million passengers yearly by the end of the century. In 1995, China's airlines accommodated only 53 million travelers, and even that was an increase of 34 percent over 1994. The year 1994 was in turn an increase of 33 percent over 1993, so the trend was both clear and alarming in terms of capacity and safety.

That period saw the worst year in Chinese aviation history as a series of crashes in a four-month period killed 276 people, many of them foreign tourists.

The similarity to thousands of military surplus helicopters being dumped into a civil airspace system could not be missed.

Several members of the U.S. Congress introduced legislation to deal with the problem, notably Senator Larry Pressler (R-SD) and Representative Robert Menendez (D-NJ), and their objective was clear: As the world enters a new millennium, it needs a single standard of aviation safety. There is no such standard as long as surplus military aircraft from many designers, nations, and quality-criteria continue to appear in civil operations, and there is no such standard when so many aircraft are exempt from the law. The wider problem ballooned outside national borders and became a UN matter.

The International Civil Aviation Organization (ICAO), an agency of the United Nations, expressed great concern over the deterioration of international safety standards, which are based upon bilateral and multi-lateral agreements. A complex set of standards had taken many years to perfect, especially regarding airworthiness and certification. In the cascading events collectively called the end of the Cold War, the set of standards was in danger of collapsing.

ICAO found the following problems in some unnamed countries, describing in uncomfortable detail the circumstances into which countless surplus military helicopters would be injected: ". . . serious deficiencies in safety oversight at dozens of national aviation authorities . . . [in] 45 nations, none identified . . . [especially] in three areas: programs of supervision and certification, national laws and regulations, and personnel qualifications and financial resources. . . . The most serious finding was a lack of qualified personnel in various countries tasked to carry out safety oversight. In most cases, the civil aviation authority designates an inspector. . . . The designated inspectors usually carry out the task under little or no government supervision. Inadequate funding of civil

A double standard of a different type is used by government agencies regarding helicopter flights over certain parks and other scenic areas. Commercial operators must constantly adhere to flight restrictions based on perceived noise and environmental impact, while federal officers using boats with outboard motors patrol the rivers in those same parks. Noise and oil seepage from an outboard engine is not considered in the same light as that from a helicopter. While trying to prevent "flight-seeing" operations over national parks, the federal government had no hesitation in contracting for private helicopters (in addition to a pair of National Guard UH-60s) to evacuate 400 people from the floor of the Grand Canyon when floods threatened an Indian village. The National Guard helicopters were unable to maneuver in the narrow lower canyon areas, so private operators were asked to bring in JetRangers.

The message to commercial operators from their government seemed to be: When we need you, we want you immediately and we want you fully prepared; when we don't need you, go away.

Around-the-world helicopter flights have an appeal that is shared by few other communities.

Two British teams accomplished the feat in 1997, one flying a piston-engine Robinson R44 and the other a turbine-powered McDonnell Douglas MD 500D.

Jennifer Murray and Quentin Smith flew the R44 through 28 countries in 97 days on their 30,000-mile trip, while Mike Smith (Quentin Smith's father) and Steve Good flew the 500D around the world via the North Pole and landed at their starting point in Seattle, Washington, about 13 days after starting.

How did Mike Smith and Steve Good do that?

By flying east from Seattle to Maine, then to Greenland and up the 16th meridian to the North Pole, down the 28th meridian and across Spitzbergen to England, then a diversion to the European continent, back across the Atlantic to the U.S., and on to Seattle.

That route satisfied all the requirements of a round-the-world trip by crossing all meridians, even though it eliminated most of the Eurasian land mass. Economics, technical requirements, and strategy forced them to find some way to avoid Russia.

Smith and Good looked at the 1996 around-the-world dash of Ron Bower and John Williams, who took the second Bell 430 ever built and zipped around the world in 17 days, and decided they could better that time.

By choosing their route carefully, they did beat it with a time of 13 days, 13 hours, and 40 minutes, totaling 230 flight hours to cover 19,982 miles.

And you always thought the earth was about 25,000 miles in circumference.

---

aviation authorities and lack of proper authority to hire, train, and compensate inspectors and support staff are other critical problems."

The report continued: "Only 31 percent have authority to refuse, revoke, or amend an air operating certificate; and a scant 20 percent of the aviation authorities have a requirement for the exchange of mandatory airworthiness information. In the legal and regulatory area, the analysis revealed that aviation authorities are established in three-quarters of the 45 countries, but only about half were properly constituted. Just 22 percent of the 45 authorities have adequate staffing and qualified inspectors; only 29 percent are adequately funded and 13 percent have adequate inspector training, and 18 percent have established a system for certifying and inspecting aviation training centers.

"About a third of the 45 nations have issued a set of basic aviation laws that can be and are amended and revised. Less than half of the aviation authorities have a code of air navigation regulations that establish operating rules for an aviation authority, and less than a quarter have an amendment procedure. Some 42 percent of the nations have regulations and orders on operations, but only 22 percent have enforcement provisions in place and 29 percent have an appropriate content and amendment procedure."

This was the real world into which thousands of ex-military aircraft, many of which were not airworthy or were of uncertain safety standards, were being dumped. The initial condition of the aircraft at the time of turnover was not the only consideration; ongoing maintenance is always necessary to retain the required safety parameters. Also the record-keeping procedures of military and civil maintenance facilities are not compatible.

ICAO teams performed safety assessments under a 1995 ICAO Assembly resolution which called on the organization to be more effective in dealing with such issues as privatization and globalization, both of which mushroomed into huge problems with Cold War changes. The nations evaluated were only those volunteering to be examined, and one could only wonder how many knowingly unqualified nations would offer to be tested.

The topic of safety was not so ambiguously treated in the helicopter industry, where critical decisions on safety are made at the top. Addressing a major national conference that drew attendees from across the aviation spectrum on the topic of safety, PHI's CEO, Carroll Wilson Suggs, said: "Safety is a strategic decision. It must be treated as a strategic initiative." She said improvements in aviation safety are blocked by the tendency of many corporate and government leaders to ignore potential problems and punish those individuals who try to bring problems to light before an accident occurs. She said they must identify safety as the true top priority of their organizations and refuse to subvert it to finances or schedules.

The official U.S. rotorcraft population when Matthew Zuccaro became HAI chairman in 1990 was about 11,220, and when Robert D. Fox took over the top job in 1991, the official registration at HAI's HELI-EXPO nearly equaled that number at 10,150. These fleet numbers, from FAA's registry, included certified, as well as experimental, home-built, and inactive machines. The industry's collective voice was gaining strength each year, and it used that strength to press for safety programs, maintenance and defect reporting systems, reduction of operating costs, and enhancement of profitability for the hard-pressed operators.

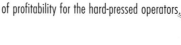

Robert B. McNab of Edwards & Associates took over the HAI chairmanship in 1992 and oversaw a continuing industry truism: the HAI HELI-EXPO was the forum in which to make major new industry announcements. The debut of American Eurocopter was announced at the HELI-EXPO, as were the introductions of the Kaman K-MAX heavy-lift utility helicopter and the Sikorsky S-92 airline-style transport helicopter.

The manufacturers get the huge majority of news media attention at any aviation show and during all the days in between. It is the operators, however, who make up the backbone of the industry. Without them, there would be no point to anything, and the manufacturers would be merely military suppliers.

Two terms were used with increasing frequency by the media in the late 1980s and well into the 1990s: Pacific Rim and emerging market.

Though a chill came over references to China in 1989 after the Tiananmen Square incident, those two interlocking terms resurfaced with increasing warmth as the 1990s progressed, until the later years of the decade saw almost the same change regarding China as had occurred with regard to the Soviet Union.

"Pacific Rim" seemed to go together with "emerging market" even more harmoniously than regards Russia, which has been the runner-up for a long time because Russia's financial health is less rosy than Asia's, or even China's.

As late in the decade as 1996, the official Xinhua news agency reported that China would invest heavily on modernizing its airport infrastructure and would build 12 new airports by the year 2000. In addition, around 100 airports would be overhauled as part of a plan costing a total of $5 billion.

China, more than most other countries, had aggressively pursued joint-venture and license-production agreements with American helicopter manufacturers.

Talk about an emerging market in just a few years.

Eurocopter's first production version EC-120B Colibri, a cooperative project of Eurocopter (61 percent), China's CATIC (24 percent), and Singapore Technologies Aerospace (12 percent), first flew in late 1997 after the first production airframe was delivered from Harbin, China, by CATIC, which was responsible for producing the entire fuselage structure. More than 100 orders were received for the light single-engine helicopter before it ever flew.

Then there was Vietnam, described by travel agencies as "a nation re-emerging on the world stage." Political progress and the restoration of international air services hastened Vietnam's rebirth.

Vietnam and Britain's John Laing International signed a deal to build a new multi-million dollar passenger terminal at Hanoi's Noi Bai airport to help with anticipated economic expansion based largely on tourism.

Promoters of tour packages said they anticipate that many American veterans of what the Vietnamese call "The American War" would be interested in helicopter flightseeing of old battlefields. It seems only a matter of time before some helicopter production activity occurs as the Vietnamese economy looks for high-technology infusions.

Agusta 109

1993 - Janet Reno becomes the first female attorney general • Movie 'Jurassic Park' debuts •

Most helicopter operators in the earliest days of the industry were one-aircraft enterprises, while toward the end of the 1990s, it is more likely that they are large corporations for whom the entire world is an operating arena.

An example is Era Aviation, as described by Carl Brady, who himself began as a one-helicopter operator in the late 1940s. In 1997, he said, "Era Aviation has several subsidiaries, including Era Helicopters, Era Aviation Services (which makes auxiliary tanks for Bell 212s), Era Aviation Center, where we service itinerant aircraft as well as our own. . . . Then we have an airline, Era Aviation.

"We go to Russia to pick up medevac people. We operate a Learjet for the local hospital under contract, and have a BO-105 for close-in problems. We've got 10 bases in Alaska and 20 in Louisiana. The Era fleet is well over a hundred helicopters and 22 fixed-wing airplanes; two Dash-8s; five Convair 580s; and 12 Twin Otters. Most of them are on the airline or charters. We have two DC-3s for sightseeing. They're old planes and need a lot of maintenance. We call the pair of them The Fun Division.

"This industry has seen some interesting people. Jim Ricklefs sold some of his equipment, I think . . . in the 1960s. He's now retired in San Francisco and rebuilds classic airplanes, like Jennys. He's a hell of a nice guy but he was a fierce competitor. My only claim to fame is that I taught Carl Agar how to fly a helicopter. Chuck Johnson is president of Era now. I hired him in 1968 or 1969 right out of the Vietnam [War]. Now he's running the company and doing a good job."

Era had bought about half interest in KLM Helikopters before eventually selling it to Schreiner Airways, and that was just about the time that North Sea refurbishment projects were nearing completion. The technology of oil field production made a big difference in the economics of support helicopter operators.

It is not possible to separate the fortunes of helicopter operators from the fortunes of the oil/gas industry. How does one refurbish an oil field and not ensure helicopter operators more years of work?

In seven years, the Brent oil field in the North Sea was overhauled and was coaxed into giving up more of its oil and gas than would normally have been the case. Shell Expro rebuilt three giant North Sea platforms while hydrocarbons continued to flow beneath them and converted the mainly oil-producing field to a long-life gas reservoir.

MBB BK 117 Space Ships

The $2 billion project by Expro, operating in the North Sea on behalf of Royal Dutch/Shell Group has extended Brent's life to at least 2010. Helicopter operators like to hear those kinds of numbers.

In the Gulf of Mexico, commercial operators were buoyed by new leases sold to major oil companies, again ensuring years of offshore support work. In August 1997, oil companies paid $939.2 million in a record-setting federal auction of rights to drill for oil and natural gas in unleased sections of the western Gulf of Mexico, some located in waters more than 10,000 feet deep. Occidental Petroleum Corp. paid $8.1 million on a section relinquished by British Petroleum about 185 miles south of Cameron, Louisiana.

Gulf of Mexico deepwater projects are surging, largely by major oil companies with the cash to produce oil and gas and move it back to shore. Along with that surge will be a late-century surge in the fortunes of commercial helicopter offshore support work.

Virtually all the trade press attention for aircraft is devoted to the manufacturers whose names appear on the aircraft, and secondly to the makers of the engines.

Occasionally there will be references to avionics manufacturers, but that's about the extent of the trickle-down effect when it comes to saying who makes the helicopter work as efficiently as it does.

Enter the companies who build specialty accessories that are not part of the helicopter's standard equipment. The auxiliary fuel tanks, wire strike protection systems, visible fuel sight gauges, cabin heaters, special exhaust ducts, Emergency Medical Services quick change kits, popout float kits, cargo hooks, additional lights, special floorboards, and dozens of other products to enhance the mission capability.

They are not as well known as the airframe manufacturers, but many helicopters couldn't do the job without them. Even many professionals in the industry know the names but not necessarily what they provide.

Advanced Technology & Research, Aeronautical Accessories, Alpine Aerotech, Apical Industries, Keystone Helicopters, Mechanical Specialties, Onboard Systems . . . their names often don't say what such firms do; but if a helicopter crew ever needs one of these products in a pinch, it will be obvious that they do it well.

Take electronic news gathering as an example of new helicopter-accessory markets, new technology, and the economic contrasts over the industry's first half-century. The first Bell 47 models sold for about $25,000, and pioneering operator Jim Ricklefs says the manufacturer apologized for that "high" 1946 price. Now the camera system allowing television or film production crews to make aerial images as good in quality as ground-based images costs quite a bit more.

FLIR Systems Inc. (FSI) in Portland, Oregon, expanded its imaging technologies into TV news, and the company delivered 50 UltraMedia film/video units in 18 months, then FSI brought out a compact version called the UltraMedia RS. The units allow long-range, broadcast-quality video cameras in five-axis stabilized mounts, allowing news helicopters to operate at long oblique ranges when airspace over a news scene is closed. They can also be used in covert investigations. The units, $150,000 to $480,000 price range would have bought as many as nine Bell 47 helicopters in 1946.

Another camera system, by Geneva Aviation of Everett, Washington, mounts in the horizontal stabilizer of a helicopter and directs a lens toward the news gathering aircraft and the ground so that the viewing audience can see the helicopter that covers the news scene. Got the picture? There is virtually no application or market for which the ingenious innovators of the helicopter industry cannot find a successful tool.

And of course there are many other entities in addition to manufacturers that are absolutely necessary to the helicopter community: aircraft brokers, finance companies, flight schools, fuel suppliers, insurers, maintenance facilities, repair stations, and safety consultants, to name a few. Their professional efforts combine to make the helicopter truly vital and versatile.

"Three years ago we were in a desperate situation," said Siegfried Sobotta, co-president and chief executive officer of Eurocopter, describing the company's fortunes in 1993. "Now that is changing." The company took a measured approach to more production capacity, Sobotta said. In that regard, Eurocopter had much in common with other manufacturers trying to break the grip of a plateau economy. Eurocopter boosted production rates for the EC-135 twice in 1997 and geared up to a rate of 50-60 of the light twin-engine helicopters in 1998, up from an initially planned rate of 20-30 at the start of 1997.

Good times were beginning to show themselves again as the millennium approached.

With global competition becoming more ferocious, the bottom line was everything.

As HAI chairman and Sun Company executive Richard Salzarulo reminded corporations in his 1994 message, "Placing a finite value upon a person's time is not a new concept. Over the years, it has been determined that an employee, if cost-effective, is worth 5.5 times his salary. Therefore every hour of that person's time that is saved by traveling in a helicopter, as opposed to ground transport, saves the company 5.5 times that person's pay."

It was that entrenched notion of a "free" bottom line that kept the "public use" aircraft at the forefront of many Helicopter Association International battles when there were other deserving challenges to be met. Still,

the issue was a bread-and-butter item to commercial operators and HAI had little choice but to continue confronting various governments. Lest it be thought that FAA was happy about thousands of helicopters and airplanes being exempted from its regulations, the aviation agency certainly was not.

HAI chairman William Wells of Cascade Helicopters noted in his mid-decade message to the membership, "Pressure mounted during this time for changes to the FAA regulations. A battle ensued over rules regarding public use aircraft and compensation for flight time. FAA regulations had evolved over decades and were working. HAI was opposed to changing the rules without justification. So was the FAA. Friends were made and lost during this disagreement."

The latest segment of the industry to protest the use of National Guard helicopters equipped with special equipment was, interestingly enough, the law enforcement community. The Bell OH-58 Kiowas used forward-looking infrared systems and night-vision goggles to help spot drug trafficking activities. The concern of law enforcement interests was that the money required for the special equipment in the National Guard helicopters would eventually reduce the amount of money available for police aviation. The police agencies argued against using military helicopters in civilian roles. This was the position HAI had held for many years; finally others had seen that "free" can involve a very high price.

On September 2, 1996, Moslem rebels and the Philippine government signed a peace pact ending 24 years of war that killed 125,000 people.

On August 27, 1997, oil companies paid $939.2 million for oil and natural gas rights in the western Gulf of Mexico. A record 1,224 bids were made on 804 tracts, some in water more than 10,000 feet deep.

1994 - The "Chunnel," tunnel 148 feet beneath the sea floor, opens linking England and France •

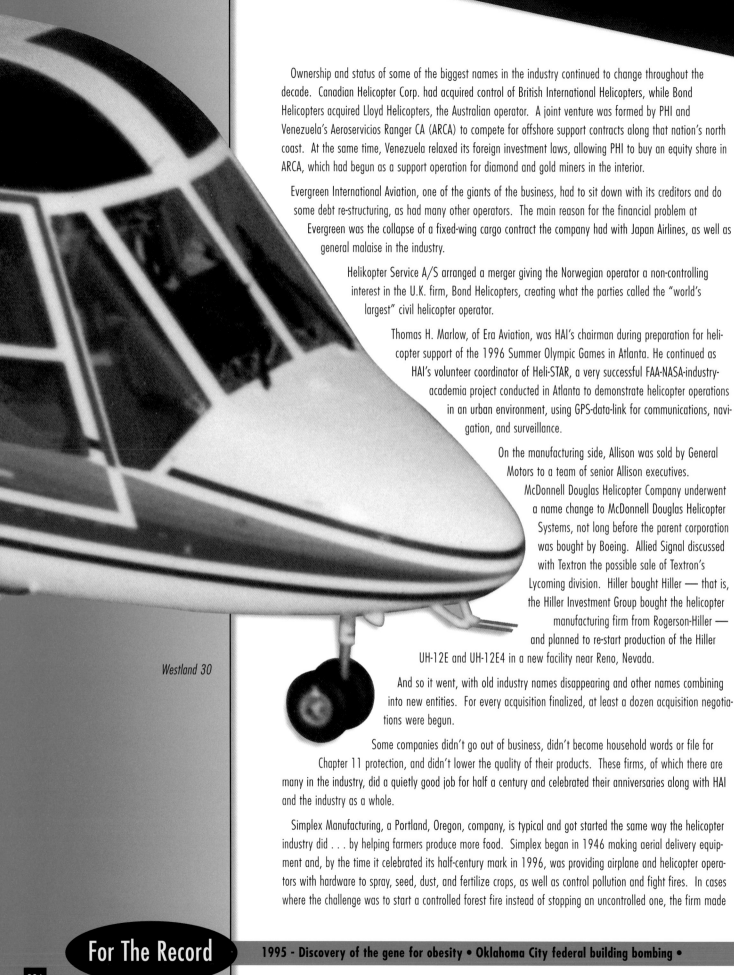

Westland 30

Ownership and status of some of the biggest names in the industry continued to change throughout the decade. Canadian Helicopter Corp. had acquired control of British International Helicopters, while Bond Helicopters acquired Lloyd Helicopters, the Australian operator. A joint venture was formed by PHI and Venezuela's Aeroservicios Ranger CA (ARCA) to compete for offshore support contracts along that nation's north coast. At the same time, Venezuela relaxed its foreign investment laws, allowing PHI to buy an equity share in ARCA, which had begun as a support operation for diamond and gold miners in the interior.

Evergreen International Aviation, one of the giants of the business, had to sit down with its creditors and do some debt re-structuring, as had many other operators. The main reason for the financial problem at Evergreen was the collapse of a fixed-wing cargo contract the company had with Japan Airlines, as well as general malaise in the industry.

Helikopter Service A/S arranged a merger giving the Norwegian operator a non-controlling interest in the U.K. firm, Bond Helicopters, creating what the parties called the "world's largest" civil helicopter operator.

Thomas H. Marlow, of Era Aviation, was HAI's chairman during preparation for helicopter support of the 1996 Summer Olympic Games in Atlanta. He continued as HAI's volunteer coordinator of Heli-STAR, a very successful FAA-NASA-industry-academia project conducted in Atlanta to demonstrate helicopter operations in an urban environment, using GPS-data-link for communications, navigation, and surveillance.

On the manufacturing side, Allison was sold by General Motors to a team of senior Allison executives. McDonnell Douglas Helicopter Company underwent a name change to McDonnell Douglas Helicopter Systems, not long before the parent corporation was bought by Boeing. Allied Signal discussed with Textron the possible sale of Textron's Lycoming division. Hiller bought Hiller — that is, the Hiller Investment Group bought the helicopter manufacturing firm from Rogerson-Hiller — and planned to re-start production of the Hiller UH-12E and UH-12E4 in a new facility near Reno, Nevada.

And so it went, with old industry names disappearing and other names combining into new entities. For every acquisition finalized, at least a dozen acquisition negotiations were begun.

Some companies didn't go out of business, didn't become household words or file for Chapter 11 protection, and didn't lower the quality of their products. These firms, of which there are many in the industry, did a quietly good job for half a century and celebrated their anniversaries along with HAI and the industry as a whole.

Simplex Manufacturing, a Portland, Oregon, company, is typical and got started the same way the helicopter industry did . . . by helping farmers produce more food. Simplex began in 1946 making aerial delivery equipment and, by the time it celebrated its half-century mark in 1996, was providing airplane and helicopter operators with hardware to spray, seed, dust, and fertilize crops, as well as control pollution and fight fires. In cases where the challenge was to start a controlled forest fire instead of stopping an uncontrolled one, the firm made

systems to do that, too. As if the helicopter industry was not specialized enough, Simplex also designed and built spray systems for blimps.

Like many providers of essential equipment to the industry, Simplex systems fit almost anything that flies including Bell, Hiller, Kamov, Eurocopter, McDonnell Douglas, and Kaman — no matter where in the world it flies.

Rod Kvamme, Heli-Jet Corporation, while HAI's Chairman 1996-1997, called upon the industry to continue its advances by flying to a higher standard.

As had other global politico-economic developments, the North American Free Trade Agreement (NAFTA) affected the industry significantly, but often indirectly. Helicopter logging operations were among the first to feel effects of the trade treaty, but caution was expressed by several operators who noted differences in airworthiness and regulatory issues. It promised to be a slow transition.

Neil Osborne, Air Logistics, became HAI's Chairman in 1997.

Other industry transitions also promise to be slow as the centuries change, and it remains to be seen whether commercial operators will benefit or suffer as a result of Europe's planned aerospace setup.

Eurocopter and other aerospace firms are established cross-border joint ventures, but the European industry still is highly fragmented, its analysts and critics say. European Community observers note that Europe's aerospace industry has nearly 7,000 companies, including about 40 medium-size and major firms.

Europe reacts only to great pressure from external forces, say European critics, and the U.S. initiatives that created giants like Lockheed Martin and Boeing/McDonnell Douglas have a strong psychological effect in Europe, where it is perceived that the newly formed U.S. industrial groups are vicious competitors. European consolidation is therefore picking up momentum and can be expected to become a strong reality.

Consumers and users of any product or service are often told that such massive corporate changes benefit the customer through "economies of scale." It remains to be seen how the fortunes of the helicopter operator emerge from recent trends.

New helicopters, new variants of existing helicopters, and new capabilities for helicopters all combined to give a boost to the demand for civil helicopters throughout the world. "Aviation Week" summed up the industry's probable future course — and simultaneously seemed to put the industry in its place — by pointing out that "the civil helicopter business, long the smallest segment of the aerospace industry, could experience pockets of sharp growth as new, highly capable models — especially the tiltrotor — enter service."

MD-500E

1996 - Clinton becomes first democratic president since FDR to win two terms ●

It was not hard to figure out that the helicopter industry was overdue for some good news, especially in light of new offshore oil and gas exploration and production activities in the North Sea and the Gulf of Mexico. Consolidation of business by several operators who joined forces also led to improved operating efficiency and financial results.

Sikorsky S-76C

The sales surge of the 1970s also meant that a large number of helicopters were now approaching 20 years of age in the late 1990s and represented the technology of an earlier era. Improvements in safety, operating efficiency, and lower direct operating costs were the order of the decade, coupled with improved stability and navigation avionics.

Every generation, whether machines or people, has a standard-bearer, even if that standard bearer is a statistical uncertainty. The technology standard-bearer of the 1940s was the Bell 47, hundreds of which were still

For The Record

1996 - Web TV introduced • The EV1 becomes the first electric commercial car •

flying as Bell Boeing rolled out their first civil tiltrotor near the turn of the millennium. The technology standard-bearers of the 1970s were the Sikorsky S-76, Bell 222, and the Aerospatiale Dauphin series.

It is generally conceded that all the manufacturers who took the road of civil-design-from-scratch models in the 1970s would not go down that road again. It was expensive for them, far more than anyone would have thought, and the payoff was simply not there to fulfill the projections.

But now that the first digit of each year was about to change from a 1 to a 2, what choices are available to commercial helicopter operators in terms of the tools of their trade?

The Bell Boeing Model 609 civil tiltrotor may be seen from a future vantage point as the technology standard-bearer of the 1990s. It may be a civil aircraft, but its parents were paid for by the military research and development budgets of the 1970s, 1980s, and 1990s. Applications for the civil tiltrotor will be created by the first operators of the 9- to 11-place aircraft after deliveries begin in 2001. Larger models are under consideration, including a 19-passenger commuter, which could take short-haul airline transport totally away from airports if the appropriate infrastructure can be created. The first Model 609 configuration offered by Bell Boeing would serve New York-to-Chicago segments quite well.

The $9 million Model 609 was introduced to the civil market with a 275-knot dash speed and 750-nautical mile range, a good search-and-rescue combination. Medevac applications are another obvious niche for the aircraft, and its range can be extended to about 1,000 nautical miles with auxiliary tanks.

While tiltrotor technology had the appeal of novelty and thus captured a large amount of ink and videotape of the news media, conventional helicopters were also doing better than in past years.

Bell had about 130 orders for its Model 407 as the industry's first half-century ended, and more than 50 orders were in hand for Bell's new light-twin called the Model 427.

By 1999 Sikorsky and its consortium partners expect to fly the first prototype of the new 19-passenger S-92 Helibus, which may replace about 350 aging S-61s. Sikorsky's production rate of 20 Model S-76s a year (at $7 million each) kept the offshore and corporate markets supplied with another workhorse.

Eurocopter's light-turbine single EC-120 is being manufactured in partnership with Singapore and China, to directly compete with the Bell JetRanger III.

McDonnell Douglas Helicopter Systems had its eight-place MD-600N in position for healthy sales at $1.25-million per copy and the firm was also making deliveries of the new MD Explorer light-twin.

At this writing, James T. Cheatham, Verticare, is HAI's Chairman-elect with term commencing July 1, 1998.

The first half-century of the commercial helicopter industry thus drew to a close, looking as different from its beginnings as it could possibly look in terms of both hardware and organizational structure.

Did You Know?

Fire season and other disasters give helicopters an opportunity to show their excellent capabilities to the general public by way of the media, despite the tragic overtones of those events. Just as fire, flood, and trauma bring out the excellence in emergency services personnel, so do those things bring out the best humanitarian attributes of the helicopter — the most useful tool in any emergency service inventory. Personnel need tools to do the job right.

During fire season anywhere in the world, transporting fire fighters (and sometimes rescuing them), dumping chemicals on the fire, and acting as the eyes of the fire boss, helicopters are absolutely unmatched for their ability to do the job. Year-round, helicopters set lookout towers in remote areas, check the dryness of trees, and maintain surveillance over campers and their fire-making activities.

Helicopters were first used for fire fighting in 1947 in California, when Rotor-Aids was approached by the Forest Service to provide a helicopter for aerial surveillance of the fire and to allow the fire boss to plan strategy.

By 1958, Okanagan was using a converted S-58 as a helicopter tanker in British Columbia to dump 225 gallons of water directly on fires. Later, more sophisticated systems for fire fighting accessories were devised. When the situation requires, a helicopter can also set a fire to destroy fuel that an uncontrolled fire might use.

Disaster planners know that most natural disasters on the planet are caused by water. There's either too much or too little of it at a given place. From the absence of water in fires and droughts to the abundance of water in floods and hurricanes, the helicopter can help re-establish the balance by bringing water to people or rescuing people from the water.

Some of the most dramatic rescues in the world have been broadcast on television: The Potomac River rescues after the Air Florida crash, lifting of passengers from burning passenger liners in Alaska waters, saving people trapped in the Manaus building of Sao Paulo, Brazil, — all these represent the helicopter's capabilities as one of mankind's most effective tools.

Helicopters didn't write that history; people wrote that history, using helicopters.

No longer a group of risk-taking entrepreneurial ex-GIs who bought a new-fangled machine with borrowed money and kept records in their back pockets, the commercial operator was, after 50 years, more likely to be a sizeable corporation with many millions in assets (and sometimes more in liabilities) operating all over the world.

Nor did the industry's collective voice remain static with a half-dozen visionary entrepreneurs sitting around an office table at the end of a day. At the half-century mark, Helicopter Association International had grown into a multi-million-dollar powerhouse of technical, financial, and political savvy that represented the industry well.

As HAI President Frank Jensen noted in his message to the membership, "HAI is the only aviation trade association having a major trade show, an annual, a magazine, and representing both aviation and small business interests." The association, he said, has members in 70 nations, and 20 percent of its membership is outside the United States.

In everything from communications with its own members to communications with the Congress and other government leaders, as well as that hard-to-define term "clout" when it matters, HAI had fulfilled virtually every promise made to its members.

HAI, in the final analysis, does not speak for helicopters . . . it speaks for the people who operate helicopters — the machine that had saved more than a million lives by the time it was 20 years old; helped raise untold amounts of food that otherwise would never have grown; helped bring ashore the mineral energy to heat, light, and operate an entire planet; doused innumerable forest fires; carried captains of industry across the landscape; and did more worthwhile jobs than many people would ever hear about. Clearly, what HAI has done for operators has benefitted the entire industry and all of society.

Looking at its history even briefly, it is remarkable what changes the helicopter industry has brought to the world in its first 50 years, and almost all those changes were for the betterment of people.

Helicopters didn't write that history; people wrote that history, using helicopters.

Sikorsky S-76
Flying passengers for Helijet

For The Record

PHI BO-105

PHI A-Star

HELICOPTER ECONOMICS

*If only a helicopter can do
a particular job, how relevant is cost?
And compared with what?*

Every aircraft has certain costs, whether the aircraft is used by or for the military, other government entities, commercial operators, or corporate or private owners. Among these costs are acquisition; fuel and expendables; pilots and other flight crew; maintenance, including parts and all ground support personnel; depreciation; and insurance. The last must be calculated, even if the operator is "self-insured," and includes insurance of hull (damage to the aircraft) and liability (any damage to persons or property that may be attributed to the aircraft).

Evaluation of the total cost of an aircraft operation vis-à-vis the benefits of such operation is not always understood and not always done.

However, someone, somewhere must pay for every one of the costs listed above, for every flight of every helicopter.

In the case of military or other government helicopter operations, all costs are ultimately paid by taxpayers. It is incumbent upon government managers and decision-makers to fully understand all the costs and to control and manage aircraft use such that minimal undue burden is imposed upon taxpayers.

In many cases, it may be much more cost-effective to contract with the private sector for necessary aircraft services. This option has several significant advantages: it reduces cost, enhances the tax base, and provides greater flexibility in aircraft, crew, and other aspects.

An example of such contracting out is the use of a commercial helicopter operator (Erickson Air-Crane) to remove and replace the Freedom Statue on the U.S. Capitol dome (see page 12) rather than allow the National Guard to do the job.

The contractor did a complete turnkey operation, including the correct type of aircraft and a highly skilled crew, with full insurance coverage, for $60,000 (1993 dollars).

ABC newsman Sam Donaldson challenged this expense as a waste of taxpayer money. Donaldson found out; however, that Texas National Guard helicopters had tried a dozen years earlier to remove and replace a statue from the Texas State Capitol, and were unsuccessful in all 18 of their attempts. The Texas National Guard was using Chinook helicopters, which are invaluable for many military and humanitarian missions, but not the one in question.

So it is often a matter of the right commercial helicopter versus the best "free" government helicopter available, especially when "free" is an illusion.

If only a certain type of helicopter can accomplish a necessary task, how relevant is cost? Furthermore, cost relative to what? If nothing else can do the job, a theoretical comparison is moot.

Running a commercial helicopter operation is a tough business. It is difficult to believe, reading the comments of pioneering helicopter operators, that they are speaking about the business in which they willingly — and usually joyfully — spent most of their adult lives.

Descriptions of the early days of the helicopter industry confirm what many other bits of evidence have revealed over the years: The early operators were persistent risk-takers and hard workers; they had good judgment, and supportive families, and they were survivors. One thing that comes through in talking with virtually all of them is that they were fierce competitors who fought each other in the business arena, then met at a Helicopter Association International (HAI) affair and had a cup of coffee together to laugh and swap stories.

Today's operators are a faster, globalized, high-technology, computerized version of the same breed.

The typical helicopter operator of the early years was neatly described in a Helicopter Association of America (HAA) report that conveyed in a nutshell the importance of the person and the machine. "The commercial operator is familiar with his parts inventory, the capabilities of the machines at his disposal, and takes an intense interest in every nuts-and-bolts aspect of his operation. He may be an adventurer at heart. But it is probable that he is tough to the core and has worked his way to affluence along a traditionally strenuous route, at least during the first four to five years of operation. Each operation is custom tailored to the needs of its market, and there are few common denominators to link one with another. Company structure, procedure, and financial policy vary markedly from one to another as a general rule."

It often seems that making money is almost a side-effect of doing what they enjoy.

How do commercial helicopter operators make money . . . if they make money?

The answer then and now is that making money in the helicopter industry is a never-ending juggling act. Machines run on fuel, people run on food, and businesses run on money. Two out of three will not sustain any industry — all three must be in the air, and the juggling must be constantly adjusted before success is in hand.

All industries have their risk-taking dreamers.

There could be no higher accolade for the businesslike performance of any commercial helicopter operator than that given to Chicago's Helicopter Air Service in 1951. At an award ceremony honoring the firm for two years of accident-free service, its insurance broker, Marsh & McLennan, told VP-Operations Wes Moore, "Not a copter has been scratched, the company's original financing has never been increased, the corporation has operated in the black since its inception, and quarterly dividends have been paid ever since flying operations commenced — all-in-all a most remarkable achievement."

In the earliest days of the fledgling industry, those words were not heard often. As Peter Wright told of his effort to start a new helicopter company in the late 1940s, "I started doing some costing and trying to get backers. Among the analyses I did, I found that hull insurance had gone up about 30 percent. . . . It might even have been more than that. When any of the investors I talked to got around to the subject of insurance, and I said it was that high, they all dropped the idea like a hot potato because they were familiar with insurance and they knew that those rates meant helicopters were a terribly risky business. I never did get it going at that time."

For the insurance companies of the day, the helicopter was just as much an unknown quantity as it was to the operators who tried to make a living with it, and the insurance companies intuitively felt that any aircraft that flailed those big rotor blades so close to trees, power lines, and other obstructions — such as the ground during agricultural operations — had to be a risky venture.

One of HAI's first involvements, in fact, came when the association was less than two years old, on behalf of a California commercial operator disputing an action of his insurance company. The association and the operator prevailed, but those early days of educating the financial and insurance communities were difficult throughout the industry. After a series of joint programs with the insurance industry over many years, HAI has succeeded in correcting much of the adversarial relationship of the early days when misunderstandings prevailed on both sides.

A major reason for the high attrition rate among early commercial helicopter operators was the difficulty of establishing the economic formulas for success when there was so little experience with this new flying machine and its various direct and indirect costs.

It was not known for certain then, but there is no single formula for success; there is no silver bullet. Only those outside the industry don't know that.

Hughes 500

"The work of the individual still remains the spark that moves mankind ahead."

Igor Sikorsky

233

The formula for success in the helicopter business varies according to the specifics of the job, the operator's overhead, the helicopter type, the location, the weather, any government agencies that may get involved, how reasonable the client is, the flexibility of the insurance carrier, how soon the mortgage is due, and many other considerations for which there is no appropriate space on the bid-estimating form.

Peter Wright, who got his start with Helicopter Air Transport (HAT) of Camden, New Jersey, described the dilemma of working with a machine having no track record: "In those early days, most estimates and rates were wild guesses. We made a little money — not very much — but setting rates was very difficult, and of course, once you set those rates, you were stuck with them. The manufacturers always give you some numbers on what things will cost, and if you don't know any better, you use those. The cost of spares went up sharply very soon. Every 25 or 50 hours we had to break the transmission open. Naturally, some of the operators' problems were simply bad judgment, not only low rates. It varied from operator to operator."

The key to success, however, was to be found in Wright's afterthought: "When the helicopter did work, however, it was very productive."

Jim Ricklefs tells of a conversation he had with Bell Helicopter president Dave Forman when he arranged to buy a pair of Bell 47s that had been repossessed. Ricklefs bought the used helicopters in 1947 because new ones were so expensive. He had been so impressed with the success of Armstrong-Flint Helicopters in California that he decided to enter the business himself.

"The new price of helicopters was $25,000. Dave Forman apologized profusely for this high price and told me that in a year or two after they got more production, the price would certainly go down. On Dave Forman's desk there was something ominous that should have told me to stay out of the helicopter business. It was a carafe of buttermilk. Every one knows the relationship between ulcers and buttermilk.

"I started in business with an invested capital of $40,000. By the end of the first year I had lost $20,000. The second year another $10,000. I started making money in the third year, just in the nick of time."

In 1948, Bell Helicopter had to drop the other shoe, and the price for a Model 47D jumped from $25,000 to $39,500.

It's hard for some people in the turn-of-the-millennium industry to visualize those early days when few people knew anything about helicopters, including the people who were making them and using them.

Joe Seward gave a graphic description of how a helicopter business evolved in the days when there was no assurance that success would come: "Roy Falconer and I had resigned as navy pilots to get into helicopters. We went into business as Rotor-Aids on March 9, 1948, when we took delivery of our first helicopter. The only application we really knew of was crop-dusting. Then there was a forest fire in Ojai, California, in September 1948 — and it's extremely mountainous country. Accessibility was next to impossible by road and they called on us to move people on the fireline. It had never occurred to us as an application. But eventually the crops were done and the fires were out, and there we were . . . pacing the floor.

"So I went down to Los Angeles in November 1948 and contacted the biggest chain of drive-in theaters and they gave us a contract to deliver Santa Claus to 27 theaters in the Los Angeles, Long Beach, Orange County area. We'd fly into the nearest vacant lot near the theater and dress up Santa Claus. That kept us busy during the Christmas season. Then it was back to agricultural work in the spring.

"What had whetted my appetite was the opportunity represented by the fact that [there] were only about a hundred helicopter pilots in the world when I got my license. I went back to my navy ship and told Roy about it so he went and got a license and we both quit the navy and started a helicopter business. It was a real gamble. We nearly starved.

"But that's what got people interested. That it was a new venture, helicopters were rare. In fact, when we moved to our first base in Ventura, California, the other women in the community looked at my wife like she was crazy to marry a guy who would fly a helicopter. Even up to 1950, we'd pay our mechanic first, then Roy and I would split what was left, and my wife and I actually turned in soda bottles so we could get the deposit money and go to a movie. There were several times I wished I hadn't resigned from the navy.

"I stopped wishing I hadn't resigned when we got an Army Map Service contract. We threw a big party in our hangar at Christmas time in 1951 because we had grossed a hundred thousand dollars. Until that year, our top gross had been around fifty thousand.

"The Army Map Service had realized the potential of helicopters and they had us mapping the entire state of Alaska. We mapped Alaska in the summers for four or five years. That's where we met up with Carl Brady of Economy Helicopters and Jim Ricklefs of Rick Helicopters, other operators on the job. Rotor-Aids would spray crops in California in the spring, map Alaska in the summer, fly Santa Claus in the winter, spray mustard weed, fight fires, and so on like that. . . . That was the sum and substance of the helicopter business in those days.

"In the early 1950s, around 1952-53, the oil exploration thing really got started. Until that time it was mainly seismic work. After the oil companies got into the seismic work, they discovered how easily they could move people around with helicopters. So the drilling rigs that were being placed offshore in Louisiana were that next big step. They started putting these rigs 10 to 15 miles out and the boat transportation was pretty slow and they had to pay the guys portal-to-portal pay. That started the offshore support business.

"Rotor-Aids got a contract with Humble Oil Company in 1956 in Louisiana, and at one time we had the largest helicopter passenger service in the world because we were carrying 15,000 passengers a month. Igor Sikorsky came down to observe our operation. The big difference with the oil business was that it was 365 days a year, versus the other jobs, which were seasonal. So we wound up primarily working on oil.

"That's how the applications developed, just as people discovered a need for the capability. When an application occurred to somebody, we'd try it."

Trying it, however, did not always ensure success.

Rotor-Aids developed into a sizable helicopter offshore passenger operation for production rigs in the early 1950s, but the seismic experts in the oil business had been using helicopters for quite a few years by then.

In the spring of 1947, barely a year after the Bell 47 was certificated for commercial operations, Helicopter Air Transport sales manager Peter Wright went down to Louisiana to introduce the oil industry to the new machine. A property owner had leased his marshland to an oil company but refused to allow marsh buggies to trek across it for fear of disturbing the muskrats. But the oil company's seismic contractor had to place gravity-meters throughout the area for exploration. What to do?

Enter a Bell 47B of Helicopter Air Transport, for which Wright had just made a deal to see what it could do. The first thing to be done was remove the wheels and replace them with floats for operation in the marshland. Writer Charles Deegan of "Oil & Gas Journal" reported on what he believed was "the first use of a helicopter for any purpose in the petroleum industry."

It is interesting to compare today's familiar ho-hum attitudes on the use of helicopters with the sense of wonder in Deegan's 1947 writing: "The speed of operations is amazing, an elapsed time of as little as five minutes having been recorded from one station to the next. The best record to date is 19 [gravity meter] stations in two-and-a-half hours." Deegan said the customer was elated to find that the helicopter — which Deegan described as "slow" and "expensive" — did the entire job at a cost one-third that of the cheap marsh

Did You Know?

As an example of the 1949 dollars involved in government contracting work, consider the Alaska surveying project of the U.S. Army Map Service let out for bids in April 1949. It required a two-place helicopter operating from Nome, Alaska, from May 15 to September 15, 1949. The job guaranteed 124 days and 250 flying hours. Bidders were required to put up a 10 percent bid-bond as well as a 50 percent performance bond.

The charge for one helicopter per day averaged about $125, and the hourly rate was estimated at $52.50. Total net price bid was listed as $25,745 after discounts.

The consensus among early helicopter operators is that the enterprise required good judgment, in addition to the willingness to take risks — and these were not always compatible.

Joe Seward tells of the most bizarre thing he ever saw: "We at Rotor-Aids had built a trailer to ferry the helicopter from job to job. In those days you could trailer them for 25 cents a mile, but if you flew them it would cost you a dollar a mile. The other operators were the same way.

"In 1951 there was a company out west that had one of the early Bell helicopters, the kind that were on wheels, before skids. The only reason for the wheels was so you could roll it out of the hangar, or move it around on the ramp, or whatever.

"The tires were therefore only two-ply and because of the light duty they were designed for, they had no tread.

"Well, in 1951 we trailered our helicopters up the Alcan highway to Alaska. We took off the tailboom and the main blades, as did other operators who worked up there.

"When we got back from Alaska, our next job was defoliating cotton in Bakersfield, California. We worked with Kern Copters, who got the jobs from the farmers and subcontracted them to us.

"So we were standing there at the airport alongside Highway 99 in Bakersfield, and that was the main artery from Northern California through to Southern California. We saw this truck coming down the highway towing this helicopter, not on a trailer, but on the helicopter's wheels. Right down the main highway.

"They were new to operating in Alaska, and they apparently came down on the boat from Anchorage to Seattle, then towed that Bell helicopter to their home base on the highway on those two-ply tires. We just shook our heads.

"So, about two weeks later, the head of the service department at Bell called me on the phone and asked if we had been having any trouble with the tires on our helicopter. When I said we were not, he told me that he was puzzled because another operator out our way had just ordered 12 sets.

"I don't believe that company is still in business."

buggies that had always set up the seismic stations, and in a fraction of the time. Such is the difference between the media and the guy who's paying the bills.

The difference was between $25 per station set by the "expensive" helicopter and $75 with the "cheap" marsh buggies; and when businessmen saw that bottom line, the term "expensive helicopter" became irrelevant. Wright noted later that the Bell 47B used on the job was down for 65 days out of the 93-day work period due to maintenance problems, but that was because the experimental operation had not been properly set up to deal with mechanical requirements. The actual maintenance downtime, he estimated, should have been closer to 15 days by today's standards. Even with those problems the Bell 47B was highly productive.

The rate for the helicopter was $75 hourly, with a guarantee of 80 hours per month. The monthly gross was therefore $6,000. Adding the cost of the geophysical crew, the total was $15,000 for the month. The final result still brought the often-grounded helicopter's cost in far lower than buggies moving at a speed of three miles an hour.

There were, therefore, many reasons it was so difficult for early operators to make a profit, not the least of which was that no one knew what kind of work to do with this new machine. The machine's potential was yet unknown, and so were its costs.

Often, operators will cooperate with each other for mutual benefit, as Carl Brady, Joe Seward, and Roy Falconer did when they formed Era Helicopters. Seward explains: "When we were flying for the Army Map Service in Alaska, Carl Brady of Economy Helicopters also had a contract with them. Occasionally, when we needed fuel, we'd fly to the other operator's camp because it was all army fuel. We met Carl Brady in his camp and took a liking to one another.

"Carl Brady pioneered winter work with helicopters in Alaska. We'd all go home but he would stay up there with his guys and fight the elements. Around 1957, Standard Oil of California came to Carl and wanted him to do some seismic work with a Sikorsky helicopter. He had never operated one. The biggest thing he had operated was a Bell. We at Rotor-Aids had been operating Sikorskys in the Gulf of Mexico as offshore support for Humble Oil Company.

"So we had the big-helicopter experience, but Brady had the offer of a job. Common sense being what it is, we got together, then took the initials from his company, Economy Helicopters, and the R and A from Rotor-Aids, and we formed Era.

"But still, we operated Rotor-Aids independently in California, and Brady operated Economy Helicopters independently on his crop-dusting business in Yakima, Washington. Era was strictly Alaska at that time when Brady, Roy, and I owned Era.

"We sold Era to Rowan Drilling Company in 1967, but that still left Rotor-Aids as a separate company outside the deal with Rowan. In the process, Brady remained with Era and Falconer and I elected to stay with Rotor-Aids. But then Rowan, which had bought Era, hired Rotor-Aids to operate two Flying Cranes on the North Slope."

Eventually, Rotor-Aids was sold to Evergreen Helicopters in 1979.

A lingering problem throughout the industry well into the 1970s was the difference in methods used to calculate costs. It caused frustration on both sides of the manufacturer-operator fence.

In one helicopter roundtable discussion, typical numbers were exchanged that show how far apart the parties once were; and though they are not yet using identical numbers, the gap has narrowed.

Bell estimated that it required about one maintenance hour per flight hour to keep a Model 47 operating. That included the 50, 300, 600, and 1,200-hour inspections. A major overhaul, said Bell, required about 300 hours. Unscheduled maintenance time was also estimated at about 300 hours. The manufacturer thus said maintenance should cost about $5 per flight hour. Engine overhaul time on the Lycoming VO435 was estimated at $2 per flight hour.

Not so fast, retorted Petroleum Helicopters, Inc.'s Bob Suggs.

"The thing you want to say is, be very careful how you accept manufacturers' figures. They are not all-inclusive — they purposely paint a very good picture. I don't blame them; they have a product to sell."

K-MAX

HAA President Cully Weadock of Chesapeake & Potomac Airways moderated the 1963 roundtable and noted that "direct expenses, as manufacturers visualize them, are limited to man-hours, parts cost, mandatory retirement items, and engine overhauls. Beyond that, we get into intangibles, which vary from operation to operation."

That exchange was typical of those between manufacturers and operators until it was eventually realized that they were using different "dictionaries" of terminology.

This problem was one of the stimuli for HAI and its industry partners to create the cost-estimating standard, the "Guide for Presentation of Helicopter Operating Cost Estimates."

As the industry's collective voice said at the time, "In recent years improvement has been seen in manufacturers' estimates, partly due to greater skill in extrapolating cost history from an expanding database of contributing operators, and partly due to the manufacturers' willingness to clarify the criteria used in estimating cost and the fact that not all cost information is available for the manufacturers to present."

What criteria are involved in helicopter operator cost estimates?

• Operating environment and climate

• Type of service

• Experience of the crew with the aircraft model

• Overall aircraft utilization

• Maintenance plan

As Carl Brady pointed out in his formula for success in the helicopter business today, "You can do it, but you need an awful lot of credit to get into the business. You know what a JetRanger costs, and that's about the smallest helicopter you can operate commercially anymore. They get more expensive as they get bigger, and I guess a Super Puma now costs between $12 and 15 million or even more. They get even more in spare parts . . . if you can get them."

Even the biggest and most efficiently run operators today often have some difficulty getting all the numbers right, but the picture is far more clear than it was in the 1940s. Analytical tools provided by HAI go a long way toward reducing some of the variables.

> On April 13, 1922, Senator Frank B. Willis said applying business methods to the federal government resulted in a savings of more than $4,000,000 a day.

From the outset there was a love-hate relationship between commercial helicopter operators and various agencies of the U.S. and state governments, and that mixed relationship continues today. Government agencies can be a source of contracts but are simultaneously a source of aggravation for operators trying to make a living within restrictive rules far from home base and probably farther from a profitable outcome.

The impact has been documented by helicopter consultant Andy Aastad, who projected a "major impact" by what he called "the mass intrusion of military surplus turbine helicopters" into the civil market.

Government agencies often launch internal air operations using "free" surplus military aircraft that impinge on both civil helicopter manufacturers and commercial operators.

There has never been a satisfactory explanation of how a helicopter costing so much for commercial operators to buy and maintain can be "free" to a government agency. Someone, somewhere is paying the costs, but this fact is often obscured in the rhetoric of something for free.

This is not a post-Cold War phenomenon, it has existed for many years and has been fought by HAI for many years. However, the sheer numbers of surplus military helicopters have increased from a trickle to a deluge, with more than 3,000 surplus U.S. Army helicopters being released.

"The operator is prone to financial limitations to which the military services and other federally funded agencies are not, as a rule, subject," wrote HAI in the 1970s, and the fact has not changed.

HAI has always been careful to draw a distinction between government competition in terms of doing commercial jobs — or injecting surplus military helicopters into what should be a commercial role — and those

*Air Logistics
Sikorsky S-76
approaching
offshore rig*

Jack Schweibold boards
a PHI BO-105

*Effective
marketing is
the usual key
to survival in
any business.*

legitimate government uses of helicopters such as law enforcement, military, and related missions like the Coast Guard. HAI truly believes in the rule of law and has always appreciated — and recognized — the contributions of its law enforcement members.

As HAI President Frank Jensen pointed out in an "Upfront" message, the "Rule of Law" involves at least two things relevant to the public aircraft situation. One is the recognition that government's job is to steer the ship of state, not to engage in competition with those who pay for that ship. Secondly, honesty — which Thomas Jefferson said is the essence of government — requires government at all levels to recognize when it is doing its job and when it is doing things that are not its job and that compete with its own taxpayers.

An example of government disregarding both these principles was the transfer of eight surplus OH-58 military helicopters from the federal government to the local government of the District of Columbia. The city had two certificated helicopters and a surplus UH-1, all of which were grounded because the local government could not afford to keep them flying. Despite this, the District succeeded in getting eight surplus army OH-58s, which were then sold for about $1.5 million. The transaction had all the trappings of a dealership in used helicopters, not that of a responsible government.

Privatization is one of the favored end-of-the-century buzzwords in the federal government, and would have great impact on commercial operations if its definition were clear and its application consistent with that definition. While President Clinton recommended a dozen privatizations in 1995, the Congress approved only three, and none were recommended to the next Congress. Increasingly, tasks that should be done by the private sector are being done by government agencies despite a drive to "downsize" the federal machinery.

In the private sector, as commercial operators struggled to find black ink for their business ledgers, the relatively small size of the industry made it difficult to generate sound business practices and strategies.

Helicopter Association International decided to do something about that and launched an annual series of management training courses. HAI, in concert with manufacturers' groups, also developed formulas and procedures for presenting helicopter operating cost estimates. This gave a commercial operator's marketing and estimating staff (which often were the operator himself) something to work with that was more tangible than wild guesses.

In 1970, Helicopter Association International held its first Helicopter Operators Management Course in mid-year and the course became a regular feature of HAI membership, being held in several countries around the world. Later in 1970, the association published its "HAA Management Guide and Operations Manual."

With the arrival of Frank Jensen as chief executive in 1982, the pace of providing more business training resources to operators accelerated, and before the 1980s had ended, HAI was scheduling a variety of seminars,

Did You Know?

Below are nominal 1985 hourly rates for several commercial operators in the Gulf of Mexico. Keep in mind that inflation and helicopter technology have a major influence on different rates charged. Actual rate schedules are very complex and contain many variables. The Bell 206B is the smallest helicopter currently operating in this capacity.

	Lowest Hourly Rate	Highest Hourly Rate
Bell 206B	$460	$575
AS-350D	$575	$575
Bell 206L	$575	$700
AS-355F	$660	$875
BO-105	$875	$980
Bell 222UT	$1,035	$1,120
Bell 212	$1,190	$1,750
Bell 412	$1,425	$1,550
S-76	$1,425	$2,300

courses, and workshops around its HELI-EXPO. A continuing effort to get helicopter operating costs under control was pressed by HAI in 1990 in developing an industry ratio for such costs.

Effective marketing is the usual key to survival in any business, and it often takes on some arcane features. To surround a business with the qualities that attract clients, there must be evidence of accomplishment, of an ability to do the job.

This evidence is often found in "being first" and that is a significant psychological factor in the marketing of helicopters or helicopter services. It should not be dismissed lightly as an influence on the prospective customer.

There are at least two facets to the question of who was first to do anything of note. There is the personal pride and recognition aspect, which most people intuitively understand, and there also is the marketing credential aspect. To be able to lay claim to being the first or the biggest or the oldest is to have a marketing edge. Potential customers feel more comfortable with a company having such credentials, and expert marketers know this.

Practical helicopters became available in the late 1930s, and were used in World War II. Immediately after the war, civilian uses of helicopters began simultaneously in several parts of the world. To positively name the "first of the first" is impossible. Thanks and congratulations to all of the pioneers.

A company can incorporate at the courthouse tomorrow morning but not begin operating for three or four years — after a new competitor has become active — leaving the way open for arguments about who was first. Or, suppose a brand-new operator has one brand-new helicopter made by, say, the Everflight Company and begins selling its services to a market sector where no other operators of Everflight helicopters are active, although lots of Bells and Eurocopters may be in that market. The new, one-helicopter operator can legitimately advertise itself as the world's oldest and largest provider of Everflight helicopter service to that market sector.

The service industry has made billions of dollars by knowing and exploiting the psychology of the customer. Helicopter operators must do no less, if they want to survive and prosper.

An example of this drive to have credentials was provided by Peter Wright, whose first job in the helicopter industry ended when Helicopter Air Transport went out of business in the late 1940s, leaving him as a sales manager with nothing to sell and nothing to manage. (He is not eager to yield the point on who was the first commercial operator, and the author of this HAI volume is prudent enough not to try sorting out all the possible claims to any "first.")

"Helicopter Air Transport was indeed the first operator, even though Leon Plympton's New England Helicopter Service might have been incorporated first. HAT bought the first three Bell Helicopters ever sold commercially, which were Bell 47Bs, and the first three Sikorskys ever sold commercially, which were S-51s."

Lee Plympton, however, says he was using an army surplus R-4 for agricultural work prior to HAT's startup, and his literature says he was the world's first commercial operator and had the world's first helicopter mechanic school. And so it goes . . .

Bell Helicopter literature on the Model 47D neutralizes the fact that Igor Sikorsky, Frank Piasecki, and Stanley Hiller all flew earlier than Bell's first helicopter by describing Bell as "Creators of the World's First Commercially Certificated Helicopter" and in another case "Still FIRST in the Commercial World!" There can be no argument because of the way the statements are phrased, and any company's marketing must exploit being first in any category that can be found.

Carl Brady described how and why he and mechanic Joe Beebe devised the first improvised skids for the Bell 47 when they were flying in Alaska. Vancouver Island Helicopters officials, however, reported that Alf Stringer, co-founder of Okanagan Helicopters, "was the first helicopter engineer to remove the wheels from a Bell 47 and replace them with what is now known as skid gear."

Such distinctions are made frequently by industry pioneers, whether it was who did the first oil industry seismic work, versus oil industry production work, versus oil industry offshore work, and so on. There is also the distinction of who did it first in a particular country, in North America, or in the world. It is a point of personal pride, as well as legitimate marketing advantage.

The critical point is the importance of marketing credentials, and being first is the first of those credentials.

With the industry becoming increasingly specialized, however, finding things to do first is not as easy as it once was.

Joe Seward remarked on specialties that once did not exist: "When I look around today, I think that there are so many applications that you cannot be in all of them. Now you have to pick a specialty within the helicopter business. When we started, it was THE helicopter business and you did everything. You can't do that now. When I look at how HAI has grown, I am so grateful they organized into committees, so operators can attend the appropriate part of their specialty within the helicopter business."

Costs of operations are among those things that keep commercial operators drinking buttermilk as an antidote for ulcers. Costs seem to be made of teflon, with no handles that an operator can firmly grip while struggling to calculate a competitive bid.

Andre Marsan, described as the "financial wizard" at Trans-Quebec Helicopters, put it well in the 1970s when Trans-Quebec operated 50 helicopters, and his analysis remains valid for almost any time period and any size operator. "The first mistake [a new operator] makes is to forget about the 1,200-hour overhaul. They get a turbine and start watching $280 an hour roll in and they spend it as quickly as they earn it. Then, when they get to the 1,200-hour overhaul, they have a cash flow problem. The second difficulty — and it's probably the same in other industries — is the profit curve. With one helicopter you can be profitable. With three helicopters, three pilots, and an engineer, you can be very profitable. The operator is one of the pilots, he can keep an eye on everything and direct his operation with a minimum of paperwork.

"But if you get five or six ships, the paperwork increases. You have to have a secretary and somebody to run the office. A couple of more machines, and there's an operations manager, a chief engineer, two secretaries, and an accountant. You find your gross going up, but your profits going down. In short, profits don't grow with the size of the fleet."

Aware that cost estimating of all kinds was critical to success of the operator, HAI pointed out: "Industry experience in recent years has certainly taught all of us two important lessons, i.e.:

"1. There is no such thing as a single representative cost of operations estimate that will suffice as serviceable for all operators. Drastic fluctuations in inflation, insurance costs, individual accident/incident history, skill of pilot and maintenance personnel, mission applications, and environment all serve to cause high variances in cost experience.

"2. 'The definition of terms is (truly) the beginning of wisdom.' The terms of costs (e.g., indirect cost, direct cost, and average cost) can mean many different things in different situations. They may seem contradictory, yet be entirely correct, depending on the facts and situations. It is extremely important that operators take the time, even absorb some expense, to come up with the most exact estimates, and to keep the most exacting cost records possible. The benefits to the whole industry through better cost awareness are as significant as the danger of treating costs, and cost estimates, too lightly."

The question of maintenance, both scheduled and unscheduled, has always been a major factor in helicopter operations. In one sense, the helicopter is a renewable resource whose components have a finite life. These "rotables" include main and tail rotor blades; main, tail-rotor, and intermediate gearboxes; engines, avionics, accessories, and other systems. Because these items can all be replaced on schedule, there is no real limit to the life expectancy of a helicopter.

The Maintenance Malfunction Information Reporting (MMIR) program is an example of an industry effort to make the most of such opportunities. The MMIR program, developed by HAI, enhances safety and reduces operating costs by sharing and automating the information available on service difficulties.

In fact, the regularity of scheduled maintenance and the reduction of unscheduled maintenance has led to the growth of an entire industry to provide maintenance, modification, and overhaul services to aircraft operators. Quite often, these are even further specialized into companies servicing main rotor blades, turbine engines, piston engines, gearboxes, avionics, and other systems.

Given the constantly escalating average age of the helicopter fleet, it is not surprising that the original equipment manufacturers (OEMs) and the user/rebuilder firms have shown great ingenuity and dedication in developing product improvements to enhance the utility and safety of the helicopter, extending its useful life well beyond what was originally contemplated. Some firms hold numerous supplemental type certificates (STCs) on helicopters. Each STC represents an item of supplemental equipment for use on a particular model of helicopter, and requires Federal Aviation Administration (FAA) approval. This is the category where wire strike protection systems, popout floats, visible fuel sight gauges, retractable doorsteps, and other add-on items can greatly boost the utility and value of the helicopter.

This sub-industry, so to speak, has more influence than might be initially apparent.

By 1994, the STC manufacturers had essentially turned the picture around and were responsible for directing the industry's course. It was a case, said Glenn Wonnacott, publisher of "Rotor Roster," in which "the technological tail wagged the dog."

"The year saw the certification, production, and deliveries of a number of new models. . . . Many of these 'new' machines were created as a result of a manufacturer recognizing the need for improvements, or, more amazingly, where a local shop had 'created' a different model with their own ingenuity, design, and construction talent."

Discussing hardware, marketing strategies, sound business practices, and other aspects of the business is all well and good, but without a foundation of safety underlying all of these, the operator has no business at all because flaws in safety have a way of catching up to all in equal measure.

To impress on the operating community at all levels how important the basic quality of safety is, HAI launched a program called "Safety Through Accurate Statistics" (STATS) in cooperation with FAA, NTSB, and the industry. The "Fly Neighborly" program by HAI was another effective effort to minimize noise complaints.

The availability of pilots is always a key issue in the industry. The helicopter industry — like the airline industry — has always depended on the military as a source of trained pilots. This situation varies occasionally, depending on several factors.

During the late 1960s and early 1970s there was concern that the large number of pilots emerging from the military were prone to risky flying — a skill they had sometimes been expected to display during combat operations — which had a clear impact on civilian insurance rates. As time passed, that problem was corrected.

As the 1990s come to an end, however, the concern is that the military-trained pilot pool is drying up because of a downsized military establishment. Some in the industry have been forced to lower the number of hours they require in order to meet their personnel requirements for pilots.

Commercial operators toward the end of the 1990s constituted about 64 percent of the total fleet, while corporate and private operators made up another 23 percent and the public service sector 13 percent.

Those 1996 figures change dramatically when the numbers of aircraft are taken into account. Commercial operators, for example, operate nearly 90 percent of the civil helicopter fleet and they expressed optimism about the future. There are two types of helicopters making up 85 percent of the commercial fleet: light turbine and light-to-medium twin-turbine helicopters.

Commercial helicopter operators can experience widely varying profitability, as Jim Ricklefs and others had discovered in the early 1950s. In 1995, for example, 23 percent said they were not profitable, while 19 percent were at breakeven, 26 percent were somewhat profitable, 16 percent described themselves as profitable, and an enviable 16 percent said they were very profitable.

By 1997, those who described themselves as unprofitable had dropped to 8 percent, the breakeven contingent came in at 11 percent, somewhat profitable was up to 35 percent, and the profitable and very profitable categories were at 26 percent and 19 percent, respectively.

Profitability, of course, varies with the type of operation. Those in agriculture, oil/gas, construction, and other industrial support applications generated the greatest revenue by a considerable margin at 64 percent of the total, while operators in emergency medical services generated 23 percent.

Profits are the positive side of the picture, but what were the costs to these same operators? More than half of total expenses of the operators went for two items: aircraft maintenance and personnel costs, each equaling one-quarter of the total operator costs.

Did You Know?

Sometimes being the first to do something is not an advantage.

Jim Ricklefs tells of a new operator who bought a Bell helicopter and was trained to fly it at the factory in Buffalo, New York, before Bell moved to Texas. He went back home to the Southwest and decided to pass along his knowledge to a pilot he had hired.

They got into the helicopter and he did a vertical autorotation like those taught at the Bell school. The new pilot-operator, however, completely forgot to allow for the difference in density altitude between Buffalo and the southwestern desert where he was based. The Bell 47 dropped out of the sky and compacted horizontally about three feet in a cloud of dust.

Bell removed vertical autorotations from its training curriculum.

The general rule of thumb in the industry has been that any helicopter that cannot be flown 500 hours a year in commercial operation should not be bought. Ideally, commercial operators try to sell helicopter time to customers in contracts of 100, 50, or even 25 hours — depending on the type of operation involved — so that the operator is ensured utilization of the aircraft and the customer gets a price break for the bulk purchase.

An interesting fact emerging from the HAI 1996 survey of operating performance was that 26 percent of the commercial operators had unproductive helicopters. These were idle or parked aircraft that had been out of service for at least six months. Reasons varied from excess capacity at 31 percent (73 percent for U.S. operators) to seasonal markets at 25 percent and insurance costs at 17 percent. Whatever the reasons, such idle helicopters amount to a great loss of revenue for the operator and of potential service for customers. The reasons are compelling, however, and represent some of the hazards of being in the business.

Aside from the obvious cost categories of initial acquisition of the helicopter, fuel, pilot, maintenance, and spare parts for airframe, engines, avionics, accessories, and special-mission equipment, commercial helicopter operators also must make allowances for the following, which are collectively called "contingencies":

- Deductibles on insurance claims
- Lost revenue due to aircraft downtime
- Incorporation of manufacturer service bulletins or FAA airworthiness directives
- Allowance for crew sick leave, overtime, and other special labor costs
- Lawsuit expenses not covered by insurance
- Environmental impact on the aircraft (e.g., corrosion, cold weather damage)
- Unanticipated expense arising from new government regulations
- Transportation costs and commissions
- Information services

- Special tools and ground support equipment
- Support vehicles and other support facilities required
- Catastrophic failure not covered by warranty or insurance
- Replacement aircraft rental cost while awaiting repairs
- Personnel recruitment and training costs due to turnover
- Supplier price increases and inflationary influences
- Various government taxes, fees, and licenses

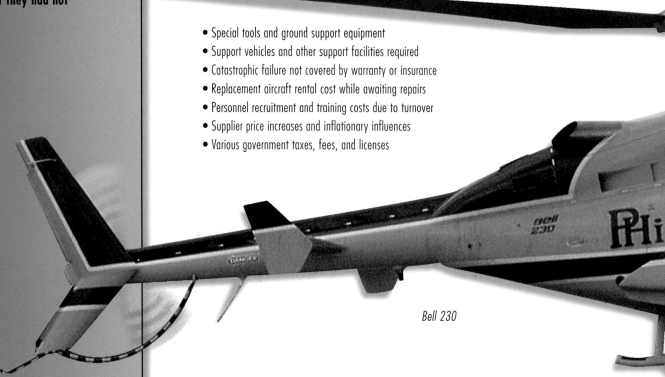

Bell 230

- Premature contract cancellation and associated costs
- Interest on financed assets and operating funds
- Cost of risk-management program (safety programs and/or recurrent training)

Where to from here?

As the millennium winds down and the helicopter industry approaches its half-century mark, one can only wonder if it is possible to separate the fortunes of individual operators in the industry from the fortunes of the association that acted as its strong right arm and its clear voice since the days when the Big Bands played the music of the land.

One of the oldest proverbs in any book says there is strength in numbers. If helicopter operators proved nothing else in their half century of service, they proved the truth of the proverb.

Predictions are a dangerous trade to ply, for who would have predicted the collapse of the Soviet Union in what seemed to be the blink of an eye? One moment Konstantin U. Chernenko was replaced by Mikhail Gorbachev in the usual way, and suddenly a man named Boris Yeltsin was defeating a vote of no-confidence by the Communist minority in the Democratically elected parliament.

The sudden glut of surplus military helicopters from both sides of the former Iron Curtain has thrown every marketing projection of the 1980s onto the trash heap.

Eurocopter AS355 N

For those interested in pursuing the history of helicopters and the industry surrounding them, there are a number of facilities available, both public and private.

Helicopter Association International has an extensive website at www.rotor.com.
Telephone: 703-683-4646
Fax: 703-683-4745

Helicopter Foundation International (HFI), housed at HAI headquarters, is dedicated to preserving vertical takeoff and landing records, documents, and related historical data. HFI also houses the world's largest public display of scale model helicopters.
John Slattery is curator
Telephone: 703-683-4646;
Fax: 703-683-4745.

The International Helicopter Museum in the U.K. has helicopters of historic significance, including the first WS-55 used by Bristow for offshore support in 1955, the Westland 30s that operated with Pan Am and AirSpur, and other notable aircraft and artifacts.
Rodney Ballantyne is director
Telephone: 44-(0)1934-822524;
Fax: 44-(0)1934-822400.

The American Helicopter Museum and Education Center in West Chester, Pennsylvania, near Philadelphia, is both a hands-on museum of actual helicopters and a repository of documents concerning the industry. Many educational exhibits are aimed at young people.
Carl Shafer is curator
Telephone: 610-436-9600;
Fax: 610-436-8642.

The prediction business, obviously, has as many contingencies as the helicopter business, and perhaps more.

A rather safe prediction, however, could have been made in 1948 when a group of people sat down in an office in California and decided that the new machine called a helicopter, which they were using in ad hoc applications, should have the benefit of united action. The prediction that such a collective effort was almost guaranteed to bear fruit would have been safe.

The effort has borne fruit, not only for the Helicopter Association International but for the individual operators of all kinds who have supported it, and have in turn been supported by it.

As 1998 HAI Chairman Neil Osborne put it, "To address the multitude of issues with the responsiveness and certainty of purpose required to help lead our industry into the future, HAI must remain focused on our stated mission 'to advance the helicopter industry, promoting the highest levels of safety and efficiency.' This mission will continue to guide our organization."

There is no shortage of challenges, as HAI president Frank Jensen pointed out in his 1997 report: "The helicopter industry has not recovered fully from the serious slump it entered into in the very early 1980s." Yet, he added, the association's regular membership, consisting of commercial operators, increased by 63 percent during the decade following that very slump, while overall membership rose 175 percent.

Growth of that magnitude during economic malaise can only indicate that the services of the helicopter are as vital to the global economy as the services of the association are to the industry.

When the first half century of the industry's growth came to a close, it was again clear that the people of the industry — using helicopters as the tools they were meant to be — amounted to a secret ingredient. The bottom line was summed up years earlier by Igor Sikorsky, the man who acted as the catalyst: "The work of the individual still remains the spark that moves mankind ahead."

It is a worthwhile benchmark for others.

*Papillon Grand Canyon
Helicopters S-55
Whisper Jet*

EPILOGUE . . . A FORWARD LOOK, AND SOME REMINDERS

With a solid, generally upbeat half century of history behind us, let's look briefly at where helicopters are, in 1998, and then project our thoughts ahead and see what the future may hold in store for helicopters and other vertical-flight aircraft.

As 1998 begins, we can see that the modern helicopter has become very safe, reliable, and practical. Even though the average age of the existing civil fleet is about 17 years, most of these aircraft are still safe, robust, and quite serviceable. Many of the newer helicopters are even safer and more efficient. Still newer, more powerful, and more versatile vertical-flight aircraft are nearing readiness for production and entry into service. The operators, support personnel, and pilots are experienced and professional.

There are some problems, including a shortage of properly located public-use heliports; increasing lack of realistic access to airspace; too many military surplus helicopters going into non-military hands; and high operating costs.

Conversely, there are some very bright considerations as well, in addition to the excellent machines and the very high standards of the industry's professionals: the outstanding safety record of helicopters, and the very wide array of vital tasks that can only be done by helicopters. In short, if there were no such aircraft as a helicopter, we would have to invent one!

Given this vitality and versatility, the future of helicopters and other vertical flight aircraft looks very promising, indeed.

Some Reminders

For all readers: As you read through this book, please make notes of any inaccuracies, omissions, or questions. Communicate these to HAI, through its Internet e-mail address: rotor@rotor.com or mail them to HAI, 1635 Prince Street, Alexandria, VA 22314-2818, Attn: Communications Department. This will help, in the event of a reprint.

For helicopter professionals: As we begin the next 50 years of helicopter service, keep accurate and detailed records of your accomplishments and achievements (along with photos with captions) and share these with HAI, in writing. This will help tremendously when the next major volume on helicopters is written.

And, in the meantime, **Fly Neighborly!**

Eurocopter A-Star

BIBLIOGRAPHY

American Helicopter, Alexis Droutzkoy, Editor, American Helicopter Magazine, New York, NY, January 1957, 20 pages. Plympton Collection.

American Helicopter Society Newsletter, H. M. Lounsbury, Editor, American Helicopter Society, New York, NY, October 1956, 20 pages. Plympton Collection.

The Bell Helicopter Textron Story, David A. Brown, Aerofax Inc., Arlington, TX, 1995, softcover, 220 pages.

A Brief History of the First Use of Helicopters in Agriculture, Dr. Carrol M. Voss, AgRotors Inc., undated, apparently mid-1960s, 30-page booklet.

The Capitol: A Pictorial History of the Capitol and the Congress, U.S. Government Printing Office, 1979, softcover, 194 pages.

"Captain John Miller Had What It Took to Fly the Weird Ones," Bud Walker, *Aviation History Magazine,* November 1996, p. 14.

Flight Handbook, Fifth Edition, Maurice A. Smith, editor, Iliffe & Sons, London, 1954, hardcover, 282 pages.

From Da Vinci to Today and Beyond, American Helicopter Society, Washington, DC, 1994, softcover, 56 pages. A compendium of expert articles and essays on the history and development of vertical-flight technology through the decades.

A Good Life: Newspapering and Other Adventures, Ben Bradlee, Simon & Schuster, New York, NY, 1995, softcover, 514 pages.

"The Greening of the Helicopter," Robert Williams, *Aviation Heritage Magazine,* March 1991, p. 24.

Guide for the Presentation of Helicopter Operating Cost Estimates, Committee on Helicopter Operating Costs, Aerospace Industries Association in Cooperation with the Helicopter Association International, 1987 (Reprinted February 1992 and currently under revision), paper, 40 pages.

HAI: 1948-1973: Photo and History Book, Jim Ricklefs, Helicopter Association International, Alexandria, VA, unpublished collection in three volumes, donated 1989.

HAI Survey of Operating Performance, Economics Committee, Helicopter Association International, Alexandria, VA, 1996, paper, 85 pages.

"Helicopter Aids Oil Search," Charles Deegan, *Oil & Gas Journal,* June 7, 1947.

Helicopter Annual, Helicopter Association International, Washington, DC, and Alexandria, VA, 1983 through 1997, softcover.

Helicopter Foundation International, John M. Slattery, Curator, Alexandria, VA, general collection and library.

"The Helicopter Goes to Work," Clive Howard, *Flying Magazine,* August 1947, p. 23.

Helicopter Guide, Charles Lester (Les) Morris, Helicopter Utilities, Inc., White Plains, NY, 1951, illus., 75 pages.

The Helicopter: Its Importance to Commerce and the Public, Ann Davis & Robert Richardson, Helicopter Association of America, Washington, DC, 1978, paper, 137 pages.

Helicopter Mechanics School, course syllabus and outline, New England Helicopter Service, Rhode Island, 1951. Plympton Collection.

"Helicopter Roundtable," *American Aviation Magazine,* American Aviation Publications, Washington, DC, July 1963, pp. 50-57.

Helicopters & Autogyros of the World (Enlarged and revised edition), Paul Lambermont with Anthony Pirie, A. S. Barnes and Company, South Brunswick and New York, 1970, hardcover, 446 pages.

Helicopters and Urban Communities, David S. Lawrence, Sikorsky Aircraft, paper presented to the Transportation Research Board, 1984, 8-page booklet.

Helicopters That Made History, David C. Cooke, G. P. Putnam's Sons, New York, 1963, hardcover, 72 pages.

Helicopters: The British Columbia Story, Peter Corley-Smith and David N. Parker, Canav Books, Toronto, 1985, softcover, 157 pages.

"Helicopters Come of Age," *Holt's Gazette* (newspaper), Stockton, CA, January 1951.

Hovering, Henry M. Holden, Black Hawk Publishing Co., Mount Freedom, NJ, 1994, hardcover, 256 pages.

In Retrospect: The Tragedy and Lessons of Vietnam, Robert S. MacNamara, Times Books/Random House, New York, NY, 1995, hardcover, 414 pages.

Ink & Avgas: Silver Anniversary History, Aviation/Space Writers Association, Washington, DC, 1963, softcover, 50 pages.

Lift, Joe Stein, The Zig-Zag Papers, Zig-Zag, OR, 1985, softcover, 210 pages.

Naval Aviation 1943, U.S. Naval Institute, Annapolis, MD, 1943, hardcover, 147 pages.

"New-Manufacture Skycranes," Paul Proctor, Industry Outlook Department, *Aviation Week & Space Technology,* August 11, 1997.

One Way Up, John F. Straubel, Hiller Aircraft Co., Inc., subsidiary of Fairchild-Hiller Corp., 1964, softcover, 40 pages. Plympton Collection.

"Operation Statistics for First Oil Survey," Peter Wright, *American Helicopter Magazine,* May 1949, p. 10.

Pioneering the Helicopter (Revised 1945 edition), Charles Lester Morris, Helicopter Association International, Alexandria, VA, 1985, hardcover, 161 pages.

Plympton Collection: An archive of historic text and photographic materials covering the commercial helicopter operating industry, with focus on New England Helicopter Services and its affiliates in the U.S. and other countries beginning in January 1946. Compiled by Leon Plympton, founder of NEHS, and donated to the Helicopter Association International.

The Presidential Character, James David Barber, Prentice-Hall, Englewood Cliffs, NJ, Second Edition, 1972-1977, softcover, 576 pages.

The Promise of Helicopter Transportation, Raymond Sawyer, Executive Director, Civil Aeronautics Board; paper presented at the Eighth Annual Convention of the Helicopter Association of America, San Francisco, January 1956.

Respectfully Quoted, Library of Congress, Washington, DC, 1989, hardcover, 520 pages.

Ricklefs Collection. A comprehensive archive of historic text and photographic materials covering the commercial helicopter operating industry from 1948 to 1973 in three volumes. Compiled by HAI's first president, James S. Ricklefs, founder of Rick Helicopters, and donated to the Helicopter Association International.

The Rise and Fall of the Third Reich, William L. Shirer, Simon & Schuster, New York, NY, 1960, softcover, 1,599 pages.

Rotor Breeze, newsletter of Bell Helicopter, Fort Worth, TX, various issues from 1951 to 1965. Plympton Collection.

ROTOR, Helicopter Association International, Alexandria, VA, various issues.

The Story of the Helicopter, Frank J. Delear, Sikorsky Aircraft, Stratford, CT, 1961, 20-page booklet.

They Filled the Skies, Richard S. Tipton, Public Relations Dept., Bell Helicopter Textron, Ft. Worth, TX, 1983, softcover, 36 pages.

Timetables of Technology, Bryan Bunch & Alexander Hellemans, Simon & Schuster, New York, NY, 1993, softcover, 490 pages.

To Fly Like a Bird, Joe Mashman as told to R. Randall Padfield, Phillips Publishing Co., 1992, hardcover, 194 pages.

Tram Book, History of the Palm Springs Aerial Tramway, George O. Wheeler, DeserTopics Publishing, Palm Springs, CA, 1950, with an undated and expanded revision, softcover, 64 pages.

Vertical Challenge: The Hiller Aircraft Story, Jay P. Spenser, University of Washington Press, Seattle, WA, 1992, hardcover, 224 pages.

Vertiflite, a publication of the American Helicopter Society, Alexandria, VA, various issues.

Voss Collection. A comprehensive archive of historic photographic and text materials covering the commercial helicopter industry, especially in agricultural applications, from the mid-1940s. Compiled by Dr. Carrol M. Voss and donated to the Helicopter Association International.

"V/STOL: The First Half Century," Michael Hirschberg, *Vertiflite,* American Helicopter Society, Alexandria, VA, Vol. 43. No. 2, March-April 1997, p. 34.

World Aircraft Recognition Manual, C. H, Gibbs-Smith & L. E. Bradford, Putnam, London, 1956, hardcover, 268 pages.

World Almanac 1963, New York World-Telegram, New York, NY, softcover, 896 pages.